SCIENTIFIC CODE

of

THE I-CHING

T. TRAN, Ph.D.

First edition 2011

Title: "Scientific Code of the I-Ching"
Author: T. Tran, Ph.D.

Science – Philosophy – Chinese Studies

Created in 2000-2003 by T. Tran, Ph.D.

First edition 2011

ISBN-13: 978-1460942314

Last Science Publishing
San Jose, California 95112
Website: www.lastscience.com
Email: lastscience@yahoo.com

Foreword

Since the time of their invention, reportedly by the Chinese king of antiquity Fu Hsi between five to six thousand years ago, the eight trigrams have always been the subjects of unabated fascination, if not reverence, in many Eastern Asian countries. While there are many applications of the trigrams, the best known application of all must be the I-Ching, whose literal English translation is "the Oracle of Change." The I-Ching is based on 64 pairs of trigrams, which are more commonly referred to as the 64 hexagrams. Each hexagram has 6 lines, either solid or broken. The solid line represents Yang, the broken line Yin. In addition to an overall meaning for each hexagram, individual lines –under special circumstances—also have their own meanings. The overall meanings for the 64 hexagrams are known as the work of king Wen (11th to 12th century BC), who reportedly wrote them when he was imprisoned by the then emperor of China. The meanings for the 64×6=384 lines have been credited to the Duke of Chou, who was one of king Wen's sons.

In recent years, the interest in the I-Ching has grown steadily in the world in general and the western world in particular. Naturally the number of questions regarding the I-Ching has also increased. There are good reasons to believe that the I-Ching was a work based on logic, and that this logic must have been known at least to King Wen and the Duke of Chou. The list of grandmasters of I-Ching logic may also have included Confucius as well as a few Taoist sages of antiquity.

Many scholars specializing in Asian studies will argue that the knowledge of the I-Ching grandmasters has been successfully passed down to us in the vast amount of commentaries by scholars from the Han dynasty onward. On this point, the writer begs to differ. One common characteristic of later I-Ching commentaries is that they are either vague or provisional, or both. Reading commentaries by the so-called later I-Ching scholars is like listening to financial analysts arguing whether the stock market will move up or down. The reality is, if there was a coherent logic behind the I-Ching, that logic was lost!

Does this mean that we can never make sense of the I-Ching? The writer doesn't think so. We have the great fortune of living in the age of science. While science is not the answer to everything, it is a product of accumulated logic. Thanks to science an average person now knows much, much more about the world, the universe than any sage of antiquity. While the scientific method may never match the insight of the enlightened sages, it may just be able to decode the scribbled messages that they left behind.

That is the whole goal of this book. The rest is up to the reader to judge and decide.

Minnesota June 9, 2002
T. Tran

Scientific Code of the I-Ching
Table of Contents

Chapter 1

Can the I-Ching be scientific?

I-Ching and the Yin-Yang theory

The I-Ching needs no introduction. It is definitely the best known of the so-called "Five Oracles" of Chinese classics, and arguably the most popular book of divination known to the world today.

In a nutshell, the concept contained in the I-Ching is a particular application of the Yin Yang theory. While the Yin Yang theory is not yet well understood (even to the Chinese), most of us have some common knowledge of Yin and Yang, such as:

Yin (broken line): Female, tentative, passive, dark, cold, dead, etc.

Yang (solid line): Male, aggressive, active, bright, warm, alive, etc.

▬ ▬   ▬▬▬▬▬   *Figure 1: Traditional*
Yin   Yang   *Yin Yang symbols*

We will see later in this book that, contrary to popular belief, the different Yin attributes are independent of one another, so are the Yang attributes. Thus, although "female," "passive," and "cold" are all Yin; "being female" does not necessarily imply "being passive." In fact, Yin Yang logic predicts that there are active females and passive males. (And yes, it also predicts that there are "hot" females.)

The I-Ching mystery

All I-Ching users know that the I-Ching is based on 64 binary variations of 6 Yin Yang lines, which are usually called "the 64 hexagrams." Most users also know that each hexagram is formed by putting two units, of 3 lines each, on top of each other. There are 8 of these 3-line units, usually called "the 8 trigrams."

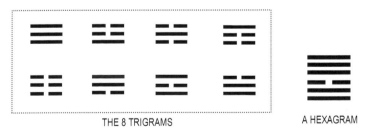

THE 8 TRIGRAMS   A HEXAGRAM

Fig 2: The 8 trigrams (left block) and the hexagram formed by putting the top left trigram on top of the bottom right trigram (right).

Each hexagram has an overall meaning. Under special circumstances, each line in a hexagram also has its own meaning. Since the total number of lines is relatively large (64×6=384), the writer has decided to focus only on the overall meanings of the 64 hexagrams in this book. He has plans for a volume II, in which the 384 individual lines will be discussed in detail.

As an example of hexagram meaning, we will pick the hexagram listed as hexagram 10 in the I-Ching. This hexagram is formed by putting the top left trigram in figure 2 (three solid lines) on top of the bottom right trigram (one broken line on top of 2 solid lines). The literal meaning for this hexagram is "Stepping on the tail of a tiger. The tiger does not bite the person. Progress." Thus, the I-Ching says that this hexagram corresponds to an extremely dangerous situation where even the smallest mistake would result in total disaster; yet it maintains that whoever is trapped in this very scary situation should escape without harm and even gain something positive.

STEPPING
CAUTIOUSLY

Fig 3: This particular hexagram describes an extremely dangerous situation where the smallest mistake would result in total disaster. It has the fitting name "stepping cautiously" and is listed as trigram #10 in the I-Ching.

It is not difficult to see that the meaning of hexagram 10 is a prediction. This is also true for the other 63 hexagrams. While some are more dramatic and some are more mundane than the others; the 64 hexagram meanings are *predictive descriptions* of 64 situations. This is one reason why the I-Ching has always been a popular book of divination.

Everything associated with divination is considered by existing science as unscientific, and the I-Ching is no exception.

The scientific argument for the Yin Yang concept

But the I-Ching is different from other divination tools because it is based on the Yin-Yang concept, which is a binary model of the universe. The current status of science and technology is in favor of such a binary model:

1. In a nutshell, science is a form of reductionism. The goal of science is to continuously reduce complex physical manifestations to the simpler rules that govern them. Thus, complex movements of the stars and planets were reduced to Newton's law of gravitation. Newton's law of gravitation and the peculiar behavior of light were reduced to Einstein's theory of General Relativity. Complex atomic phenomena were reduced to the laws of Quantum Mechanics. The

problem is, as things stand today, General Relativity is in severe conflict with Quantum Mechanics. This suggests that, in order to reconcile General Relativity and Quantum Mechanics, at least one more step is necessary in the reduction process of science.

2. The computer, which grows more and more powerful every day and seems to have no future limit, is based on the binary system of 0 and 1.

While it is impossible to guess what must be involved in the reduction step that reconciles General Relativity and Quantum Mechanics, it is clear that no further reduction is possible beyond a binary system. At the same time, as seen with computers, even the most complex phenomena could be described by a binary system.

Adding all these together, there is no reason to rule out the possibility that Yin-and-Yang is the ultimate model of the universe, and theories such as General Relativity and Quantum Mechanics are simply partial theories that can be reduced to Yin-and-Yang.

However, as it is today, the Yin-Yang theory is still a pseudo-science. Since the I-Ching is based on the Yin Yang theory, we have no choice but to justify the Yin Yang theory before going any further. This will take a considerable amount of effort, and the readers are asked to be very patient. The writer promises that their patience will pay off handsomely.

A proposed naming system for the eight trigrams

Since the building blocks for the Yin Yang theory are the eight trigrams, we need to know something about them.

The eight trigrams are usually called by the English sounds of their Chinese names; but in this book the writer will propose a different naming system. The first reason for this rather unusual proposal is that the Chinese names for the trigrams are exotic and incomprehensible to even Chinese natives. The second reason is that the proposed system is very easy to remember and yet, as the reader will find later, it contains all necessary information. Thus, this is the lazy person's first step to become an I-Ching expert (or Yin Yang expert, for that matter.)

The proposed naming rules are:

1. Trigrams with odd number of solid lines are Yang, with odd number of broken lines are Yin.
2. The trigram with three solid lines is "All-Yang."
3. The trigram with three broken lines is "All-Yin."
4. The other six trigrams are differentiated by the order of the odd line. Starting from the bottom, the order is: Max, Mid, Min.

The trigrams are listed in figure 4. By noticing the position of the "identity line" (marked with an "x") and with the help of rule number

4, the average reader should be able to remember the names of all eight trigrams within 5 minutes. This feat should not be underestimated, considering that differentiating the eight trigrams has always been a very difficult task for Yin Yang beginners and even for some intermediate Yin Yang students.

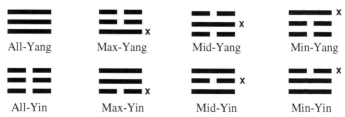

Fig 4: The proposed naming system for the 8 trigrams

Serious students of the Yin Yang theory will recognize that the proposed naming system is an abstraction of the symbolisms invented by King Wen (12th century BC). The reason why we modified King Wen's system instead of using its original form will be evident later.

The 64 hexagrams and the 384 lines
There are two main parts in the I-Ching:
1. The 64 hexagrams: Each hexagram has a meaning. It is believed that these meanings were written down by King Wen in the twelfth century BC, which was more than three thousand years ago. Two hexagrams are shown in figure 5 as examples.

Fig 5: One difference (in line 5 counting from bottom) changes the meaning of a hexagram completely.

2. Individual lines: Under certain circumstances, a Yang line is considered "too Yang" and has the potential to change to Yin. Likewise, when a Yin line is "too Yin" it has the potential to change to Yang. It is under these circumstances that the individual lines have meanings.
It is believed that the meanings of the individual lines were the works of the Duke of Chou. He was one of King Wen's sons and arguably the most well respected political figure in Chinese history. Theoretically the number of changing lines in a hexagram could vary

anywhere from zero to six. Thus, in theory, each hexagram could change to any of the other 63 hexagrams.

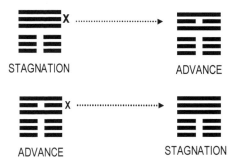

STAGNATION   ADVANCE

ADVANCE   STAGNATION

Fig 6: Changing lines have special meanings. They also cause hexagram transformation (changing one hexagram to another)

Yin Yang and I-Ching questions

The traditional step at this point is to spell out the textbook meanings of the trigrams, then follow up with the meanings of the 64 hexagrams and 384 individual lines. The writer, however, has chosen not to do this yet, because in his opinion –and he trusts that most readers will agree with him—the existing Yin Yang theory is not in a satisfactory state. Worse, while the meanings of the 64 hexagrams and 384 of their individual lines are known (in archaic ancient Chinese, which differs from current Chinese in many cases) and can be trusted to be original, the logic behind them is a total mystery.

The easiest approach is to accept things as they are without asking questions. While this approach is obviously non-scientific, it has been the status quo. Some Yin Yang masters even expressed the opinion that, since the Yin Yang theory is a part of mysticism, it is beyond the grasp of science.

The scientific community, on the other hand, holds a very low opinion for the Yin Yang theory, and not without good reasons. Except for a few mavericks such as Carl Jung, it is fair to say that most scientists consider the Yin Yang theory, at best, an object of curiosity, on the same level as the concept of reincarnation.

The writer believes that, while science is the most reliable tool to acquire and accumulate knowledge, there are special cases where science still lags behind mysticism. Further, he believes that the Yin Yang theory is one such special case. At the same time, the writer agrees that the burden of proof lies squarely on the shoulders of mysticism. In order to be accepted by the scientific community, the I-

11

Ching must pass the tests common to all scientific hypotheses. In particular, the following questions will have to be answered before the Yin Yang theory in general and the I-Ching in particular can be seriously considered as scientific knowledge:

1. Is there any scientific reasoning behind the Yin Yang concept?
2. Why are the trigrams the building blocks of the Yin Yang theory? Specifically, why are these building blocks based on three lines instead of say two lines, four lines, five lines, etc.?
3. It is known that there are two major trigram classifications. Former Heaven trigrams (credited to Fu Hsi, a legendary Chinese king believed to have lived between 4000 BC and 3000 BC) and Later Heaven trigrams (credited to King Wen, 12th to 11th century BC). How did these classifications come about and what is the significance of each? Why are Mid-Yang and Min-Yang considered Yin in Former Heaven and Yang in Later Heaven? Why are Mid-Yin and Min-Yin considered Yang in Former Heaven and Yin in Later Heaven?
4. What are the scientific meanings of the trigrams?
5. Why in the I-Ching only two trigrams are combined at a time to get 64 hexagrams? Isn't 64 too small a number to describe the complexity of our world? Why not combining three trigrams or four trigrams to get more possibilities?
6. What is the logic behind the overall meaning of each hexagram?
7. What is the logic behind the meanings of the 384 individual lines?
8. On which ground or grounds that the I-Ching connects the 64 hexagrams and 384 lines to human beings?
9. Is the Yin Yang concept consistent with natural science? Can it explain natural science (to the same extent as say Newtonian or Einsteinian physics)?

We will seek answers to these questions in the following chapters. The exceptions are question 7 and a part of question 8, which will be addressed in volume II.

First written March 2002
Completed May 2002
© T. Tran

Chapter 2
Space-time logic
of the Yin Yang theory

The incompleteness of existing science

The description of existing science requires the patching of two paradigms that are diametrically opposite to each other. On the one extreme is classical physics, which claims that all physical phenomena are completely deterministic. On the other extreme is quantum mechanics, which claims that all physical phenomena are indeterminate. Since these two hypotheses are mutually exclusive of each other, at least one of them has to be wrong or incomplete. It can be shown that both theories are incomplete *(see Appendix I at the end of this book.)*

Einstein's spacetime continuum

A very brief summary of the historical evolution of the concept of space and time is sufficient for our purpose. It was first thought by Newton in the 17th century that space and time are independent of each other. However, Minkowski pointed out in 1908 that time must be connected to space to be consistent with Einstein's Relativity theory. Specifically, in Einstein's Relativity theory, the quantity "ict" (where i is the square root of -1, c the speed of light, and t time) must be treated mathematically as another dimension of space *(see reference 1).*

Minkowski's argument gave rise to the so called "Einsteinian spacetime continuum," which consists of 4 dimensions: The x, y, z dimensions of space that we all are familiar with, plus the (ict) dimension, which must be considered mathematically equivalent to each of x, y, z. Thus, space and time were united by Einstein's Relativity theory into one self-connected entity known as spacetime.

The incompleteness of Einsteinian spacetime

Actually there is one thing that classical physicists and quantum mechanicists can and do agree on, namely the Einsteinian spacetime concept that we have just presented. As a matter of fact, Einstein's spacetime is currently a part of the foundation of both classical physics and quantum mechanics.

But the concept of a spacetime continuum is not without problem. If time is, in the sense implied by Einstein's Relativity, equivalent to space, then from the fact that space travel is possible, time travel –i.e., moving backward or forward in time- must also be possible. We will not go into detail here, but it suffices to say that the idea of time travel has many paradoxical consequences.

While many science enthusiasts and even some scientists embrace the paradoxical possibility of time travel, we will revert to common sense (despite the fact that it has been abandoned and even attacked by many modern scientists.) Common sense tells us that it is almost impossible for a highly successful theory to be completely wrong, but it is entirely possible for such a theory to be incomplete. We will therefore ask the question: "Could the Einsteinian spacetime model be incomplete?"

Incredible as it seems, the answer comes right from Einstein's theory of Special Relativity, according to which length is shortened along the direction of motion. For example, Special Relativity predicts that if a stationary box with measurements of 1m×1m×1m is put in motion, the side parallel to the direction of motion would be shortened to 0.6m at velocity equaling 80% the speed of light, while the other two dimensions are unaffected. Since lengths are the manifestations of space, and since we can arbitrarily choose the direction of motion as one of the three spatial dimensions, it is clear that –as long as motion exists, i.e., the velocity v is different from zero - the three spatial dimensions are not equivalent. Since all existence is reducible to the atomic scale, and in the atomic realm there is always some form of motion, the three spatial dimensions are _always_ not equivalent.

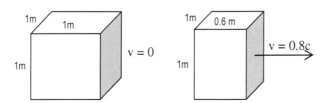

*Figure 1: Length is shortened in the direction of motion
(from 1m down to 0.6m at 80% the speed of light c), but
not in the two directions perpendicular to it.*

The curious fact is that, while this spatial inequivalence was a direct result of Einstein's Relativity theory, it was never accounted for in the Einsteinian spacetime continuum, where the three spatial dimensions are taken for granted as being equivalent *(see appendix II)*. The conclusion is obvious: The Einsteinian spacetime continuum is an incomplete description of space and time.

The incompleteness of Einstein's spacetime continuum has great implications on the "time travel" paradox. Regrettably the subject of time travel is outside the scope of this book. The writer hopes to return to it in another book in the future.

The complementary roles of space and time in microscopic entities

It can be shown that time t and the direction of motion z are complementary factors in the total existence of a microscopic entity such as a photon or an electron, and can be combined geometrically as a circle drawn by the tip of a rotating arrow *(see appendix III at the end of this book)*. Specifically, the t and the z components of existence change in sympathy of each other (i.e., increase and decrease together.) This means we only need to analyze one factor to understand both. Since it is more natural to associate existence with time, we will choose the time component.

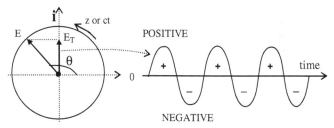

Figure 2: The time component of existence alternates between being positive and being negative. Since the direction of time is arbitrarily chosen as positive, the "positive existence" agrees with the direction of time, the "negative existence" is reverse to the direction of time.

As shown in *Appendix III*, the time component of existence E_T is an alternating series of increases and decreases. In mathematical language we say that E_T is a periodic function of time. Taking zero as our reference, there will be periods when E_T is positive, and there will be periods when E_T is negative.

A qualification must be made at this point. The description just given applies only to a very large collection of microscopic entities, and it is impossible to predict whether E_T is positive or negative for an individual microscopic entity at a given moment in time. This point was elaborated in detail in an earlier book by the writer "Symmetry and The End of Probability" *(see reference 2)*. For those who have not read this book, the following analogy will be helpful. When a three year old child tosses an unbiased coin repeatedly, we can safely bet that the counts for heads and tails will be more or less equal in the long run, but we cannot predict whether heads or tails will turn up in the next toss. Positive and negative E_T's are the counterparts of heads and tails in this analogy.

Yin Yang as a complexity theory

This section requires some basic knowledge of the Central Limit theorem of statistics. Readers who are not familiar with this theorem can either trust the writer or consult *Appendix IV* before continuing.

One of the hottest scientific concepts at the time of this writing is that of complexity. In a nutshell, complexity is the overall order that may take place when a large collection of unpredictable units are combined together.

As far as the value of E_T is concerned, each individual microscopic entity is an unpredictable element. However, most microscopic entities do not exist separately, but are combined into more complex entities such as atoms, molecules, and compounds; which we will refer to by the generic name of "groups." Groups, in turn, may combine with microscopic entities or other groups to form even more complex entities. If this combining effect keeps going, at some point the condition of the Central Limit theorem will be met, giving rise to a new existence *(see Appendix IV)*. For our present purposes, it suffices to say that this aggregate existence is a perfect application of the Central Limit theorem, which states that the distribution of the mean value of many random factors has the form of a (bell-shaped) normal curve.

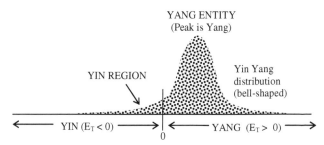

Fig 3: Yin and Yang are two possible states of a complexity that covers a range of possible values. Here each dot in the bell-shaped curve represents an occurrence. While most occurrences are in the Yang region, some of them are in the Yin region.

When we say an entity is Yang, all we mean is that the peak of the bell-shaped curve, which is a record of all occurrences experienced by the entity, is in the Yang region, as shown in the picture. It is clear from the picture that a Yang entity may have Yin occurrences.

Since most possibilities center around the mean value of the aggregate existence, if the mean value is positive we will say that it is a positive existence, if the mean value is negative we will say that it is a negative existence. The Yin Yang concept arises naturally by defining "Positive E_T = Yang" and "Negative E_T = Yin"

The fact that the aggregate existence emerges from many random individual factors makes it fit the definition of "complexity" exactly. Thus, Yin and Yang are two faces of a complexity, and the Yin Yang theory is a complexity theory.

The temporary nature of Yin and Yang

To have a feeling for the meaning of Yin and Yang, let's consider the simplified example:

Yin   = "being sick"

Yang = "being healthy"

Think of the (bell shaped) Yin Yang distribution in figure 4 as a graphical presentation of the physical makeup of a 20-year-old person. Since the expected value of the distribution is on the healthy side, the person is considered "healthy" by medical standards. If we limit ourselves to a period of time without any dramatic events, so that there is no significant change in the physical makeup of the person, we can assume that the Yin Yang distribution of his health will stay more or less constant. During this period we may find that, despite being described as being "healthy," the person could actually get sick at times. That is because the Yin Yang distribution for this healthy person does include a small but non-zero possibility for sickness.

Because the physical makeup of this person is strong, when he gets sick we know almost with certainty that he will soon become healthy again. This same conclusion can also be reached by realizing that only a very small part of the Yin Yang curve is in the "sick" region.

Yin and Yang, then, are temporary states; and there is no rule that says that Yin and Yang cannot switch back and forth. Thus, an entity that has been Yang many times in the past could be Yin the next time, and vice versa.

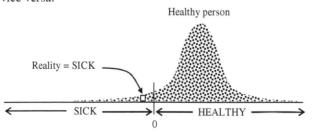

Fig 4: A "healthy" person (peak of curve in "healthy" region) should be understood as a person who is healthy most of the time. This means he or she could still be sick at times (then recovers and becomes healthy again.) This example shows that Yin (sick) and Yang (healthy) are dynamic, not invariant states.

17

In the field of criminology, it is well known that many individuals who commit hideous crimes show no prior signs of such cruel tendency. The after-the-fact account is that these individuals "snapped." The Yin Yang theory offers a more scientific view. For the sake of demonstration let's simplify the situation so that we can use figure 4 again. Now we will equate Yang with "being mentally healthy," Yin with "being mentally sick." As seen in figure 4, a "mentally healthy" person (expected to be Yang) could, in rare occasions, becomes "mentally sick" (Yin in reality).

It is therefore possible for a "normal" person to murder the innocent. On the other hand, it is also possible for a "cruel" person to risk his life to save a little child from a burning house. It is this kind of unpredictability that makes life perplexing and hopeful at the same time. It forces us not to take a good person for granted, and at the same time it gives us hope that conscience may exist even in a criminal mind.

The time factor in macroscopic existence

Our bodies are examples of macroscopic entities. Macroscopic entities are collection of microscopic particles such as electrons, protons, neutrons, and photons.

Then why microscopic particles keep on "living" while our bodies (and other macroscopic entities) eventually die? This question is sometimes referred to as the "time puzzle" (time seems to matter only to macroscopic entities, not microscopic entities.) The "time puzzle" is a great mystery of contemporary physics.

The time puzzle is easily solved by the Yin Yang theory. Macroscopic entities are complexities that come to existence only because of the averaging process of the Central Limit theorem (CLT). The CLT averaging process requires that the random factors together meet certain set of criteria. While such a set of criteria could be quite liberal, it is nevertheless necessary for the random factors to be considered loosely as a "qualified system" so that the CLT averaging process could take place. When the required set of criteria is not met, the random factors are no longer recognized by the CLT averaging process as parts of a "qualified system," and a CLT distribution cannot be formed. Since the CLT distribution _is_ existence, without it the macroscopic entity ceases to exist.

A fictitious example is given in figure 5 to illustrate this point. Here the CLT process requires that the square contains at least 3 units. Case A (3 units), case B (5 units), case C (4 units) all meet this requirement. Each of them should correspond to a state of existence. Case D, on the other hand, cannot be a state of existence because it only involves 2 units.

18

| A (3 units) | B (5 units) | C (4 units) | D (2 units) |

Fig 5: Here the set of criteria for existence is "must have at least three units inside the square." Cases A, B, C are three states of existence (which could be either Yin or Yang), but case D is a state of non-existence.

Return to the example of the human body. Blood circulation must be within certain range. While this range may be quite loose for some individuals, when blood circulation wanders outside it, the normal functions of the body will stop, bringing down with it all Central Limit Theorem averaging processes associated with life; and the result is death. *(Also see Appendix IV).*

Yin Yang symbols

Earlier we have chosen to define "Yang = positive E_T" and "Yin = negative E_T," which seem to be arbitrary choices as "being positive" and "being negative" are but conventions. To be more universal, we note that, in the same convention, time is taken as positive. We therefore revise our definitions as follows:

Yang   = E_T agrees with the direction of time.

Yin   = E_T is reverse of the direction of time.

Since circles must be used to represent the combined effect of t and z *(see Appendix III at the end of this book)*, circles of equal sizes are the proper geometrical shapes for both Yin and Yang. Clockwise arrows can be used to signify agreement with time (Yang), counterclockwise arrows disagreement (Yin). Alternatively we can use light circles to signify Yang, dark circles Yin. Visually, the later alternative is more convenient. It will be used throughout this book.

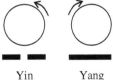

Yin   Yang   Yin   Yang

Fig 6: Two methods to describe Yin and Yang as circles. The second method (dark and light circles) is preferred because of its simplicity. Traditional symbols for Yin and Yang (broken line and solid line) are included for comparison.

Light circles (associated with increases) will be called Yang circles. Dark circles (associated with decreases) will be called Yin circles.

Yin Yang as the measures of all existence

Since motion makes z different from x and y, the only way for the three spatial dimensions to be equivalent to one another is that there is no motion. But as we know from modern physics, there is no meaningful existence when there is no motion. Furthermore, since motion necessarily leads to changes, we arrive at the first result of the Yin Yang theory: "Existence is CHANGE!"

Since Yin and Yang are the elements of change, all phenomena in the universe can be described in terms of Yin and Yang!

Yin Yang as the logic of life

All of us should be very familiar with comparative logic, i.e., the logic based on qualitative relations "greater than," "smaller than," "equal to," etc. Thanks to comparative logic we know why the two final basketball scores 116-115 (very close) and 150-50 (very lopsided) imply the same outcome, with the first team winning and the second team losing. We also know why team B wins the following best-of-seven series despite the fact that their overall score is much less than that of team A in the following table:

Game	Team A	Team B	Outcome
1	100	50	A wins
2	100	50	A wins
3	100	50	A wins
4	100	101	B wins
5	100	101	B wins
6	100	101	B wins
7	100	101	B wins
OVERALL	700	554	B wins

The problem with comparative logic is that it requires at least one extra condition to be meaningful. For example, the basketball team that scores 116 points beats the team that scores 115 points because of two conditions:

1. Comparative logic: $116 > 115$
2. According to the rule of basketball, the team with the higher score wins.

If the scores were from a friendly 18-hole golf tournament, the situation would be reverse, with 115 being the winning score instead of

116. This dependency on extra conditions imposes a severe limit on the applicability of comparative logic.

We will see in later chapter that Yin Yang is also a form of comparative logic. The big difference is that Yin Yang is a complete logic, requiring no extra condition. For this reason, Yin Yang logic is a powerful tool in our search for an understanding of many complex real-life situations that are clearly outside the reach of the existing methods of science.

The natural match between Yin Yang and life

One of the most amazing properties of the Yin-Yang concept is that it has a natural match with many realities in Nature and in life. A few examples of this natural match:

Two basic physical make-ups of all living beings are female and male, fitting Yin and Yang.

Human thinking, including the decision making process, is strongly binary, which is a natural match with the Yin-Yang concept. This can be seen most clearly in the way we formulate our adjectives: Good vs. bad, rich vs. poor, high vs. low, hot vs. cold, etc.

It must be emphasized that such natural match is completely absent in existing scientific theories. For example, it is impossible to deduce from any known scientific laws that humans should exist in two biological forms: Male and female. The male-female differentiation therefore has to be made after the fact and accounted for in an *ad hoc* manner.

Thus, at least at the starting point, the Yin-Yang theory outperforms all other scientific theories known to mankind. The big question is whether the Yin-Yang theory has enough predictive power to stand alongside known scientific hypotheses such as Newtonian mechanics. In subsequent chapters, we will see that it does indeed have this power.

First written April 2002
Completed June 2002
© T. Tran

References:

1) "Space and time," Minkowski, H. Address delivered at the 80th Assembly of German Natural Scientists and Physicians at Cologne, September 21, 1908. Reprinted English translation, pp. 73-91, "The Principle of Relativity," Einstein, 1952, Dover, New York (1923, Methuen and Co.)

2) "Symmetry and the End of Probability." Tran, T., 2011 (2nd ed.), 2003 (1st ed.), Last Science Publishing, San Jose, California, USA.

Chapter 3
Logic of the eight trigrams I
The Four Symbols and the Four Elements
Solution to the three-line puzzle

Yin and Yang, as defined in the last chapter, are relationships between the spatial dimensions of motion and time, at a moment in time. Still missing are:

1. The two spatial dimensions in the plane perpendicular to the direction of motion.
2. The (non-zero) time duration, without which no meaningful existence could be defined.

By ignoring the first factor, we will obtain the Yin Yang rule for "temporal existence" (i.e., existence seen from a time-only perspective.) This method gives the "Four Temporal States," which we will discuss briefly.

By ignoring the second factor, we will obtain the Yin Yang rule for "spatial existence" (i.e., existence seen from a space-only perspective). This method gives the "Four Spatial States," which we will also discuss briefly.

The Four Temporal States and the Four Symbols

Each Yin and Yang circle represents a deviation from zero at a moment in time, which by definition has zero duration. Since existence with zero time duration is meaningless, more than one Yin Yang circle is required to describe existence.

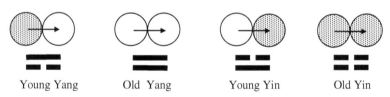

| Young Yang | Old Yang | Young Yin | Old Yin |

Fig 1: The Four Temporal States are 4 permutations of two Yin Yang circles with the direction of time pointing from the left circle to the right circle. Note that the left circle corresponds to the bottom line (in traditional notation). In traditional Yin Yang theory, the Four Temporal States are called "The Four Symbols."

Since each circle represents a moment in time, two circles in contact represent a non-zero time duration. This can be seen mathematically as follows: Time is a dimension, and it takes two points (i.e., two moments in time or two circles) to define a dimension.

Thus, two Yin Yang circles are required to represent time, giving rise to the "Four Temporal States." To follow tradition, we will call them by familiar names: Old Yang, Old Yin, Young Yang, and Young Yin.

Naturally, a direction of time is required to distinguish Young Yang and Young Yin. Young Yang means the Yang circle is newer than the Yin circle; the reverse is true for Young Yin. In the traditional line notation, the convention is that the lower line exists before the upper line. It follows that the proper notation for Young Yang is a Yang line (solid) on top of a Yin line (broken), the proper notation for Young Yin is reverse (see figure 1).

Readers who are familiar with the Yin Yang theory will realize that we have just settled an academically important disagreement among Yin Yang masters. There are many masters who believe that the notations for Young Yang and Young Yin should be reverse of what we have presented. The reader may want to read the "Special Section" at the end of this chapter to confirm to him or herself that the notations that we presented make more sense.

The Four Temporal States serves as a simple but powerful example of the Yin Yang theory. Increases cannot be maintained forever, and will eventually become decreases. Decreases cannot be maintained forever, and will eventually become increases. (In between the changes from increases to decreases and vice versa are states of non-existence that escape our attention because, after all, they are non-existence.)

The first Yang circle of Old Yang appears first, therefore it will change to Yin first. When this happens Old-Yang, which is a purely Yang state, becomes Young Yin, which is a mixed state where Yin starts to manifest itself but not very strongly. Next, the second circle of Young Yin switches from Yang to Yin, giving rise to Old Yin, which is a purely Yin state. Then the first circle of Old Yin switches from Yin to Yang, giving Young Yang, a mixed state where Yang starts to manifest itself.

The cycle of change is completed when the second circle of Young Yang switches from Yin to Yang to give back Old Yang, the purely Yang state. These four states take turn to appear, one replacing the other, and the same cycle keeps repeating itself ad infinitum.

Two best known examples of the Four Temporal States are:
1. The four stages of life: Birth and young age is Young Yang, early adulthood is Old Yang, middle age is Young Yin, old age and death is Old Yin.

2. The four seasons: Spring is Young Yang, Summer is Old Yang, Autumn is Young Yin, and Winter is Old Yin.

In the traditional Yin Yang theory, the Four Temporal States are called "The Four Symbols." Since "Four Symbols" is not a very descriptive name, we prefer "The Four Temporal States."

Implications of the Four Temporal States on world affairs

The Four Temporal States have great implications when we apply them to world affairs. Take a civilization, for example. According to the logic of the Four Temporal States, no matter how glorious a civilization is, it will eventually crumble when the time of Old-Yin comes. In the subsequent stage of Young Yang, such a civilization either goes through a renaissance (and then eventually crumbles again), or it will disappear to leave room for another civilization (which will achieve its height at Old Yang, degenerate at Young Yin, and crumble at Old Yin.) The same with ideologies. Even the teaching of a "perfect" sage will eventually be badly misunderstood, forgotten, forsaken, or even abused.

In fact, the Four Temporal States applies to all developments in the universe. It tells us that all states of existence in this universe are transitional and temporary. That is because existence is the manifestation of Yin and Yang, which are themselves impermanent.

The Four Spatial States and the Four Elements

If we ignore time and only concern ourselves with space, we will notice that each Yin Yang circle corresponds to only one point in the traverse plane (i.e., the plane perpendicular to the direction of motion).

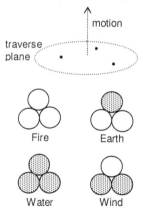

Fig 2: Each Yin Yang circle represents only a single point in the traverse plane. Since it takes 3 points to define a plane (i.e., two dimensions), it takes three Yin Yang circles to complete the description of space, giving the Four Spatial States.

The Four Spatial States are Yin Yang states that would not be affected by time. They are perfect Yin Yang descriptions of the Four Elements, believed by old western philosophy to be the building blocks of the universe. Interestingly, the Buddha also referred frequently to the "Four Agents," which are also Water, Earth, Wind, and Fire.

Since it takes three points to define a plane, it takes three Yin Yang circles to complete the description of space. Since the two dimensions x and y are equivalent there are only four distinguishable spatial states, which we will call "The Four Spatial States":

1. Three Yang circles.
2. Two Yang and 1 Yin circles.
3. Two Yin and 1 Yang circles.
4. Three Yin circles.

The proper geometrical presentation of each of the Four Spatial States is a set of three contacting circles as this is the only arrangement that possesses a sense of a unit and has no preferred direction in the x-y plane.

Readers who have some familiarity with the old western theory of the Four Elements will notice the perfect correspondence between the Four Spatial States and the Four Elements. This fact allows us to use the Yin Yang theory to establish the validity as well as the inherent limits of the pseudo-science of western astrology, which is based completely on the Four Elements. Regrettably, the writer must refrain himself and delay this exciting topic until a more appropriate opportunity presents itself in the future.

Yin Yang logic of the eight trigrams

We are now ready to solve one of the most baffling puzzles of the Yin Yang theory. As we all know, the building blocks of the Yin Yang theory are the eight trigrams, each with three Yin Yang lines. The question is, why 3 lines? Why not stopping at the Four States (with 2 Yin Yang lines)? If the reason for not choosing 2 lines is because 2 is not enough, then why is 3 enough? Why not 4 lines, 5 lines, 6 lines, 7 lines, etc.?

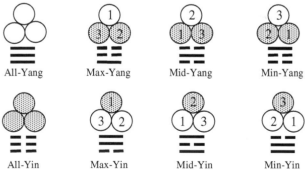

Fig 3: The eight trigrams with proposed new names. Following convention, the time order of the circles is chosen to be clockwise and that of the lines from bottom to top. The reader is advised to become familiar at least with the convention of the line order, as this is the convention used in the I-Ching.

Some of the traditional answers are:
1. "Because 3 is the number for Yang, where everything originates from."
2. "Because space has 3 dimensions."
3. "Because 3 stands for the three sacred positions in Chinese philosophy: Heaven, Earth, and Man."

The problem is that none of these three qualifies as a scientific answer. Therefore we have to look for a new logic.

Fortunately, the new logic can be derived by simply putting the existing pieces together. Since real-life existence must take place within the frame of space and time, the correct Yin Yang description for existence is obtained by combining the logic of the Four Temporal States and that of the Four Spatial States. This means:
1. Three contacting circles are required to describe a Yin Yang entity.
2. A time direction is required to describe the existence of a Yin Yang entity.

Since time flows in only one direction, this combination gives rise to exactly 8 combinations. The reader will recognize immediately that these are the eight trigrams (see figure 3).

While our reasoning is very short, its theoretical value should not be underestimated, because this is the first time ever that the 8 trigrams are shown to be legitimate scientific entities.

The completeness of the 8 trigrams

The 8 trigrams contain all elements of space and time:
1. The complementary relationship between time and the spatial dimension of motion (direction of change) is contained in the Yin and Yang qualities of the circles.
2. The equality of the other two spatial dimensions (in the plane perpendicular to the direction of change) is contained in the spatially equivalent configuration of the three circles.
3. The time duration (required for existence) is contained in the direction of time that connects the three circles.

Since all meaningful entities in the universe must manifest themselves within the domain of space and time, the eight trigrams are the complete set of all entities in the universe. Thus, all entities, from a simple photon to a complex organization or even the whole universe can be understood in terms of the logic of the 8 trigrams. This makes the Yin Yang theory a complexity theory that can be applied to all real-life phenomena. And most remarkably, it achieves this very general goal with just 8 building blocks!

But we are still a long way from being able to declare that the Yin Yang theory is a complete scientific theory. The reader may be surprised to learn that no Yin Yang masters of today can offer a coherent explanation for the meanings of the 8 trigrams. In fact, it is not an exaggeration to say that there is no coherent understanding whatsoever in any part of the Yin Yang theory. Starting with the next chapter, we will try to rectify this situation.

First written April 2002
Completed June 2002
©T. Tran

SPECIAL SECTION
Settling the Young Yin & Young Yang disagreement

Yin Yang scholars are split equally when it comes to line notations for Young Yang and Young Yin. In the body text of this chapter, we presented Young Yang and Young Yin as:

Young Yang   Young Yin

Fig 1: Young Yang and Young Yin according to this book.

This is only one of two schools. The other school would switch everything around, like figure 2. We will call these the alternative notations:

Young Yang   Young Yin

Fig 2: Alternative notations for Young Yang and Young Yin.

Our goal is to show that the notations that we proposed make more sense.

We will choose Old Yang for the starting point. Old Yang has two Yang lines, the bottom line formed at time t_0, the top at time t_1, which is later than t_0. It is clear that the line formed at time t_0 is the one that switches when Old Yang becomes Young Yin. Let the time of the switch be t_2. The thinking that led to the alternative notation is shown in figure 3A. The bottom line is (correctly) taken as the line that will be switched. The problem is, the newly formed line (Yin) is allowed to replace (the switched line) at the bottom, which violates the time convention (older line at bottom, newer line on top).

The corrected sequence is shown in figure 3B, starting with Old Yang having 2 Yang lines formed at time t_0 and t_1 respectively.

At time t_2, when Old Yang becomes Young Yin the Yang line formed at time t_0 must disappear to leave room for a new Yin line. The situation for Young Yin then is:

Yang line formed at time t_1

Yin line (newly) formed at time t_2

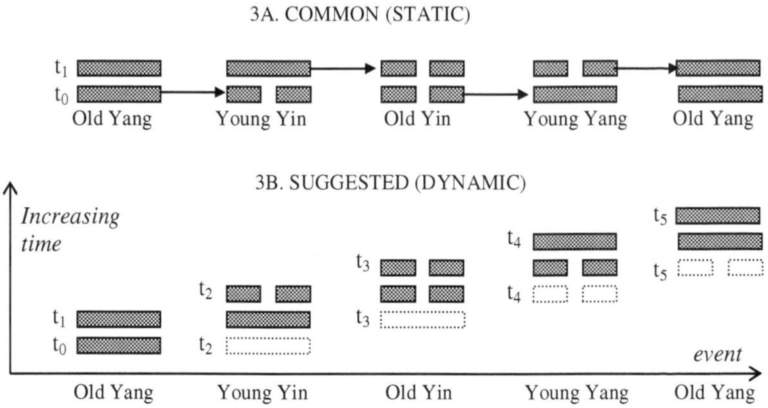

3A. COMMON (STATIC)

3B. SUGGESTED (DYNAMIC)

Fig 3: The sequence that leads to the alternative notations for Young Yin and Young Yang is shown in 3A (top). The sequence that leads to the notations used in this book is shown in 3B (bottom).

Since t_2 happens after t_1, by the time convention the Yin line (formed at time t_2) must be the top line, the Yang line (formed at time t_1) must be the bottom line. We conclude therefore that the top line of Young Yin is Yin, and its bottom line Yang, not the other way around (as in the alternative notations).

By default, the top line of Young Yang has to be Yang, and its bottom line Yin.

This so-called "Young Yin / Young Yang" controversy has been around for as long as the Yin Yang theory itself. While this controversy has only academic value, its presence is a bad sign, pointing to the possibility that the Yin Yang theory is incomplete. Hopefully we have just settled this issue once and for all!

Chapter 4

Logic of the eight trigrams II

Solution to the "Former and Later Heaven" puzzle

Trigrams of Former Heaven and Later Heaven

In the last chapter we have solved one mystery of the Yin Yang theory by explaining why the building blocks of the theory consist of exactly 3 lines, not 2 or 4 or 5 or 6. In this chapter we will solve the next great mystery: The differentiation of trigrams of Former Heaven and Later Heaven.

"Former Heaven" and "Later Heaven" are literal English translations from original Chinese words. According to prevailing Yin Yang theory, there are two sets of trigrams. "Former Heaven trigrams" according to Fu Hsi, "Later Heaven trigrams" according to King Wen. With the naming system proposed earlier in this book, these are:

TABLE 1: Two trigram classifications

Trigram		Former Heaven	Later Heaven*
All-Yang	☰	Yang	Yang
Max-Yang		Yang	Yang
Mid-Yang		Yin	Yang
Min-Yang		Yin	Yang
All-Yin		Yin	Yin
Max-Yin		Yin	Yin
Mid-Yin		Yang	Yin
Min-Yin		Yang	Yin

*Note: Naming system agrees with Later Heaven classification

The alert reader may have noted from table 1 that Mid-Yang and Min-Yang are Yin in Former Heaven but Yang in Later Heaven, Mid-Yin and Min-Yin are Yang in Former Heaven but Yin in Later Heaven. These Yin Yang switches between the two Heavens have been a source of great confusion, even to Yin Yang experts. Some of the (unsatisfactory) explanations are:

1. (It is explained that) As the names imply, Former Heaven should occur before Later Heaven; thus (it is believed that) Former Heaven trigrams are the trigrams as created, Later Heaven trigrams are the trigrams as applied to life.

2. (It is explained that) Former Heaven signifies "Form" (such as a knife), Later Heaven signifies "Utility" (such as the particular usage of a knife). Thus (it is believed that) the trigrams take

29

their forms in Former Heaven, and their utilities are manifested in Later Heaven.

In addition to being vague, these explanations are not even useful. Adding to the confusion, there exist two trigram orders also named "Former Heaven" and "Later Heaven." Since these two orders are not relevant to our understanding of the I-Ching, the writer has decided to present his explanation for them in another book in the future.

On the other hand, as it will become clear later, a scientific investigation of the I-Ching is impossible without a thorough understanding of Former Heaven and Later Heaven trigram classifications. Our immediate objective, therefore, is to find the solution to this great mystery of the Yin Yang theory.

Three binary properties of the trigrams

Anyone who reviews the various explanations for Former Heaven and Later Heaven trigrams will discover that they all assume that a trigram can only be either Yin or Yang, but never both.

At a quick glance, this assumption seems to make sense as it appears paradoxical for a trigram to be both Yin and Yang at the same time.

But common sense also tells us that a trigram must be more complex than a single line; because if a trigram can only be Yin or Yang, then how can we say that it is different from a single line? In brief, the Yin Yang characteristic of a trigram must be more complex than the simple "Yin or Yang" binary choices of a single line.

Let's start with a single line. A single line can only have two cases. We can say that it has only one property, and this property has two values Yin and Yang. By adding the second line we get the Four Symbols, which we covered in the last chapter. If each symbol must be either Yin or Yang, then by symmetry there have to be 2 Yin symbols and 2 Yang symbols. We do have two Yin symbols "Young Yin" and "Old Yin," and two Yang symbols "Young Yang" and "Old Yang." But is "Young Yin" exactly the same as "Old Yin"? Is "Young Yang" exactly the same as "Old Yang"? The obvious answer is No. More clearly, Old Yin is "more Yin" than Young Yin, and Old Yang "more Yang" than Young Yang. Therefore it is incomplete to describe each symbol simply as "Yin" or "Yang."

The solution is simple: Each member of the Four Symbols must have two Yin-Yang properties. The first property has two values "Yin" and "Yang," the second "Less" (Yin) and "More" (Yang). In other words, two Yin-Yang properties are required to fully describe the Four Symbols.

Extending the argument to the case of the trigrams, each trigrams must have three Yin-Yang properties, which we will temporarily refer to as properties 1, 2, and 3.

TABLE 2: Generic properties of the trigrams

Trigram's Yin-Yang	Property 1	Property 2	Property 3
(Yang, Yang, Yang)	Yang	Yang	Yang
(Yang, Yang, Yin)	Yang	Yang	Yin
(Yin, Yang, Yang)	Yin	Yang	Yang
(Yin, Yang, Yin)	Yin	Yang	Yin
(Yin, Yin, Yang)	Yin	Yin	Yang
(Yin, Yin, Yin)	Yin	Yin	Yin
(Yang, Yin, Yang)	Yang	Yin	Yang
(Yang, Yin, Yin)	Yang	Yin	Yin

Trigram magnitudes

Recall that each circle in a trigram represents a moment in time, with the first circle occurring first and the last circle occurring last. A trigram, then, is like a snap shot of the 3 circles after the last one has come to existence.

Let's examine the Yang and Yin snap shots with the aid of figure 1. Since Yang represents increases, its reference point (Yang = 0) is the lowest point of the curve. Likewise, since Yin represents decreases; its reference point (Yin = 0) is the highest point of the curve.

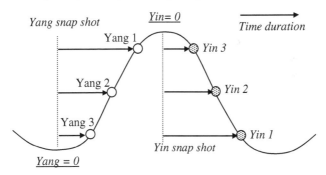

Fig 1: Yang (increases) can be divided in two three stages with respect to time duration (1 has largest duration). The same with Yin (decreases).

When the Yang snap shot is taken, due to the time difference, the last Yang circle (Yang 3) is still near the bottom, while the first Yang circle (Yang 1) has climbed almost to the top of the curve. We say that Yang 3 is least Yang, Yang 1 is most Yang, and Yang 2 intermediate.

Similarly, by examining the Yin snap shot we find the last Yin circle (Yin 3) is very close to the top of the curve, while the first Yin circle (Yin 1) has dropped close to the bottom. We say that Yin 3 is least Yin, Yin 1 is most Yin, and Yin 2 intermediate.

Each circle in a trigram carries an essence (Yin or Yang). The intimate contacts make each circle a member of a three-circle team *without losing its Yin Yang essence.* This point is extremely important, as many beginning students of the Yin Yang theory tend to assume that Yin and Yang, when combined, would cancel each other out. To see why this assumption is erroneous, imagine putting a good person and a bad person in the same team. Sometimes the bad person will get his way, and sometimes the good person will get his. In the long run the good and the bad outcomes of this team may average out, but the good and the bad elements always co-exist.

A trigram with one Yin and two Yang circles is similar to a divided team with one member on the Yin side and two members on the Yang side. This does not necessarily mean that the Yang side, by sheer number, will overwhelm the Yin side. The analogy can be drawn directly from life. When all other factors are more or less equal, the majority will certainly dominate; but a weak majority will be dominated by the so-called movers and shakers, who are always a minority.

When a team is divided, the dominant side will win and their opinion emerges as the opinion of the group while the opinion of the weaker side is ignored. Similarly, since Yin and Yang are mutually exclusive of each other, the dominant essence represents the trigram while the recessive essence is suppressed.

Internal conflicts weaken the effectiveness of a team when it faces the external environment. We deduce therefore that All-Yang and All-Yin are the most effective of the trigrams, as they are the only two trigrams that have only one essence and therefore are free of internal Yin-Yang conflicts. Moreover, since there is no logic to support the idea that Yang is more effective than Yin or vice versa, All-Yang and All-Yin must be considered as being equally effective.

To facilitate further discussion, we will assign the following "Yin Yang magnitudes" to the circles according to their essence and order of occurrence:

First Yang:	$F1 > 0$
Second Yang:	$F2 > 0$
Third Yang:	$F3 > 0$
First Yin:	$-F1 < 0$
Second Yin:	$-F2 < 0$
Third Yin:	$-F3 < 0$

With the side condition that came from the order of time duration:
F1 > F2 > F3

The first two properties of the trigrams

A lengthy but straight forward argument (Special Section I at the end of this chapter) gives us the first property of the trigrams, based on their overall algebraic values:

Yin = Overall algebraic sign of the trigram is negative.

Yang = Overall algebraic sign of the trigram is positive.

To make the theory more accessible, we will replace "Yin" and "Yang" by more descriptive qualities. Since the first property is based on the algebraic values of the trigrams, we will call Yin "negative" and Yang "positive."

FIRST PROPERTY *(based on overall algebraic value)*
Negative: All-Yin (least negative) > Mid-Yang > Min-Yang > Max-Yin.
Positive: All-Yang (least positive) < Mid-Yin < Min-Yin < Max-Yang.

Another argument (Special Section II at the end of this chapter) gives us the second property, based on the number of Yin or Yang circles:

Yin = Containing odd number of Yin circles (1 or 3)

Yang = Containing odd number of Yang circles (1 or 3)

We will replace the generic qualities "Yin" and "Yang" of the second property by "Feminine" and "Masculine" for reasons that will be clear later:

SECOND PROPERTY *(based on the number of Yin or Yang circles)*
Feminine: All-Yin (3), Max-Yin (1), Mid-Yin (1), Min-Yin (1)
Masculine: All-Yang (3), Max-Yang (1), Mid-Yang (1), Min-Yang (1)

Solution to the Former Heaven – Later Heaven trigram puzzle

The following table lists the two properties we have just derived:

TABLE 3: Activity and identity properties of the trigrams

Trigram		Property 1	Property 2*
All-Yang	☰	Positive *(Yang)*	Masculine *(Yang)*
Max-Yang	☱	Positive *(Yang)*	Masculine *(Yang)*
Mid-Yang	☲	Negative *(Yin)*	Masculine *(Yang)*
Min-Yang	☳	Negative *(Yin)*	Masculine *(Yang)*
All-Yin	☷	Negative *(Yin)*	Feminine *(Yin)*
Max-Yin	☶	Negative *(Yin)*	Feminine *(Yin)*
Mid-Yin	☵	Positive *(Yang)*	Feminine *(Yin)*
Min-Yin	☴	Positive *(Yang)*	Feminine *(Yin)*

*Note: Naming system agrees with property 2

33

For reference purposes, we re-list table 1:
TABLE 1: Two trigram classifications

Trigram		Former Heaven	Later Heaven*
All-Yang	☰	Yang	Yang
Max-Yang	☱	Yang	Yang
Mid-Yang	☲	Yin	Yang
Min-Yang	☳	Yin	Yang
All-Yin	☷	Yin	Yin
Max-Yin	☶	Yin	Yin
Mid-Yin	☵	Yang	Yin
Min-Yin	☴	Yang	Yin

*Note: Naming system agrees with Later Heaven classification

The amazing fact is, property 1 of table 3 matches the Former Heaven classification of table 1 exactly. Likewise, property 2 of table 3 matches the Later Heaven classification of table 1 exactly!

Former Heaven = Property 1
Later Heaven = Property 2

Property 1 is based completely on the first line of the hexagram (Yang = first line Yang, Yin = first line Yin). Since the first line is the first one to appear in a hexagram, the name *Former Heaven* is very appropriate.

Property 2 is based on the essence that appears in odd number (1 line or 3 lines). Since this can only be determined after all 3 lines have appeared, the name *Later Heaven* is also appropriate.

Thus, we have finally solved the three-thousand-year-old Former Heaven – Later Heaven trigram classification puzzle and spared future generations the confusion that it may create. *Former Heaven and Later Heaven* are simply two properties of the eight trigrams, not two sets of trigrams or two situation-dependent properties as alleged in many existing teachings of the Yin Yang theory.

Property 1 as trigram "activity"

Depending on time order, the same one-Yin two-Yang combination could be Max-Yin (order 123, bottom left of figure 2), or Mid-Yin (order 312), or Min-Yin (order 231); and the same one-Yang two-Yin combination could be Max-Yang (order 123, top left of figure 2), or Mid-Yang (order 312), or Min-Yang (order 231).

Imagine 4 males, one in his early teens, one in his late teens or early twenties, one in his late twenties or early thirties, and one in his forties or fifties. Because of the age factor, each male would tend to assume a different level of activity. The male in his early teens tends to be very tentative because his family still has a strong influence on him. The male in his late teens or early twenties is in his transition period with many decisions to make. While one of his feet is still in the family, his other foot is in the society. Most likely he will be somewhat tentative, but less so compared to the first male. The male in his late twenties or early thirties is completely free to exercise his potential. He would tend to overcompensate by being too active. The male in his forties or fifties has gone through all developmental stages of life. Experience taught him that he has to optimize his actions to achieve the best results. He would be active, but less so compared to the third male. (Not surprisingly, we will find out that females tend to develop differently, but that detail is saved for another book dedicated to the Yin Yang theory.)

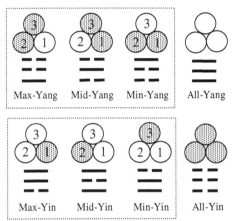

Fig 2: The eight trigrams with proposed new names. Note that Max-Yang, Mid-Yang, Min-Yang are three permutations of one Yang two Yin. On the other hand, Max-Yin, Mid-Yin, Min-Yin are permutations of two Yang one Yin.

These examples tell us that property 1 is a measure of the activity level taken by a trigram; therefore we will call it the "activity property."

Property 2 as trigram "identity"

If the time factor is ignored, Max-Yang, Mid-Yang, and Min-Yang will appear identical because each trigram has one Yang and two Yin circles. Max-Yin, Mid-Yin, and Min-Yin will appear identical because each trigram has one Yin and two Yang circles.

Return to the example of the four males. Regardless of age they have the same identity of "being male." Thus, "being male" is the inherent "identity" of these 4 persons. By analogy, since property 2 only depends on the number of Yin and Yang circles in a trigram regardless of time order, it gives us the timeless "identity" of the trigrams. For this reason, we will call property 2 the "identity property" or simply the "identity" of the trigrams.

The "minority rule" of the identity property

It is interesting to note that except for All-Yang and All-Yin, the identity is decided by the essence in the minority, not the majority. This is the well-known but intriguing "minority rule" of the Yin Yang theory. (All-Yang and All-Yin are exceptions to the minority rule, but that is because the minority/majority differentiation is meaningless for both of them.)

Real-life applications of the identity property

While the Yin Yang theory applies to all existence, its most important application to date is the I-Ching, which is a treatise on human interactions. We are therefore interested in applying the identity property specifically to the set of human beings.

The only significant factor that decides the identity of a newborn baby is its sex organ. The male sex organ suggests excess and is therefore Masculine, the female sex organ suggests deficiency and is therefore Feminine. The sex organ is only the most recognizable indicator of an encompassing dichotomy that develops into differences in body shape, body size, physical strength, endurance, psychological perceptions, and many other parameters that combine to give each individual a very strong sense of identity.

It is expected, therefore, that gender is the most dominant identity in the set of human beings. Keep in mind, however, that being dominant is not the same as being exclusive. In their interactions people may perceive Feminine/Masculine identity in many different ways, depending on, among other things, their own experience and immediate situation. For example, a homosexual couple may perceive each other as having Feminine and Masculine identities respectively in their romantic relationship, though both are of the same sex.

The best way to determine human identity, therefore, is to determine the roles played by the respective individuals or groups *in a given situation*. It is true in most cases, however, that "being female" and "being male" are the same as the two identities (Feminine/Masculine) for the set of human beings.

Before leaving this section, we must re-emphasize that the Yin Yang theory is the only theory that anticipates the existence of males and females; while all other theories miss this very obvious reality and have to account for it after the fact.

Real-life application of the activity property

We will be very careful in choosing words to describe the Yin Yang states of the activity property. While the easiest choice is to keep Yin = passive, Yang = active, the word "passive" has bad connotation and therefore may give the false feeling that the negative trigrams are somehow inferior to the positive trigrams. We will therefore choose Yin (negative activity) = tentative, Yang (positive activity) = aggressive as these two words are relatively neutral.

TABLE 4: Identity and activity properties

Trigram		Activity	Identity
All-Yang	☰	Aggressive	Masculine
Max-Yang		Aggressive	Masculine
Mid-Yang		Tentative	Masculine
Min-Yang		Tentative	Masculine
All-Yin	☷	Tentative	Feminine
Max-Yin		Tentative	Feminine
Mid-Yin		Aggressive	Feminine
Min-Yin		Aggressive	Feminine

From table 4, we see that a woman (whose dominant identity is usually "being feminine") could be aggressive (positive activity), while a man could be tentative (negative activity). This dispels a misconception that has been perpetrated for many centuries, that –as a general rule- women are passive and men are active. We know that this rule is not correct, as life teaches us that there are very active women and very passive men.

We still need to determine one more property to complete our understanding of the eight trigrams. This will be done in the next chapter.

First written April 2002
Completed June 2002
©T. Tran

SPECIAL SECTION I
The first property of the trigrams

To facilitate further discussion, we will assign the following "Yin Yang magnitudes" to the lines according to their essence and order of occurrence:

First Yang: $F1 > 0$
Second Yang: $F2 > 0$
Third Yang: $F3 > 0$
First Yin: $-F1 < 0$
Second Yin: $-F2 < 0$
Third Yin: $-F3 < 0$

With the side condition:

$$F1 > F2 > F3 \qquad (1a)$$

Recall that both Yin and Yang are imbalanced states. Imbalance leads to inefficiency. It follows that the effectiveness of a trigram runs in reverse of its overall magnitude.

Being the most effective trigrams, All-Yang and All-Yin must be the least imbalanced (with equivalent magnitudes of opposite algebraic signs). Quantitatively, the overall magnitudes for Yin and Yang must be closer to zero than those of the other six trigrams. The reader can verify that the only way for this to work is to define the overall magnitude of a trigram as the average (linear average or geometrical average) of individual magnitudes of the dominant essence.

We know from arithmetic:

Linear average of A and B = $(A+B)/2$. Linear average of A, B, and C = $(A+B+C)/3$

Geometrical average of A and B = $(AB)^{1/2}$. Geometrical average of A, B, and C = $(ABC)^{1/3}$

Since our only interest is to rank the trigrams, we will choose linear averages to simplify matters. The reader can verify that geometrical averages will lead to the same conclusions. The rule is that if the average Yang magnitude is larger than the average Yin magnitude, the dominant essence is Yang; and if the reverse is true, the dominant essence is Yin.

Working out the arithmetic we obtain the following results:

All-Yang   ≡≡≡
$F(+)$ $= (F1+F2+F3)/3$
$F(-)$ $= 0$
$F= F(+)$ > 0 (positive)

Max-Yang   ≡ ≡
$F(+)$ $= F1 > (F2+F3)/2$
$F(-)$ $= -(F2+F3)/2$
$F= F(+)$ > 0 (positive)

Mid-Yang   ≡≡
$F(+)$ $= F2$
$F(-)$ $= -(F1+F3)/2$

If $(F1+F3)/2 < F2$, then $F = F(+) > 0$ (positive)
If $(F1+F3)/2 > F2$, then $F = F(-) < 0$ (negative)

Min-Yang　☲☲
  $F(+)$　$= F3$
  $F(-)$　$= -(F1+F2)/2$
  $F = F(-) < 0$ (negative)

All-Yin　☷☷
  $F(+)$　$= 0$
  $F(-)$　$= -(F1+F2+F3)/3$
  $F = F(-) < 0$ (negative)

Max-Yin　☶☶
  $F(+)$　$= (F2+F3)/2$
  $F(-)$　$= -F1$
  $F = F(-) < 0$ (negative)

Mid-Yin　☵☵
  $F(+)$　$= (F1+F3)/2$
  $F(-)$　$= -F2$
  If $(F1+F3)/2 < F2$, then $F = F(-) < 0$ (negative)
  If $(F1+F3)/2 > F2$, then $F = F(+) > 0$ (positive)

Min-Yin　☳☳
  $F(+)$　$= (F1+F2)/2 > F3$
  $F(-)$　$= -F3$
  $F = F(+) > 0$ (positive)

From the calculations above, we get the following algebraic order, listing top down from most positive to most negative:

TABLE 1A: Algebraic magnitudes of the trigrams

POSITIVE	Dominant side	Recessive side
Max-Yang *(most positive)*	F1	$-(F2+F3)/2$
Min-Yin	$(F1+F2)/2$	$-F3$
(Mid-Yin or Mid-Yang)	$(F1+F3)/2$ or F2	$-F2$ or $-(F1+F3)/2$
All-Yang	$(F1+F2+F3)/3$	0
NEGATIVE		
All-Yin	$-(F1+F2+F3)/3$	0
(Mid-Yang or Mid-Yin)	$-(F1+F3)/2$ or $-F2$	F2 or $(F1+F3)/2$
Min-Yang	$-(F1+F2)/2$	F3
Max-Yin *(most negative)*	$-F1$	$(F2+F3)/2$

At this point the algebraic signs of Mid-Yang and Mid-Yin are still unclear. We have to consider two possible cases:

CASE 1: $(F1+F3)/2 < F2$

TABLE 2A: Algebraic magnitudes of the trigrams if $(F1+F3)/2 < F2$

Positive	Dominant essence	Recessive essence
Max-Yang (positive)	F1	-(F2+F3)/2
Min-Yin	(F1+F2)/2	-F3
Mid-Yang	F2	-(F1+F3)/2
All-Yang	(F1+F2+F3)/3	0
Negative		
All-Yin	-(F1+F2+F3)/3	0
Mid-Yin	-F2	(F1+F3)/2
Min-Yang	-(F1+F2)/2	F3
Max-Yin (most negative)	-F1	(F2+F3)/2

POSITIVE	All-Yang	Mid-Yang	Min-Yin	Max-Yang

NEGATIVE	All-Yin	Mid-Yin	Min-Yang	Max-Yin

CASE 2: $(F1+F3)/2 > F2$

TABLE 3A: Algebraic magnitudes of the trigrams if $(F1+F3)/2 > F2$

Positive	Dominant essence	Recessive essence
Max-Yang (positive)	F1	-(F2+F3)/2
Min-Yin	(F1+F2)/2	-F3
Mid-Yin	(F1+F3)/2	-F2
All-Yang	(F1+F2+F3)/3	0
Negative		
All-Yin	-(F1+F2+F3)/3	0
Mid-Yang	-(F1+F3)/2	F2
Min-Yang	-(F1+F2)/2	F3
Max-Yin (most negative)	-F1	(F2+F3)/2

POSITIVE	All-Yang	Mid-Yin	Min-Yin	Max-Yang

NEGATIVE	All-Yin	Mid-Yang	Min-Yang	Max-Yin

Comparing case 1 against case 2, counting from the bottom:

1. First line: Three Yang one Yin for case 1 positive, three Yin one Yang for case 1 negative. Four Yang no Yin for case 2 positive, four Yin no Yang for case 2 negative. *Conclusion: The first line is consistent with the positive/negative distinction of the 8 trigrams.*

2. Second line: Three Yang one Yin for case 1 positive, three Yin one Yang for case 1 negative. Two Yang two Yin for case 2 positive, two

Yin two Yang for case 2 negative. *Conclusion: Case 2 possesses Yin Yang symmetry, case 1 does not.*

3. Third line: Three Yin one Yang for case 1 positive, three Yang one Yin for case 1 negative. Two Yang two Yin for case 2 positive, two Yin two Yang for case 2 negative. *Conclusion: Case 2 possesses Yin Yang symmetry, case 1 does not.*

4. First line and second line together: For case 1, positive and negative each has 3 distinct combinations, with one combination occurring twice, the other two each occurring once. For case 2, positive and negative each has 2 distinct combinations, with each combination occurring twice. *Conclusion: Case 2 possesses Yin Yang symmetry, case 1 does not.*

5. First line and third line together: For case 1, positive and negative each has 3 distinct combinations, with one combination occurring twice, the other two each occurring once. For case 2, positive and negative each has 2 distinct combinations, with each combination occurring twice. *Conclusion: Case 2 possesses Yin Yang symmetry, case 1 does not.*

6. Second line and third line together: For case 1, positive and negative each has 3 distinct combinations, with one combination occurring twice, the other two each occurring once. For case 2, positive and negative each has 4 distinct combinations, without any repeat at all. *Conclusion: Case 1 is more asymmetric than case 2. Another way to look at this is: case 2 is more symmetrical than case 1.*

It is a well known fact that Nature prefers symmetry; so if we have to choose between two otherwise equal descriptions of Nature, the clear choice is the more symmetrical one. We conclude therefore that Case 2 is the correct description. It follows that $(F1+F3)/2 > F2$.

This allows us to update table 1A to get table 4A:

TABLE 4A: Algebraic magnitudes of the trigrams

POSITIVE	Dominant side	Recessive side
Max-Yang *(most positive)*	F1	$-(F2+F3)/2$
Min-Yin	$(F1+F2)/2$	$-F3$
Mid-Yin	$(F1+F3)/2$	$-F2$
All-Yang	$(F1+F2+F3)/3$	0
NEGATIVE		
All-Yin	$-(F1+F2+F3)/3$	0
Mid-Yang	$-(F1+F3)/2$	F2
Min-Yang	$-(F1+F2)/2$	F3
Max-Yin *(most negative)*	$-F1$	$(F2+F3)/2$

By inspection, we immediately recognize that trigrams are divided into two equivalent groups according to their magnitudes, and the binary difference is their algebraic signs. This gives us the first binary property: Positive vs. Negative.

"Being positive" and "being negative" constitute the first property of the trigrams. This property indicates the "activity property" of the trigrams. The reasons for the name "activity property" are cited in the main text of this chapter.

SPECIAL SECTION II
The second property of the trigrams

Since Yin and Yang values correspond to decreases and increases, the first property reflects the (dominant) cumulative changes of the hexagram. But changes with respect to what? A reference point, of course. Unfortunately, the reference point of Yin and Yang is a subjective choice. As far as any observer is concerned, the reference point is where there is neither Yin nor Yang. The cumulative changes, then, are subjectively perceived to be the Yin Yang deviation from zero.

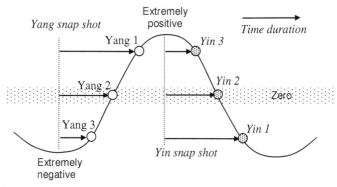

Fig 1A: Yang (increases) can be divided in two three stages with respect to time duration (1 has largest duration). The same with Yin (decreases).

Figure 1 in the body text has been redrawn as figure 1A. The Yin Yang deviations are:

TABLE 1A: Yin Yang deviation and minority line

Single line	Deviation	Similar to	Minority line
Yang 1	Positive	Max-Yang	Yang 1
Yang 2	Close to zero	Mid-Yang	Yang 2
Yang 3	Negative	Min-Yang	Yang 3
Yin 1	Negative	Max-Yin	Yin 1
Yin 2	Close to zero	Mid-Yin	Yin 2
Yin 3	Positive	Min-Yin	Yin 3

The first two columns describe the situation of figure 1A. The third column is the trigram that has the same (qualitative) deviation as the single Yin or Yang line of column 1. The fourth column is the minority line in the trigram of column 3. We note the perfect agreement between column 1 and column 4. Thus, the minority line reflects the deviation of the whole trigram, as if it is standing alone as a single line.

42

In the clockwise direction arbitrarily chosen for time, the same set of one Yang and two Yin circles gives Max-Yang (order 123), Mid-Yang (order 312), and Min-Yang (order 231). We will call this group the "one Yang triplet." Since the three trigrams in the "one Yang triplet" are so similar, they must share at least one Yin Yang property. Similarly, the "one Yin triplet" must also share at least one Yin Yang property. The obvious suggestion from table 1A is that, if we call this property 2, then property 2 for the "one Yang triplet" is Yang, and for the "one Yin triplet" is Yin.

If we switch one circle from Yin to Yang, a trigram in the "one Yang triplet" will be switched to a trigram in the "one Yin triplet." This is a switch from Yang to Yin, and it is caused by a one-circle switch. It logically follows that, since the switch of the only Yang circle in the "one Yang triplet" to Yin is also a one-circle switch, the resulting trigram should also be Yin. Since the resulting circle is All-Yin, we conclude that the property 2 of All-Yin is Yin. By a similar argument, the property 2 of All-Yang is Yang.

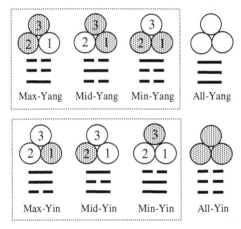

Fig 2A: The eight trigrams with proposed new names. Note that Max-Yang, Mid-Yang, Min-Yang are three permutations of one Yang two Yin. On the other hand, Max-Yin, Mid-Yin, Min-Yin are permutations of two Yang one Yin.

PROPERTY 2:
Yin: All-Yin, Max-Yin, Mid-Yin, Min-Yin
Yang: All-Yang, Max-Yang, Mid-Yang, Min-Yang

The alert reader will notice that the proposed naming system was chosen in anticipation of property 2 (the second word of each name is also the "Yin Yang value" of the property in question.)

Property 2 is called the "identity property" of the trigrams because it gives the identity of the circle that, if standing alone, would have the same deviation as the trigram.

Chapter 5

Logic of the eight trigrams III

The ability property of the eight trigrams

Conventions for trigram names

For simplicity, from here on we will identify trigrams of masculine identity as masculine trigrams, trigrams with feminine identity as feminine trigrams. Thus, when we say All-Yang, Max-Yang, Mid-Yang, Min-Yang are masculine, we mean that the identity of each of these trigrams is masculine. Likewise, when we say All-Yin, Max-Yin, Mid-Yin, Min-Yin are feminine, we mean that the identity of each of these trigrams is feminine.

This convention happens to be in agreement with how trigrams are often referred to, without clear reasoning, in current Yin Yang literature.

As mentioned in the last chapter, positive trigrams will be called "aggressive" and negative trigrams "tentative." These choices are to avoid the bad connotations in the more familiar passive/active differentiation.

Figure 1: Trigrams classification according to activity and identity properties

The ability property of the trigrams

In the last chapter, we used the criterion of effectiveness to arrive at the conclusion that All-Yang and All-Yin, being the two most effective trigrams, must also be closest to the true center line, where the identity value is zero (neither Feminine nor Masculine). A lengthy but straightforward argument *(see Special Section at the end of this*

44

chapter) leads to the result that the third and last property of the trigrams is the "Ability Property," so named because it groups the 4 trigrams closest to zero magnitude as the "powerful group" or "power group," and the other 4 trigrams the "common group."

Since effectiveness is intimately linked to the ability to achieve success, the Ability property of the eight trigrams is associated with the potential to succeed. In this respect the power group (All-Yang, All-Yin, Mid-Yang, and Mid-Yin) outperforms the common group (Max-Yang, Max-Yin, Min-Yang, Min-Yin).

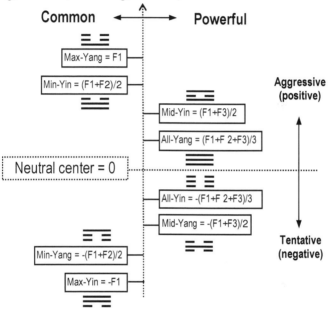

Figure 2: The third property divides the eight trigrams into the Powerful group and the Common group, each with 4 members.

Using distances from the center line as the yardstick, we rank the trigrams by their potential for success as follows:

Highest potential: All-Yang and All-Yin (most powerful)
High potential: Mid-Yang and Mid-Yin (powerful)
Low potential: Min-Yang and Min-Yin (common)
Lowest potential: Max-Yang and Max-Yin (most common)

Strength and limits of the Yin Yang theory

It is necessary to emphasize that, because Yin and Yang are measures of worldly existence, "success" must be interpreted strictly by its worldly meaning, which is usually but not always in agreement with social standards, and could be very subjective. For example, a poverty-stricken monk who has just achieved enlightenment without any one else's knowledge will most likely be considered a failure by all (ignorant) observers; while he alone knows that he is a success. Paradoxically, this kind of subjectivity makes the Yin Yang theory superior to the existing method of science –which is based on objectivity- when it comes to the investigation of human behavior. That is because subjective judgments, which could be either right or wrong, are used as the basis of decision making by all human beings.

On the other hand, the presence of subjectivity means that the Yin Yang theory can never go beyond the judging ability of the person or group of persons that applies it. This point has to be made so that we are aware of the limits of the Yin Yang theory and its applications such as the I-Ching. The Yin Yang theory can help us to live in harmony with the world, but only the world *as we perceive it to be*. Since our perception of the world could be wrong in many occasions, the Yin Yang theory falls short of the way of the saints or the Buddhas. It would be a big mistake to equate living in Yin Yang harmony with enlightenment.

Connections between trigram names and their three properties

In an earlier chapter we have come up with the following table to describe the three Yin-Yang properties of the trigrams in a generic way:

TABLE 1: Generic Yin-Yang properties of the trigrams

Trigram's Yin-Yang	A	B	C
(Yang, Yang, Yang)	Yang	Yang	Yang
(Yang, Yin, Yang)	Yang	Yin	Yang
(Yin, Yang, Yang)	Yin	Yang	Yang
(Yin, Yin, Yang)	Yin	Yin	Yang
(Yang, Yang, Yin)	Yang	Yang	Yin
(Yang, Yin, Yin)	Yang	Yin	Yin
(Yin, Yang, Yin)	Yin	Yang	Yin
(Yin, Yin, Yin)	Yin	Yin	Yin

By filling in the details, we get the following table:

TABLE 2: Detailed properties of the trigrams

Trigram's Yin-Yang		Activity	Ability	Identity
All-Yang	☰	Aggressive	Powerful	Masculine
Max-Yang	☱	Aggressive	Common	Masculine
Mid-Yang	☲	Tentative	Powerful	Masculine
Min-Yang	☳	Tentative	Common	Masculine

46

All-Yin	☷	Tentative	Powerful	Feminine
Max-Yin		Tentative	Common	Feminine
Mid-Yin		Aggressive	Powerful	Feminine
Min-Yin		Aggressive	Common	Feminine

The results are summarized graphically in figure 3, which shows all three properties. The reader is reminded that activity property (aggressive and tentative) is the intended meaning of "Former Heaven," identity property (Yang and Yin) is the intended meaning of "Later Heaven."

The advantage of the proposed naming system (as opposed to the traditional naming system) now becomes evident:

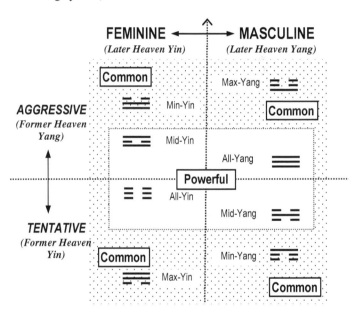

Figure 3: The activity property splits vertically (top/bottom for aggressive and tentative), the identity property horizontally (Feminine on left and Masculine on right), the ability property radially (Powerful inside and Common on the edges). Note that the activity property is the same as "Former Heaven" and the identity property the same as "Later Heaven."

1. The identity property is spelled out in the names. For example Max-Yang is Masculine, Min-Yin is Feminine.
2. With the convention Max = First circle (bottom line), Mid = Second circle (center line) and Min = Third circle (top line),

47

each name suggests the Yin Yang arrangement of the corresponding trigram. For example All-Yang indicates that all three circles (or lines) are Yang, Min-Yang indicates that the (main) Yang line occupies the Min position (i.e., top line), therefore the two Yin lines have to occupy the Mid position (center) and Max position (bottom).

3. From step 2 the essence of the first circle (bottom line) is known. This is the activity property of the trigram in question. For example, All-Yang must be positive (aggressive) because all three of its circles (or lines) are Yang, Min-Yang must be negative (tentative) because its first circle (bottom line) is Yin.

4. "Max" and "Min" are deviations from the center, therefore all trigrams with these prefixes are common trigrams (Yin ability). Moreover, "Max" suggests excess (which is considered very bad in Yin Yang theory) therefore "Max" implies lower potential than "Min."

5. "Mid" suggests the idea of a center, where power usually lies; therefore Mid-Yang and Mid-Yin are power trigrams (Yang ability). "All" suggests power (which is a major measure of success), therefore All-Yang and All-Yin are also power trigrams. Moreover, "All" suggests something stronger than "Mid," therefore "All" implies more power than "Mid."

The proposed naming system not only allows us to recognize trigram symbols (drawn as three Yin Yang lines) quickly, but also enables us to identify the three properties from either trigram symbols or trigram names. In other words, we can deduce all we need to know about a trigram once we know its symbol or its name. The proposed names are definitely more meaningful than the existing names, which are English approximations of the 8 original names in archaic Chinese (i.e., Chinese characters so old that they are incomprehensible even to the native Chinese of present time.)

More on the Activity Property (Aggressive vs. Tentative)

Our ultimate goal in this book is to approach the I-Ching scientifically. Since the I-Ching is a specific application of the Yin Yang theory to the set of human beings, we will need to expand our general knowledge to the specifics of human nature. When moving from the general to the specific, there is always the risk of misinterpretation. To minimize this risk, it is necessary to achieve a more in-depth understanding of the three properties.

When applied to the set of human beings, "Aggressive" and "Tentative" have been chosen to describe the activity property. In aggressive trigrams the Yang essence is dominant, while the Yin essence lies dormant (or is completely absence in the case of All-Yang). The reverse is true for tentative trigrams.

Aggressive trigrams represent individuals or groups that are action oriented and tend to react relatively quickly to changes. Tentative trigrams represent individuals or groups that are tentative in their actions and reactions.

Arguably the biggest difference between eastern thinking and western thinking is that the East leans strongly toward a tentative approach to life, while the West an aggressive approach. How or why the same human race, with supposedly similar goals, came up with these opposing approaches is a puzzling question that the writer will return to in a future book. For now it suffices to say that the existence of these approaches justifies our decision to describe the activity property by "aggressive" and "tentative."

More on the Identity Property (Feminine vs. Masculine)

We have mentioned in an earlier chapter that the Masculine identity usually means "being male," and the Feminine identity "being female." We also mentioned that there are exceptions to this rule. This is admittedly confusing. It is necessary, therefore, to find a logical method for the determination of the identity property.

As its name indicates, the identity property should be the most recognizable property of an entity. For this reason, the proper identity property is the first property that an objective observer would use to classify the entity in question in relation to other entity or entities. Since each situation tends to amplify a different side of the same entity, the identity property will be situation dependent.

Feminine identity usually means "female" and Masculine identity "male" because the biological difference between the two sexes is a real and significant one. Historically the world has always been plagued with violence, varying from large scale wars to individual disputes. In violent wars or physical confrontation between two persons, males are definitely masculine and females feminine as the condition makes physical strength a big factor. Even in peaceful times of the past, the constant threat of war was a good excuse for the males in power to place women below men. This excuse was effective because most victims would agree, albeit reluctantly, that the possibility of being humiliated or/and killed by brutal enemies is much worse than being mistreated by one's own kind. As long as wars could happen without notice and without reason, and as long as the rule for the losers is that all males might be executed and all females might have to serve the victors as sex slaves or house slaves; the social structure would force males to be masculine and females to be feminine with very few exceptions.

But the opinion of the world has changed. While there is no doubt that wars and violence will remain a fact of life, the human right movement has made it increasingly difficult for groups or nations to stage wars and for individuals to inflict injuries to their weaker fellow human beings. Although physical makeup is still a dominant factor, there are more and more situations where gender has no significant impact.

Since human beings tend to play out the roles that they choose or are assigned to them, when gender is not a factor, the key in determining the identity property is "role playing." Thus, on a dance floor in a gay bar, men that prefer to assume the female position are feminine, those who prefer the male position masculine. In daily interactions, the fragile looking but important senator is masculine while his huge but very replaceable bodyguards are feminine. When there is an assassination attempt the roles are switched, the senator - who must rely on his bodyguards to stay alive- becomes feminine while his bodyguards –with the ability to help their boss escape death— become masculine. When a female CEO gives orders to a group of male middle managers, she most likely will assume a masculine role while the managers the feminine role. The very last example was intentionally chosen to show that even in male/female interactions, it is possible for males to be feminine and females to be masculine.

With all that said and done, since it is very difficult psychologically to ignore the biological factor, we would seldom be wrong by "labeling" females as feminine and males as masculine.

The skeptical reader may ask "There are women who are physically stronger than average men, shouldn't these women be considered as masculine?" Objectively speaking, they should be. The problem is, the Yin Yang world is a subjective world. The biological factor makes it natural to group all men together as one group, all women together as another group; leading to the social norms of the "average man" and "average woman." Since the "average woman" is physically weaker than the "average man," a hasty generalization leads to the faulty conclusion that "all women are weaker than men." While this hasty generalization is faulty, it is very much how the human mind operates. This is the reason why when we are introduced to a woman for the first time, if the thought of comparing strength crosses our mind, we will automatically assume that she is physically weaker than most men (unless she wears a blackbelt or stands 7 feet). Thus, as we have stated earlier, women should be considered as feminine in most cases.

We will return to the identity property in a later chapter when our understanding of the trigrams is more complete. Readers who still find the subject confusing are asked to hold on to their questions until that time.

More on the Ability Property (Powerful vs. Common)

"Occupying the center" is one of the golden rules for success in life. This rule definitely works in real wars as well as simulated wars (that we call "games") played in a boxing ring, on a tennis court, on a football field, on a basketball court, on a pool table, on a chessboard, etc. It even works in the sacred game of romantic relationships.

The Ability property of the trigrams anticipates this reality. The four most effective trigrams (i.e. symmetrical trigrams) cluster around the center (of the property chart in figure 3), while the four less effective trigrams (asymmetrical) wander at the four edges.

An interesting question to ask at this point is, "Of the two approaches 'aggressive' and 'tentative' that respectively characterize the West and the East, which one has the higher potential for success?" Not quite unexpectedly, the Yin Yang answer is that they are equivalent in potential (each has two equivalent powerful trigrams and two equivalent common trigrams.)

Another amazing fact about the Yin Yang theory is that it can predict how each approach would affect the development of male and female members of the society. We will return to this topic later.

A personal thought on the three properties

While the usual interpretations of "Former Heaven trigrams" and "Later Heaven trigrams" –as passed down to us today- are erroneous, the very existence of these two classifications gives us good reasons to believe that they were fully understood (as activity and identity properties of the trigrams) at least at the beginning of the Yin Yang theory. For whatever reason or reasons, somehow the logic for the activity and identity properties was lost.

Serious students of the I-Ching will notice that The Book refers to the word "center" very frequently as an auspicious sign or a position of power. However, I-Ching discussions of "center" are very much limited to only the lines in the two trigrams that form a hexagram (line 2 of the lower trigram and line 5 of the upper trigram), and not the trigrams themselves. While everyone agrees that All-Yang and All-Yin are power trigrams, the other two power trigrams, namely Mid-Yang and Mid-Yin, have been put at the same level as the four common trigrams. This fact tells us that the logic of the Ability property was also lost.

51

With the clear understanding that, at some point in ancient time, the trigrams must have been correctly interpreted, the writer claims no originality in his analysis of the three properties and is greatly humbled by the opportunity to rediscover these incredible inventions by the Yin Yang sages of antiquity.

First written April 2002
Completed June 2002
©T. Tran

SPECIAL SECTION
The third trigram property

We already know of two trigram properties: The activity property, which happens to be based on the first line of the trigrams, and the identity property, which is based on the essence occurring in odd number.

There are 5 methods of binary division that have not been explored, each could qualify as the third property:

1. Binary division based on the 2nd line.
2. Binary division based on the 3rd line.
3. Binary division based on the 1st and 2nd lines.
4. Binary division based on the 1st and 3rd lines.
5. Binary division based on the 2nd and 3rd lines.

These 5 methods are presented in figures 1A through 5A. Methods 1 and 2 are immediately disqualified because, in each case, the sum of activities of the Yin group is positive while that of the Yang group negative. This contradicts the fundamental meaning of Yin and Yang. As a comparison, in the identity property, the activity sum of the Yang group is slightly positive and that of the Yin group is slightly negative.

In methods 3 through 5, the activity sum for both sides is exactly zero. However, we note that method 4 is the only one that classifies the trigrams by symmetry. In addition, the group of 4 trigrams that possess symmetry (i.e., All-Yang, All-Yin, Mid-Yang, Mid-Yin) cluster around the center, while the group of 4 trigrams that do not possess symmetry (i.e., Max-Yang, Max-Yin, Min-Yang, Min-Yin) wander at the edges. Since both Yin and Yang are imbalances, the center positions must be more desirable than the edge positions.

We conclude that method 4 is the proper method to classify the trigrams, giving the third property of the trigram, which we will call the "Ability property."

References: *See figures 1A to 5A in subsequent pages.*

52

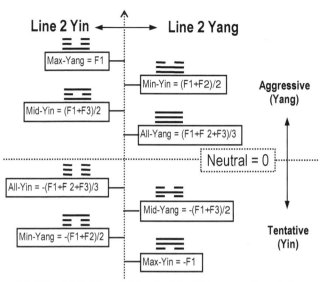

Figure 1A: If line 2 (of a trigram) determined the third property, the activity sum of the group based on the Yin line would be positive while that of the group based on the Yang line would be negative. This is inconsistent with the fundamental meaning of Yin and Yang. Not qualified as a property.

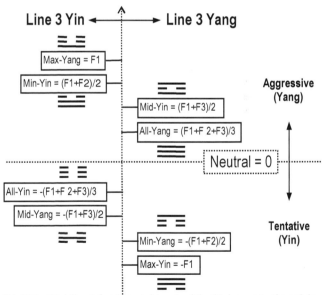

Figure 2A: If the third line (of a trigram) determined the third property, the activity sum of the Yin side would be very positive, and that of the Yang side very negative. This is inconsistent with the fundamental meaning of Yin and Yang. Not qualified as a property.

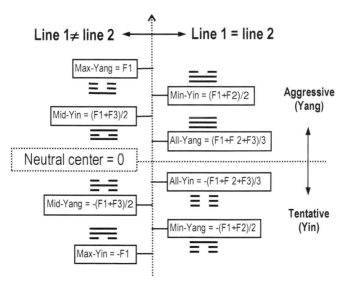

Figure 3A: Division using lines 1 and 2 gives two groups (left and right) with no particular characteristic. <u>Not qualified as a property.</u>

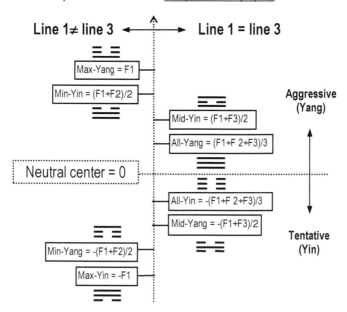

Figure 4A: Division using lines 1 and 3 gives a common group (left) which is far away from the center, and a power group (right) which is close to the center. In addition, all members of the power group are symmetrical, while members of the common group are not. CHOSEN AS THE "ABILITY" PROPERTY.

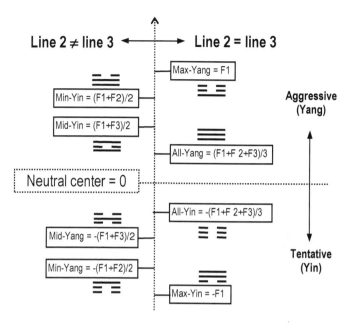

Line 2 ≠ line 3 ← → **Line 2 = line 3**

Max-Yang = F1

Min-Yin = (F1+F2)/2

Mid-Yin = (F1+F3)/2

All-Yang = (F1+F 2+F3)/3

Aggressive (Yang)

Neutral center = 0

All-Yin = -(F1+F 2+F3)/3

Mid-Yang = -(F1+F3)/2

Min-Yang = -(F1+F2)/2

Max-Yin = -F1

Tentative (Yin)

Figure 5A: Division based on lines 2 and 3 also produces 2 groups (left and right) with no particular characteristic. <u>Not qualified as a property</u>.

Chapter 6

Trigram symbolisms

Trigrams symbolisms

As mathematical entities, trigrams are difficult to visualize. To work around this problem, the Yin Yang theory devises real-life equivalents of the trigrams and deals with them instead. Since the trigrams are themselves "symbols," to avoid confusion their real-life equivalents are often called "trigram symbolisms."

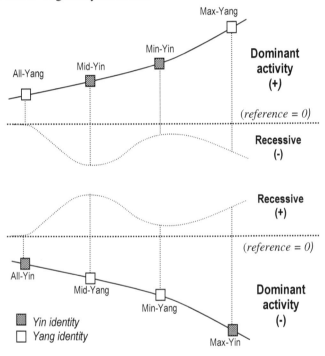

Figure 1: Activities of aggressive trigrams (top) and tentative trigrams (bottom).

Symbols: Mathematical notations of the trigrams.
Symbolisms: Real-life equivalents of the trigrams.

Although it is much more convenient to work with symbolisms than with symbols, extreme care must be taken in the creation of symbolisms otherwise some symbolisms may not be equivalent to the trigrams that they represent.

As seen in figure 2:

1. All-Yin and All-Yang: These are the two most powerful trigrams because there is no conflict between identity and dominant activity (dominant activity agrees with identity, and recessive activity does not exist.)

2. Mid-Yin and Mid-Yang: Identity is in conflict with and weaker than the dominant activity, but the difference in magnitude is small and therefore reconcilable. This is why Mid-Yin and Mid-Yang also belong to the power group along side All-Yang and All-Yin. Understandably, Mid-Yin and Mid-Yang are not as powerful as All-Yin and All-Yang.

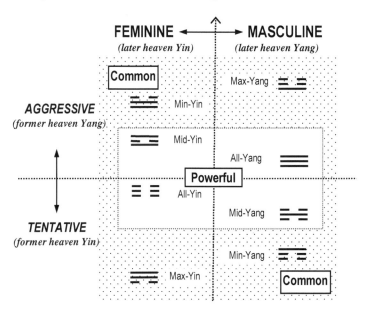

Figure 2: Geometrical orders of the three properties

3. Min-Yin and Min-Yang: Identity is in conflict with and weaker than the dominant activity. In addition, the magnitude difference between identity and (dominant) activity is significant. As a result, the activity property is expressed while the identity is suppressed. This makes Min-Yin and Min-Yang much weaker than the 4 power trigrams (enumerated in 1 and 2 above). They belong to the common group.

4. Max-Yin and Max-Yang: Identity is in agreement with the dominant activity, which leads to consistency. Unfortunately, the activity magnitude deviates too far from the reference line,

which is very bad news because in the Yin Yang theory, magnitude is the measure of (undesirable) imbalance. Entities represented by Max-Yin and Max-Yang therefore tend to border on the extremes: Excellent at something and terrible at something else. This contrast keeps them in the common group.

HISTORICAL SYMBOLISMS

Historically the two best known sets of symbolisms are the Nature set and the Family set. The "Nature set" drew its symbolisms from natural phenomena and is believed to have been invented by Fu Hsi (between 4000 and 3000BC.) The symbolisms for the "Family set" are members of a family. This set has always been credited to King Wen (12th century BC.)

THE "NATURE" SYMBOLISMS

☰ All-Yang (aggressive powerful masculine): Heaven

All-Yang is the most powerful Yang trigram. Its aggressiveness is the most effective, as evident from the fact that its (positive) activity level is closest to the center. Heaven is the fitting symbolism for All-Yang because Heaven is considered the Force that initiated the universe.

☷ All-Yin (tentative powerful feminine): Earth

All-Yin is the most powerful Yin trigram. Its tentativeness is the most effective, as evident from the fact that its (negative) activity level is closest to the center. Earth is a fitting choice for All-Yin because Earth is considered the Mother of all forms of life in our world.

☳ Max-Yang (aggressive common masculine): Thunder

Max-Yang is the most aggressive Yang trigram. However, being the extreme common trigram, it is not effective at all. Thunder is the fitting symbolism for Max-Yang because thunder is definitely extreme Yang, but its effect is minimal.

☴ Max-Yin (tentative common feminine): Wind

Max-Yin is the most tentative Yin trigram, and being the extreme common trigram, it is generally not effective at all. The choice of Wind is very fitting for two reasons. First, wind is generally flexible and weak, which fits the image of (tentative common Yin). Second, Max-Yin has a very unique characteristic that we will discuss in a later chapter. It suffices to say for the moment that Max-Yin is the only trigram that could reverse its Yin character and become very Yang under special circumstances, just like a gentle wind that could transform itself to a tornado.

≡⚏ Mid-Yang (tentative powerful masculine): Water

Mid-Yang is one of the two trickiest trigrams (the other is Mid-Yin). Being a powerful trigram, with Yang identity slightly overshadowed by negative activity, it is tentative but at the same time possesses a powerful masculine identity. Water is the fitting symbolism for Mid-Yang as water is inactive in appearance, but it is one of the most powerful (constructive as well as destructive) forces of nature. The apparent tranquility of a body of water is like the calm composure of a general who may decide to attack the enemy without notice.

NOTE: The "former heaven & later heaven" puzzle makes Water a very confusing entity. If asked "Is water Yin or Yang?" most of us would answer "Yin," which is correct (because tentative = Yin). The problem is that such an answer is incomplete. The complete answer is: "Water has three Yin Yang properties. *If only the activity property is considered, Water is Yin.* If only the identity property is considered, Water is Yang. If only the ability property is considered, Water is Yang."

⚏≡ Mid-Yin (aggressive powerful feminine): Fire.

The other tricky trigram is Mid-Yin. Being a powerful trigram, with Yin identity slightly overtaken by positive activity, it is aggressive but at the same time possesses a powerful feminine identity. Fire is the fitting symbolism for Mid-Yin as fire is aggressive in appearance and is also one of the most powerful (constructive as well as destructive) forces of nature. The eye-catching movements of fire can be compared to expressive feminine beauty, whose incredible ability to seduce and destroy is well known throughout the history of mankind. (This is why war is another symbolism for Mid Yin.)

NOTE: The "former heaven & later heaven" puzzle also makes Fire a very confusing entity. If asked "Is Fire Yin or Yang?" most of us would answer "Yang," which is correct (because aggressive = Yang). The problem is that such an answer is incomplete. The complete answer is: "Fire has three Yin Yang properties. *If only the activity property is considered, Fire is Yang.* If only the identity property is considered, Fire is Yin. If only the ability property is considered, Fire is Yang."

≡⚏ Min-Yang (tentative common masculine): Mountain.

In Min-Yang, the Yang identity is so weak that it is overshadowed by inactivity. Mountain is the fitting symbolism, as the mountain gives us a very strong impression of inactivity, yet its protruding and massive form reminds us that it possesses a masculine identity.

☱ Min-Yin (aggressive common feminine): Marsh.

In Min-Yin, the Yin identity is overshadowed by the manifestation of activity. The marsh is the fitting symbolism, as the marsh is the active and sometimes very noisy feeding ground for many species of small birds, mammals, and fish. Despite these activities, the small size of the marsh reminds us that it possesses a feminine identity.

THE "FAMILY" SYMBOLISMS

☰ All-Yang (aggressive powerful masculine): Father

The father is visibly the most powerful person in the house. He is therefore the fitting symbolism for All-Yang.

☷ All-Yin (tentative powerful feminine): Mother

The mother plays the role of the complementary leader of the house. Compared to the father, the mother actually could have more power over the children if she plays her role correctly, although this power may not be visible to an outsider.

☳ Max-Yang (aggressive common masculine): Eldest son

While the eldest son in a traditional family has considerable power over his younger brothers and sisters, he is also burdened with responsibilities. For this reason he is better fit for action and tends to be less capable than the middle son when it comes to matter that requires thinking and planning.

☴ Max-Yin (tentative common feminine): Eldest daughter

The eldest daughter has passed the age of innocence and is anticipating marriage. In a traditional society, marriage changes a girl's life completely. Worries about the unknown future make the eldest daughter thoughtful, reflective, and rather inactive. But it would be a major mistake to think that she is always passive. If pushed too far, she could become active to the point of excess. (The reason for this peculiar behavior will be accounted for in a later chapter.)

☵ Mid-Yang (tentative powerful masculine): Middle son

The middle son is old enough to take care of himself, and has the advantage of being free from real-life responsibilities. This allows him to think and plan for future success. However, he must be careful. Too much thinking and planning could hamper his ability to grasp opportunities at the present.

≡≡ Mid-Yin (aggressive powerful feminine): Middle daughter
The typical middle daughter should have a good time because her beauty is like a flower in full bloom. She has been popular long enough to know that her femininity is a powerful weapon; and she will not be hesitant to use it to her advantage.

≡ ≡ Min-Yang (tentative common masculine): Youngest son
The youngest son has just reached puberty and he has many reasons to be confused. In his family he is nobody. In the world outside, the girls his age have grown prettier and, worse, they seem to have surpassed him in maturity. He must take one step back to clear his confusion and adjust to this transition stage of his life.

≡≡ Min-Yin (aggressive common feminine): Youngest daughter
The youngest daughter has just reached puberty and is learning to adjust to her new found femininity. She realizes fully now that she is a member of the fair sex, and boys will have to compete for her attention. A few boys that have approached her were so clumsy that she could not help but feel a sense of superiority over them. In contrary to the youngest son, puberty helps build confidence for the youngest daughter. Understandably her outlook on life is rosy, and she actively participates in all the fun and games that it provides.

MODERN SYMBOLISMS

The writer has created several new sets of symbolisms. The first purpose of this exercise is to demonstrate that symbolisms are no more than practical tools that help us solve Yin Yang problems in ways that are closer to how our mind operates. The second purpose is to encourage the reader to devise his or her own set(s) of symbolisms as a means to master the meanings of the 8 trigrams.

The usefulness of symbolisms will be evident when we put together the meanings of the 64 hexagrams.

THE "ENCHANTED KINGDOM" SYMBOLISMS

≡≡ All-Yang (aggressive powerful masculine): King
The king is the fitting symbolism for All-Yang because he is the most powerful person of the kingdom. But since the kingdom is enchanted he does not stay put in his throne and tends to get into other

people's business. He does this in an aggressive but dignified manner fitting a king.

☷ All-Yin (tentative powerful feminine): Queen

The queen of the enchanted kingdom is not satisfied with being the most powerful woman of the land. She also gets involved in other people's business. Understandably, the queen is much more discreet than the king, but this does not mean that she is less effective.

☳ Max-Yang (aggressive common masculine): Knight

The knight's agenda is simple. He helps those in trouble and at the same time hopes to make a name for himself. Being all-man, he obviously has an eye for women, for better or worse.

☶ Max-Yin (tentative common feminine): Maiden in distress

Max-Yin is usually the maiden in distress that we read about so much in "knight in shiny armor" stories. However, if pushed too far she could become extremely active, for better or worse. (This peculiar behavior of Max-Yin will be accounted for in a later chapter.)

☵ Mid-Yang (tentative powerful masculine): Powerful duke

The duke is the second most powerful man in the kingdom, but this is a position that he is not satisfied with. A complex and capable man, he may engage himself in dangerous games of power against the king.

☲ Mid-Yin (aggressive powerful feminine): Beautiful duchess

She could be the duke's beautiful wife, or she could earn the duchess title on her own. With stunning beauty and an aggressive style of diplomacy, Mid-Yin is the ambitious woman in the enchanted kingdom. Her arch enemy is the (more) powerful queen.

☴ Min-Yang (tentative common masculine): Young boy

Being a powerless and inexperienced male in an enchanted kingdom is tough. Min-Yang is well aware of his inability to perform chivalrous tasks. A sense of inferiority makes him tentative.

☱ Min-Yin (aggressive common feminine): Pretty girl

Min-Yin does not have to deal with the inferiority complex that bothers Min-Yang. After all, she has the right to dream that a knight in shining armor will kneel down and ask for her hand some day. The sweet dream makes her happy and active. She takes life as it comes to her.

THE "MODERN LIFE" SYMBOLISMS

☰ All-Yang (aggressive powerful masculine): Male millionaire

In this material world the male millionaire is the envy of many. He has the power to affect others and he is very active in exercising this power.

☷ All-Yin (tentative powerful feminine): Female millionaire

Compared to her male counterpart, the female millionaire tends to be more tentative in her approach. Being very practical, she understands that this is still a man's world. Her strategy to keep on being rich is to get a male partner that she can rely on.

☳ Max-Yang (aggressive common masculine): Male entrepreneur

Max-Yang is the perfect example of a male entrepreneur: Capable and aggressive, but short of the means to realize his big dream. Although he is forceful and decisive, the lack of resources may be too difficult to overcome.

☶ Max-Yin (tentative common feminine): Working woman

Max-Yin is much more conservative than her male counterpart Max-Yang. She has seen enough of life and does not see why one should gamble the present for an unknown future. Being tentative common, she would settle for a steady job, knowing that it will not pay well.

However, if Max-Yin's patience is overextended, she may turn around 180 degrees and make shocking decisions. (This abrupt behavior will be accounted for in a later chapter.)

☵ Mid-Yang (tentative powerful masculine): Young heir

Being a young heir automatically gives Mid-Yang a sense of self importance. However, he realizes that he can only feel good when he can stand on his own. Being too busy thinking of great future plans to prove himself, Mid-Yang may end up missing opportunities within his grasp at the present.

☲ Mid-Yin (aggressive powerful feminine): Young heiress

Contrary to her male counterpart, being a young heiress does not bother Mid-Yin one single bit. After all, she thinks she deserves to get all the money in the world. Being an heiress enhances her importance, and she enjoys every minute of it.

☷ Min-Yang (tentative common masculine): Male high school drop-out

Min-Yang cannot help it. Everyone around him considers him a failure, and he has to agree with them. He cannot see any future in his dead-end job. Getting married is an unrealistic dream. Who would want to get married to a male high school drop-out with no potential to raise a good family? Min-Yang naturally becomes withdrawn.

☶ Min-Yin (aggressive common feminine): Female high school drop-out

Min-Yin also has a dead-end job, but she is not worried. This is only temporary, she thought. With her look she could be an actress; and if everything fails, there is always the chance to redeem herself by getting married to "Mr. Right." This thinking gives her a positive outlook, and there is a clear reason for her active style with men.

THE "WORK PLACE" SYMBOLISMS

☰ All-Yang (aggressive powerful masculine): Male CEO

The male CEO is decisive and tends to be dictatorial at times. He has no apology as he believes this is the only right way to run a business.

☷ All-Yin (tentative powerful feminine): Female CEO

In contrast to her male counterpart, the female CEO's secret of success is her ability to listen to the right people and create a sense of trust among her staff.

☳ Max-Yang (aggressive common masculine): Male old-timer

The male old-timer is good in what he does. This makes him a valuable resource for other employees. However, his style of communication is too straightforward and considered by many as abrasive. This is a serious barrier in his career.

☱ Max-Yin (tentative common feminine): Female old-timer

In contrast to her male counterpart, the female old-timer knows how to adjust to different personalities and therefore gets along well with everyone. The problem is, she is not very good in carrying out tasks assigned to her.

If put under pressure she will surprise everyone with her ability to survive by bending her way to fit the situation. This peculiar behavior will be covered in a later chapter.

☶ Mid-Yang (tentative powerful masculine): Male manager
The male manager knows that in his job as a boss, he has to be careful in dealing with other people. He decides to suppress some of his "male" tendencies and conduct himself as a gentleman.

☱ Mid-Yin (aggressive powerful feminine): Female manager
The female manager knows that the burden is on her shoulders to prove that women can manage as well as men. She may as well prove that women _are_ better than men in management. She believes that to achieve her purpose she has to play the "male" game of being very aggressive.

☵ Min-Yang (tentative common masculine): Male apprentice
The male apprentice knows that in his job he must listen and obey. For a male, this is a difficult adjustment to make. He therefore appears clumsy and tentative.

☲ Min-Yin (aggressive common feminine): Female apprentice
The female apprentice feels perfectly at home. She has always enjoyed working on small projects that she can handle on her own. Here she is doing exactly that, and even getting paid for it. She feels happy and that is reflected in her upbeat behavior.

THE "ROMANTIC" SYMBOLISMS

☰ All-Yang (aggressive powerful masculine): Male celebrity
The male celebrity has all the attention. He could get all the girls he wants (except maybe the very girl that he is in love with.) He is in a very powerful position of being one of the most eligible bachelors, and he will not hesitate at all in exercising and enjoying this power.

☷ All-Yin (tentative powerful feminine): Female celebrity
The female celebrity is not overwhelmed by the number of well qualified suitors that are going after her. She could take her pick, literally. However, being the symbolism for All-Yin, the most powerful Yin trigram, she wants to maintain her power. Naturally she has to be very careful, because she knows that once a choice is made, the fantasy is over and she will have to deal with reality.

☰ Max-Yang (aggressive common masculine): Masculine man
He is very masculine and is very protective. Almost the perfect man, except for one big problem: He does not understand how a woman feels.

☷ Max-Yin (tentative common feminine): Feminine woman
She is all feminine: Demure and appreciative of the protection provided by the men surrounding her. A very understanding woman, she can get along well with anyone. The problem is, her outlook on life is too pessimistic and she takes relationships too seriously. This turns away a lot of good men.
    Beware! If put under pressure this feminine woman will figure out a way to get what she wants. This peculiar ability will be covered in a later chapter.

☳ Mid-Yang (tentative powerful masculine): Thoughtful man
This thoughtful man knows how to read a woman's mind; which explains why women like him. The problem is, he goes too far with this "mindstuff" and any woman that knows him for a long time cannot help but suspect that his feelings for her are not genuine.

☱ Mid-Yin (aggressive powerful feminine): Beautiful woman
As a beautiful and aggressive woman, she is the life of the party. She is always surrounded by men, and she knows how to make the crowd around her grow bigger. The problem is, she may be considered by many to be a tricky woman who enjoys manipulating men.

☶ Min-Yang (tentative common masculine): Shy boy
Although the shy boy knows that in the game of love the male player has to make the first move, this is extremely difficult for him. In his effort to figure out what to do next, he appears pensive and tentative.

☴ Min-Yin (aggressive common feminine): Aggressive girl
The young girl is free of the problem that bothers her male counterpart. After all, she does not have to make the first move in this tricky game of love. All she has to do is to attract the attention of the male person she has in mind with conversation, body language, and maybe even inviting gestures. By doing all of these, she appears aggressive.

First written April 2002
Completed June 2002
©T. Tran

Chapter 7

Yin Yang and trigram dynamics

Feminine/Masculine identities and the female/male correspondence

Recalling that the three trigram properties are:

1. Identity: Feminine (Yin) and Masculine (Yang)
2. Activity: Tentative (Yin) and Aggressive (Yang)
3. Ability: Common (Yin) and Powerful (Yang)

Because of its strong correlation with human gender, identity is the most important (and also the most confusing) of the three trigram properties. In the construction of symbolisms in the last chapter, we have followed tradition and assumed that Feminine=Female, Masculine=Male. It will be seen later that this is not true for all cases. However, for the purpose of discussing the gender factor in the Yin Yang theory, this assumption is adequate.

We will use the now familiar diagram of all three properties as reference (see figure 1).

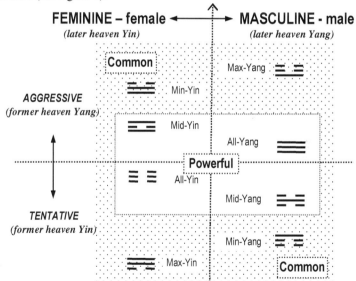

Figure 1: The relationship between Identity and the other two trigram properties. Here the Feminine (Yin) and Masculine (Yang) identities are taken to be Female and Male respectively.

The Yin Yang law of gender equality

We have established in an earlier chapter that the order in likelihood to success runs from the center outward. From figure 1, the order is:

Very likely (most powerful): All-Yin (female) and All-Yang (male).

Likely (powerful): Mid-Yin (female) and Mid-Yang (male).

Unlikely (common): Min-Yin (female) and Min-Yang (male).

Very unlikely (most common): Max-Yin (female) and Max-Yang (male).

We summarize these perfect symmetries between female and male in the following law:

THE YIN YANG LAW OF GENDER EQUALITY

As far as potential for success is concerned, there is no difference whatsoever between males and females!

The Yin Yang law of gender equality dispels the myth that the Yin Yang theory was devised by men to belittle women. This law is remarkable for two reasons. First, it is the only known scientific law, old or new, that states explicitly that females are equal to males in potential. Second, because it is a logical conclusion, we can rest assured that it is scientifically sound to treat both sexes equally.

The Yin Yang predictions of gender differences

The Yin Yang theory also anticipated a reality that experimental science finally confirmed in the later part of the 20th century, that males and females are psychologically different and even tend to excel in different academic subjects[1]. Although this reality is obvious to many, it had been a very controversial subject as late as the 1980's. Many women's right activists were concerned, and rightly so, that evidence of gender differences would be used as excuses to perpetuate the mistreatment of women. Some therefore insisted that all differences in psychology and task performance between the two sexes were long-term consequences of male domination over females. For example, it was argued that men tend to be less emotional and more aggressive than women only because they had been taught "to act like a man;" had they not been taught this way men would be as emotional as women, and women as aggressive as men. We now know, however, that the brain develops differently in the two sexes, and this difference accounts for the high level of emotional expression in women and aggressiveness in men[2, 3].

There are two tentative Yang trigrams (Min-Yang and Mid-Yang); implying that men could be quite tentative. There are two aggressive Yin trigrams (Min-Yin and Mid-Yin); implying that women could be quite aggressive. The most tentative of all trigrams is the Yin trigram

Max-Yin, implying that women dominate the extreme end of emotion. The most aggressive of all trigrams is the Yang trigram Max-Yang; implying that men dominate the extreme end of aggressiveness.

The Yin Yang theory therefore predicts that there are tentative men and aggressive women; but most of the extremely tentative people are women and most of the extremely aggressive people are men. These predictions are in perfect agreement with empirical data.

Yin Yang dynamics

Since the Yin Yang tendency of each circle in a trigram is only an instantaneous state within a distribution, it is entirely possible for a Yin circle to change to a Yang circle and vice versa.

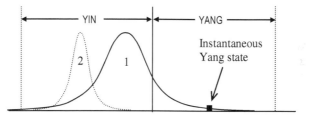

Figure 2: Since Yin and Yang form a distribution, when a circle is Yang, it only means that it is Yang at the moment we observe it. It could change to Yin the next moment.

Understandably the Yin Yang distribution for a circle may lean toward one side of the Yin Yang spectrum. Curve 1 in figure 2 is an example where the tendency is toward Yin. The circle associated with curve 1 would be Yin for a majority of cases, but the possibility for it to be Yang cannot be ruled out (black dot on the right side of curve 1). A rare exception is curve 2. Since this curve is completely in the Yin region, the circle associated with it can never be Yang.

The possibility that a circle could switch between Yin and Yang is called "Yin Yang dynamics."

Objective trigram dynamics

Since each trigram is formed by three circles, Yin Yang dynamics implies that the trigrams themselves would change over the course of many events. Since each macroscopic entity has at least one trigram associated with it at a given moment in time, multiple trigrams will be needed to fully describe the various states of a macroscopic entity over time. The need for multiple trigrams to describe each macroscopic entity is called "trigram dynamics."

So far we have the impression that, in the set of human beings, females always correspond to the 4 trigrams with feminine identity, and males to the 4 trigrams with masculine identity. Now with the understanding of trigram dynamics, we see that these rules are only approximately correct. Although most females are feminine, there exist a small number of females who are masculine. Likewise, while most males are masculine, there exist a small number of males who are feminine.

If we narrow our examination to the case of one female person whose general identity is feminine, we will find that she could, in rare occasions, exhibit a masculine identity. That is because the total identity of a person is not a fixed point in the feminine/masculine scale, but a distribution curve (see figure 3). By symmetrical reasoning, a male whose general identity is masculine could exhibit feminine tendency in selected circumstances.

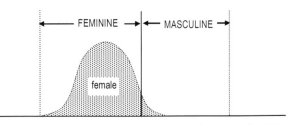

Figure 3: As the right part of the curve indicates, a feminine female person may exhibit masculine tendency (likewise a masculine male may exhibit feminine tendency at times).

By extending our logic to the activity and ability properties of the trigrams, we reach the conclusion that all three trigram properties could change, either singly or in unison. Since trigrams are mathematical counterparts of human character, the switching of personality is not just a possibility, but a reality in most of human beings. This reality explains not only a peculiar phenomenon known as split personality (e.g., "Dr. Jekyll and Mr. Hyde") but also more common behavioral changes that are considered "inexplicable" by existing theories of psychology.

The above are trigram dynamics as seen by an objective observer. For this reason, we will refer to them as "objective trigram dynamics."

The Yin Yang logic of psychological types

One important discovery in the field of psychology is that people are not all the same, but can be classified into a number of psychological types. Binary properties such as mental/emotional, extrovert/introvert have been used to classify types. The problem is that there is no universal set of binary properties that all psychologists could agree on.

With the trigrams, this issue is settled. Since trigrams are the only proper representatives of physical entities, and since there are only eight trigrams, there are only eight major psychological types.

But the trigrams have implications beyond the current status of psychological understanding of types.

The reality of trigram dynamics implies that constant change is the rule of life. Thus, while it is true in general that each person has a personality that is more or less constant, it is only the manifestation of his or her dominant psychological type, while other types wait for their chances to appear. Under proper situation or/and with proper stimulus, a personality can switch suddenly to another personality, and the switch could be so dramatic that it shocks everyone. We have seen how differently some people behave when intoxicated. We have heard about people with split personality or multiple personalities. We have read about Good Samaritans who turned into blood craving serial killers, or killers who repented and followed the path of saints. These are examples of the switch in psychological types that is best explained in terms of the eight trigrams.

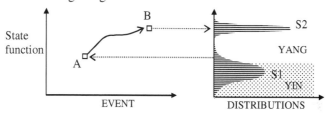

Figure 4: When a property is Yin (curve S1) it only means that there are more Yin possibilities compared to Yang possibilities, and the actual occurrence may be Yang, not Yin. Here a Yang possibility occurs. This occurrence triggers an event (A-B) that leads to a new distribution (curve S2). Note that S1 and S2 are two distinct curves, and the entity has switched from Yin (curve S1) to Yang (curve S2). Had a different possibility (in the same S1 curve) been realized, most likely the corresponding event would not be A-B, and the resulting distribution would not be the curve S2. This example typifies the dynamics of the Yin Yang theory.

Example of Yin Yang dynamics

To make our point clearer we will choose an example in which Yin is equated with "being a bad person," and Yang "being a good person." Let's consider the fictitious case of a person whose "character" distribution is curve 1 at the time we start our investigation. Since the general tendency of curve 1 is Yin, the person would tend to do more bad things than good things, which would make him a bad person in the eyes of the society.

We will assume that the person takes an action that corresponds to point A in figure 5. This action is possible because curve 1 does include it. Action A may or may not trigger an event or a series of events of significance. If there is no significant event or events following A, the "character" distribution curve will stay as curve 1. But if A triggers an event or series of events of great significance to the person, it is entirely possible for the character distribution to redefine itself and become a different curve (curve 2 in this example).

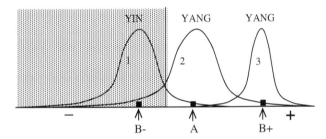

Fig 5: The character distribution could be very dynamic. In this example the person starts with curve 1, moves to curve 2, then either back to curve 1 or forward to curve 3.

The next action by the person (who is now considered good because his character distribution is curve 2) could be B- or B+, among others. Note that B- is a bad action (Yin), while B+ is a very good action (highly Yang).

First, we will assume that B- is the action taken. Further we will assume that B- triggers a series of unfavorable events, leading to the return of the person to his former character distribution. The parallel in life is the case of a person changing from a criminal tendency to a caring tendency, then back to criminal tendency.

Next, we will assume that B+ is the action taken. Further we will assume that B+ triggers another favorable series of events, leading to another redefinition of the person, and his character distribution becomes curve 3, which includes no possibility for bad action. The parallel in life is the case of a person changing from a criminal tendency to a caring tendency, then to a saintly tendency.

In conclusion, it is possible for an entity which is generally Yin to be Yang at a particular moment. It is also possible for an entity to change from being generally Yin to being generally Yang, and vice versa.

Trigram transformation

Because of trigram dynamics, each human being will undergo a series of "trigram transformations," which only ends when he or she ceases to exist in this world.

We will go through the logic for the transformations from two base trigrams: All-Yin and All-Yang. The reader can apply the same logic to the 6 remaining base trigrams.

If the base trigram is All-Yang (most powerful aggressive masculine) the person is most likely a male, generally known to be mildly aggressive with a strong drive to be in a position of power.

1. His most natural switch is Mid-Yang (powerful tentative masculine) because he still maintains some power, although it is a step back.

2. A switch to Max-Yang (most common aggressive Yang) can only happen when he could not control himself, becoming overly aggressive and losing the central position in the process.

3. A switch to Min-Yang (common tentative Yang) almost means that he has been defeated, because he has lost not only his tendency to act, but also his ability.

4. It will take dramatic circumstances for him to switch to one of the Yin trigrams. However, if he does so, his most natural choice is Mid-Yin (powerful aggressive feminine), because although this trigram requires a dramatic change of approach from masculine to feminine, it promises some power and it fits his aggressive style.

5. Next is All-Yin (most powerful tentative Yin), because the extreme sacrifice of character (changing from aggressive to tentative and from masculine to feminine) does have the reward of power.

6. Next to last is the switch to Min-Yin (common aggressive feminine), where he is still aggressive and optimistic, but has very little chance for success.

7. Last is the switch to Max-Yin (most common tentative feminine). This is a highly unusual switch because he has given up his personality completely (changing from moderately aggressive masculine to highly tentative feminine). The consequence is the severe loss of power (from most powerful to most common).

If the base trigram is All-Yin (most powerful tentative feminine) the person is most likely a female, generally known to be mildly tentative with a strong drive to be in a position of power.

1. Her most natural switch is Mid-Yin (powerful aggressive feminine). This allows her to maintain some power, although it is a step back.

2. A switch to Max-Yin (most common tentative feminine) only happens when she gives up her power, or it is taken away from her.

3. A switch to Min-Yin (common aggressive feminine) is very unusual but could happen (when she is intoxicated in a wild party, for example).

4. It will take dramatic circumstances for her to switch to one of the Yang trigrams. However, if she does so, her most natural choice is Mid-Yang (powerful tentative masculine), because although this trigram requires a dramatic change of approach, it promises some power and it fits her tentative style.

5. Next is All-Yang (most powerful aggressive masculine), because the extreme sacrifice of character (changing from tentative to aggressive and from feminine to masculine) does have the reward of power.

6. Next to last is the switch to Min-Yang (common tentative masculine). This switch is a sign that she is no longer sure of herself and has made the mistake of switching from a feminine approach to a masculine approach. The consequence is the loss of power.

7. Last is the switch to Max-Yang (most common aggressive masculine). By making this switch she deviates too far from what she is good at (switching from her familiar ground of being moderately tentative feminine to the unknown territory of being highly aggressive masculine). The consequence is the severe loss of power (from most powerful to most common).

Subjective trigram dynamics

Objective trigram dynamics are like real objects, while our perception of them is like images seen through an observing tool. The only way for an image to look the same as the original object is that the observing tool is perfect. Prior to the advent of quantum mechanics, science believed that it was in the process of converging to perfect measurements. Quantum mechanics refuted this view with the Heisenberg's uncertainty principle, but so far has not been able to come up with a coherent explanation as to why a convergence to perfect measurements would not be possible.

In this respect, the Yin Yang theory is superior. According to the Yin Yang theory all physical existence in the universe, including observing tools, are combinations of Yin and Yang. Since Yin and Yang are deviations from a "perfect" state, there can never be a perfect measurement tool.

We already know that Yin are negative changes and Yang are positive changes. To be more precise we should say that *Yin are negative changes as measured by an observer*, and *Yang are positive changes as measured by an observer*. Let the observer be A, the observed B, the following table shows that the discrepancies between the actual state and the observed state of B disappears only when A is neutral (neither Yin nor Yang).

TABLE 1: Yin Yang judgment errors by a biased observer

A, observer	**B,** object	Yin Yang state of **B (errors in bold)**	
(actual state)	*(actual state)*	*(neutral observer)*	*(as observed by A)*
-4	+2	Yang (+2)	Yang, **strong (+6)**
0	+2	Yang (+2)	Yang (+2)
+4	+2	Yang (+2)	**Yin (-2)**
-4	-2	Yin (-2)	**Yang (+2)**
0	-2	Yin (-2)	Yin (-2)
+4	-2	Yin (-2)	Yin, **strong (-6)**

The non-physical requirement of perfect observers

Since perfect measurement tools do not exist, each observation is a distorted record of the original. Depending on the observer and the observed, there are four possibilities:

1. Observations of innate phenomena by innate instruments have the lowest level of distortion, because innate objects are not interactive beings.
2. Observations of organic objects (such as human beings) by innate instruments have some level of distortion because organic objects may interact with the measurement instruments.
3. Observations of innate phenomena by organic instruments (e.g., a human being observing a rainbow) have high level of distortion because organic instruments could interact with innate phenomena, and are very subjective.
4. Observations of organic objects by organic instruments (e.g., human-to-human observations) have the highest level of distortion because both sides tend to interact with each other, and the (organic) observer tend to add subjective judgment to his or her final observation.

Since the main focus of this book is the I-Ching, we are only interested in the last case. For obvious reasons, the observed trigram dynamics of interest will be call "subjective trigram dynamics" (in contrast with the "objective trigram dynamics" discussed earlier.)

Although the Yin Yang theory applies to all existence, its main goal is to make sense out of the arbitrariness of human-to-human observations, which are better known generically as "human judgment." To see how arbitrary human judgment could be, take the case of a young female secretary who is also a single mother. As far as society is concerned, the trigram that best fits her is possibly Max-Yin (most common tentative feminine). But to her little son, she is the all powerful mother All-Yin (most powerful tentative feminine), and to her dominant and rich father, she may be the frivolous little girl Min-Yin (common aggressive feminine) when she calls and asks him to send more money. How about her own assessment? She may honestly believe that she has the ability to change things around her. For this reason, in her opinion, the fitting trigram for her is Mid-Yin (powerful aggressive feminine).

| Original object | Distorted image | Badly distorted image |

Figure 6: Since observing tools are also governed by the Yin Yang laws, observed images will be distorted. The difference is only a matter of degree (center image may be acceptable, but right image is badly distorted.)

Because of our subjectivity and our tendency to generalize from the incomplete information available to us, our judgment about any person or group of persons will be either incomplete or incorrect, or both. This applies even when we judge ourselves. The reason is that, although a great amount of information about ourselves is available to us, our subjectivity would interfere with the selection and interpretation of this information. As a result, the advantage of having easy access to information is compromised by a much higher level of subjectivity.

In conclusion, it is impossible for most of us to have an accurate understanding of human characters, our own characters included.

(While the writer was working on this very section of the book, Minnesota public radio reported an embezzlement in a rural community in Ohio, resulting in the loss of millions from a bank. The bank had to close down, and many projects that would benefit the public had to be cancelled or put on hold indefinitely. This callous crime shocked everyone because the criminal reportedly had been a very well trusted symbol of volunteerism and reliability in the community. This real-life tragedy shows how wrong everyone of us could be in judging human character.)

The Yin Yang view of mistakes and "The Middle Way"

Earlier we have established that we (human beings) are very unreliable observers of life phenomena. Specifically, the images recorded in our observations are all distorted, each may be to a different degree, but distorted nevertheless. The problem is that we have no other choice but to rely on these distorted images to make real-life decisions. This is why we make so many mistakes, as acknowledged in the well-known saying "To err is human."

By definition mistakes are bad. No one wants to make mistakes, so it would be great to prevent mistakes from happening in the first place. But how? Since "making a mistake" means "taking the choice with undesirable consequences" the obvious strategy is to avoid choices that have high probabilities of leading to undesirable consequences. Real-life experience taught us that all those choices that are considered "extreme" by common standards fall in this category. In each individual case under consideration, extreme choices usually occupy two ends of a spectrum of choices. It follows that the right choice must lie somewhere in the middle of the two extreme ends.

What about cases when a mistake has already been made? There are two possible extremes: The first is to react instinctively to the aftermath of the mistake without thinking; the second is to suffer the aftermath passively (without attempting anything). Again life experience taught us that the best choice lies somewhere in the middle of these two extremes.

In brief, real-life experience taught us to always pick a choice somewhere in the middle of the extremes. This agrees with a well-known spiritual approach to life known as "the Middle Way[4]." Both Buddhism and Confucianism teach that the Middle Way is the path to correct actions. The concept of the Middle Way fits common sense, but so far no one has offered a scientific reason for it. We now can use the Yin Yang theory to suggest the reason: Since Yin and Yang are states of undesirable negative and positive deviations, correct actions must lie somewhere between the extreme Yin and Yang deviations.

Distorted observations revisited

A well known saying of modern time is "knowledge is power." A long time ago, the Buddha preached that "human misery is a consequence of ignorance." Both statements stress the paramount importance of (true) knowledge.

As we will see in the next chapter, the I-Ching is a logical system that reveals to us possible outcomes of interactions between trigrams. Since all macroscopic existence can be described logically by the eight trigrams, the I-Ching provides us a method to predict possible outcomes in real-life interactions. This kind of knowledge is incredibly powerful, but in order to acquire it we must first correctly identify the trigrams associated with the different entities and situations that we encounter in life.

As elaborated in the last section, by default our "knowledge" is plagued with distortions. While distortion-free knowledge may not be attainable, we must try to make sure that our knowledge is the best possible. Since the best knowledge is the knowledge with minimum distortion, we must try to minimize the distortions. Interestingly, a way to achieve this goal has been outlined thousands of years ago in "The Great Learning," one of the best known Confucian classic texts *(words in parentheses are Yin Yang interpretations by the writer):*

"By stopping *(i.e., minimizing the undesirable effects of Yin and Yang on one's own ability to observe),* one can attain stability. With stability in place, one can attain tranquility. With tranquility in place, one can attain *(inner)* peace. With *(inner)* peace in place, one can attain *(correct)* thinking. With *(correct)* thinking in place, one can attain the objective."

Equating thinking with the mental construction of the trigrams, this is a valuable guide for those who want to take advantage of the wisdom contained in the I-Ching.

Just imagine a person who has the ability to point out correctly that such and such macroscopic entity (e.g., a person, a war, an election process) should correspond to such and such trigram or set of trigrams. If this person also understands the logic of the I-Ching, theoretically he or she should be able to apply it to the known trigrams and predict the development of any phenomenon in the universe! This is how powerful the I-Ching is.

We will cover the logic for trigram-trigram interactions in the next chapter.

First written April 2002
Completed June 2002
Revised May 2011
©T. Tran

NOTES:
[1]For more indepth accounts of these differences, see for example: "Boys and Girls Learn Differently" (book), Michael Gurian and Patricia Henley, Jossey-Bass, 2002.

[2]"The Female Brain" (book), Louann Brizendine, M.D., Crown Publishing, New York, 2006.

[3]"The Male Brain" (book), Louann Brizendine, M.D., Crown Publishing, New York, 2010.

78

[4]Confucius complained that he had never known anyone, including himself, who could follow the Middle Way consistently. While Confucius' complaint could be a statement of modesty, it does tell us that eliminating Yin and Yang is an extremely difficult task.

The next best thing is to minimize Yin and Yang, which is the same as minimizing subjectivity, so that our observations can become good approximations of reality. Several methods have been employed for this purpose:

- Meditation: This method has always been practiced in the East and is becoming popular in the West. In addition to mental health benefits, it is believed that meditation can bring us to a spiritual plane free of physical factors (i.e., Yin and Yang).

- Self examination: This method is a central part in the teaching of Confucianism, but practiced by very few people, possibly because human beings are, in general, afraid that they would lose self-esteem if too many flaws are discovered. The lack of self examination means that Yin Yang subjectivity will forever be a reality for most people.

Chapter 8

The 64 hexagrams I

Subjectivity and Yin Yang inequality

The unsolved secret of the I-Ching

In chapter 1 we used hexagram 10 in the I-Ching as an example of the unsolved mystery of the I-Ching. This hexagram is formed by putting trigram All-Yang on top of trigram Min-Yin. The I-Ching says that this hexagram has the meaning: "Stepping on the tail of a tiger (but) the tiger does not bite. (There will be) progress." The catch is, the I-Ching offers no logical reason for this statement as well as statements that it made for the other 63 hexagrams and the 384 lines. Over the years many commentaries of later-day Yin Yang masters have been added, but they are no more than elaborations of the original meanings.

All-Yang
Min-Yin

STEPPING
CAUTIOUSLY

Fig 1: The I-Ching says that All-Yang on top of Min-Yin is analogous to an extremely dangerous situation where the smallest mistake would result in total disaster. It has the fitting name "stepping cautiously" and is listed as trigram #10 in the I-Ching.

This is the main reason why many serious students of the I-Ching, especially those with scientific inclination, find The Book frustrating. It is believed that King Wen worked out the meanings of the 64 hexagrams in the 12th century B.C. while he was imprisoned by the then emperor of China. It is safe to assume that King Wen's work was guided by a logical system that he possibly invented himself. The problem is, King Wen's logical system is now lost.

Can this logical system be rediscovered now after so many Yin Yang masters either have not tried to do so or have tried and failed? The task seems impossible, but we should keep in mind that we have the advantage of having gathered an incredible wealth of scientific knowledge that was not available to the Yin Yang sages of the old past.

Equipped with the powerful tools of modern science, we will start our search for the meanings of the 64 hexagrams. As we have mentioned in an earlier chapter, the heavier task of rediscovering the meanings of the 384 individual lines will have to be delayed to a future opportunity.

Trigram interactions

First, we notice that, if there were nothing going on in the universe, there would be no way for us to differentiate one macroscopic entity from the others. Thus, it is through interactions with their environment that the properties of the various entities are manifested and become known to us.

As far as the Yin Yang theory is concerned, the 8 trigrams constitute the complete set of all entities in the universe. We will call an individual or group acting in unison as a "Yin Yang unit" or simply a "unit." A unit may switch from entity to entity depending on situation, but at a given moment in time it can only assume one entity. This allows us to represent each unit by the trigram that best describes it for the situation under consideration.

Since the only meaningful representatives for anything that possesses a sense of existence on its own account are the 8 trigrams, not only a unit must be represented by a trigram, but also the "environment" that it interacts with. In other words, trigram-trigram interactions are the Yin Yang parallels of real-life interactions between a unit and its environment.

Trigram interactions and real-life phenomena

The word "interactions" reminds us of "reactions," a key word in the science of chemistry. So instead of re-inventing the wheel we will attempt to apply what is known in chemical reactions to the Yin Yang world of trigram interactions.

Let's start with the basic case: Interactions involving two trigrams.

Similar to two chemical substances in a reaction, in order for two trigrams to interact with each other, they must be in contact. Recall that in our trigram model:

1. Each line is represented by a circle.
2. Each trigram is represented by three circles in mutual contact with one another. Needless to say, these 3 circles have to be in the same plane (which we may refer to as the Yin Yang plane).
3. In each trigram, the first circle appears first, followed by the 2nd circle, then the 3rd.

Inspecting the time sequence of the 3 circles in any arbitrary trigram, we notice that the two bonds 1-2 and 2-3 both possess time continuity because circle 2 occurs right after circle 1, and circle 3 occurs right after circle 2. In contrast, bond 1-3 does not possess time continuity because circles 1 and 3 are not consecutive in time. This makes 1-3 the weakest link in each trigram. As a consequence, bond 1-3 is more "reactive" than 1-2 and 2-3, and tends to "react" with another trigram to form a temporary "compound" of 2 trigrams or 6 circles.

81

When two trigrams are combined, the 6 circles must also follow a time sequence (see figure 2). Let the trigram that appears first be 1-2-3 and the one that follows 1'-2'-3'. If we identify two parties in real-life interactions as "the host" and "the guest," it is most natural for the host to show up first and play the role of the initiator. To utilize this analogy, we will call 1-2-3 the host trigram and 1'-2'-3' the guest trigram in the Yin Yang world.

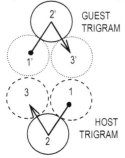

GUEST TRIGRAM

HOST TRIGRAM

Fig 2: Two trigrams could interact via their reactive sides 1-3 and 1'-3'. Their interaction is the geometrical presentation of a phenomenon. The interaction is asymmetrical because one trigram must appear before the other. The trigram that appears first is called the "Host trigram," the other the "Guest trigram."

Each trigram interaction in the Yin Yang world is supposed to represent a phenomenon in real life. Since existence without time duration is meaningless, all real-life phenomena must have time duration. To state this another way, all real-life phenomena, including phenomena that come to pass, must possess certain degree of stability.

Guest trigram B
(outer trigram)

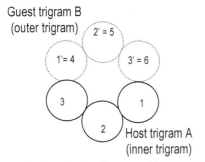

Host trigram A
(inner trigram)

Figure 4: When two trigrams interact, the most likely configuration of the Yin Yang circles is an equilateral hexagon. This configuration is exactly that of Benzene C_6H_6, one of the most stable organic compounds.

Let's take the key word "stability" back to the Yin Yang world of trigram interactions. Readers who are familiar with chemistry know that benzene C_6H_6 is one of the most stable organic compounds. Scientists have long established that in benzene the 6 carbon molecules (C) occupy 6 vertices of a planar hexagon. They concluded that the hexagonal configuration is very stable thanks to the resonant interactions inherent with this geometry.

Interestingly, the interaction of 2 trigrams involves exactly 6 circles, which allows the formation of the planar hexagonal configuration just like that of benzene. We conclude that the interaction of 2 trigrams is a reasonable model of real-life phenomena because the resulting hexagonal formation possesses inherent stability.

By simple arithmetics, the number of circles involving in a n-trigram interaction is 3n. The benzene formation that we have just discussed corresponds to n=2. Once we go beyond n=2 there is no known unit formation whose stability level is comparable to that of benzene. Therefore we will eliminate all possibilities with n > 2.

Since all interactions must involve at least 2 trigrams, the only solution is n=2. In other words, all interactions in the Yin Yang world must involve exactly two trigrams!

The I-Ching as a complexity theory

Since there are only 8 trigrams, and there are only 64 ways for 8 trigrams to interact with one another, the Yin Yang theory predicts that there are only 64 types of interactions in the real world. Thus, all possible real-life interactions, from the simplest to the most complex, are mathematically reducible to the 64 hexagrams in the I-Ching!!!

One of the "buzz words" of modern science is "complexity theory," i.e., the investigation of possible order in apparently chaotic situations. The I-Ching is amazing because *it was invented as a complexity theory* more than three thousand years ago.

Fundamental logic of the 64 hexagrams of the I-Ching

The interaction of two Yin Yang entities can be described in words as: "A interacts with B, producing outcome Ψ." Mathematically:

$A \oplus B => \Psi$

The outcome Ψ depends on:

-The properties of A

-The properties of B

-The relationship $\oplus$

We already know that A and B each has three properties: Activity, Identity, and Ability. The relationship $\oplus$ is a new factor that we must now discuss.

Let (1, 2, 3) and (1', 2', 3') be the three circles of trigram A and B respectively. In an interaction, a sense of continuity must exist among all circles. Because of this condition, only two time sequences are possible: (1, 2, 3, 1', 2', 3') and (1', 2', 3', 1, 2, 3). This means either A occurs before B or B occurs before A. Since the labels A and B are arbitrary, we will choose the convention that A occurs before B to match the convention used in the I-Ching, where the lower trigrams corresponds to A, the upper trigram to B.

A and B are sometimes called the inner and outer trigrams in I-Ching books. As mentioned earlier, our preferred names are "host trigram" for A and "guest trigram" for B; as these names specify the relationship between A and B.

The deciding role of time in host/guest relationship

One simple way to visualize the I-Ching is that it is a comprehensive list of Yin Yang logic that covers all possible real-life situations. This logic has been lost for several thousand years; but now we are ready to rediscover it.

Even without knowing anything about the Yin Yang theory, we all could feel that timing is one of the deciding factors in life. For example, there are times when action is necessary, and there are times when inaction is the best strategy. Good result is expected if action is taken when action is necessary; and bad result is expected if action is taken when inaction is the best strategy.

Since it is timing that decides the host/guest roles of two interacting trigrams, timing is, not surprisingly, the central factor in the Yin Yang logic of the I-Ching. By setting the time that A occurs as 0 and the time that B occurs as Δt, it is clear that A beats B by the time duration Δt, which is a positive number. In other words, timing is the factor that differentiates the host from the guest. The host always appears before the guest.

The subjective meanings of the 64 hexagrams of the I-Ching

As we have discovered in the last chapter, only enlightened sages who know the Middle Way can have objective views of the Yin and Yang of the world. To these sages, the host and the guest are differentiated by their order of occurrence, and the meaning of the resulting hexagram is the overall outcome of the mutual interaction between the two interacting trigrams.

Unfortunately, almost 100% of the world population is not enlightened. From the standpoint of an unenlightened person who is involved in an interaction, his or her existence precedes all other existence because it has _always_ been present and is therefore must be the first to occur. Thus, _he or she always is the host or hostess_!

While this subjective view may be scientifically inaccurate, it is the view that we use to make most, if not all, of our decisions. In fact, our subjective view is the basis of _all of our crucial decisions_.

Thus, as far as non-spiritual existence is concerned, the only view that matters is the subjective view. Since the I-Ching describes non-spiritual existence, it must also reflect this (subjective) reality. A hexagram, then, has the meaning of *the situation as seen from the subjective view of the host trigram in its interaction with the guest trigram.*

The I-Ching law of Yin Yang inequality!!!

From a Yin Yang standpoint, "being the host" and "being the guest" have to be judged relative to the Middle Way of "being neither the host nor the guest," which makes the host the early comer and the guest the late comer. Since the early comer must have positive acceleration while the late comer must have negative acceleration, we conclude that "being the host" and "being the guest" correspond to Yang and Yin respectively. Moreover, from common sense we know that "being the host" is an active role and "being the guest" is a reactive role.

Host = Active role (Yang)

Guest = Reactive role (Yin)

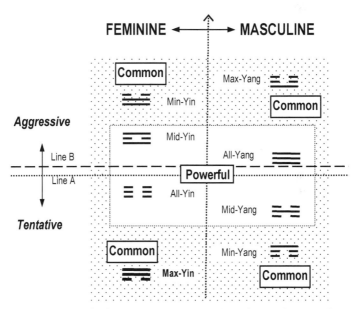

Figure 3: Because the host position is Yang, the reference horizontal line will be subjectively raised from line A to line B. This makes All-Yin less powerful than All-Yang, Mid-Yin more powerful than Mid-Yang, and Max-Yin the most common trigram.

Since "being the host" is a Yang state, the correct horizontal center line (line A in figure 3) will be mistakenly raised to a measurably higher level (line B in figure 3). This leads to the following consequences:

1. All-Yin appears less powerful than All-Yang because the shift makes her appear further away from the reference line, while All-Yang appears to be closer.
2. Mid-Yin appears more powerful than Mid-Yang because the shift makes her appear closer to the reference line, while Mid-Yang appears further away. This makes Mid-Yang the weakest of the power group (consisting of All-Yang, All-Yin, Mid-Yang, and Mid-Yin).
3. Max-Yin becomes the most common trigram (instead of sharing this dubious honor with Max-Yang).

All of these form the basis for a very significant conclusion. Although Yin and Yang _are_ equals, the subjectivity of human observation makes them unequal. The world that we live in, then, is a place where inequality will forever be a reality. We may be able to reduce inequality, but (because of our subjectivity) we can never get rid of it completely.

We will see how this apparent inequality plays out in the meanings of the 64 hexagram, which will be the focus of the next chapter.

First written May 2002
Completed July 2002
©T. Tran

Chapter 9
The 64 hexagrams II
A scientific approach to hexagram meanings

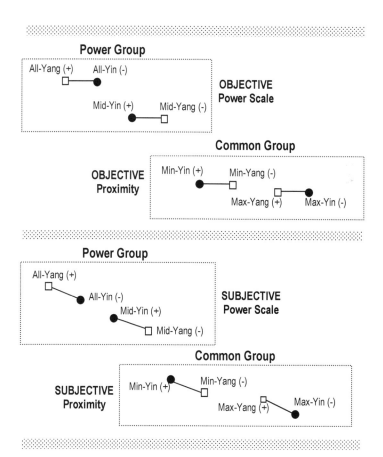

Figure 1: If the observer were objective, all solid line segments would be horizontal (top picture). But because human beings are subjective, all segments appear slanted (lower picture). In the powerful group, where power is a strong factor, All-Yang is perceived as being more powerful than All-Yin, and Mid-Yin more powerful than Mid-Yang.

The common group (Min-Yin, Min-Yang, Max-Yang, Max-Yin) are also polarized, in order Min-Yin, Min-Yang, Max-Yang, Max-Yin. However, the concept of a power scale is meaningless in the common group. It is more appropriate to think of a "proximity scale."

Hexagram meaning

Recall from the last chapter that the meaning of a hexagram is: "The outcome Ψ of the host trigram A in its interaction with the guest trigram B." Mathematically:

$A \oplus B => \Psi$

The outcome Ψ depends on:

-The properties of the host trigram A

-The properties of the guest trigram B

-The trigram relationship $\oplus$

The trigram relationship connects the two trigrams and decides the meaning of the hexagram. It is the focus of this chapter.

The significance of identity lines

At this point we will introduce the concept of "identity line," which is important in the understanding of hexagram meaning. An identity line is the line that defines the identity of a trigram. From previous discussions:

THE 8 TRIGRAMS IN HOST POSITION (Top) AND GUEST POSITION (Bottom)

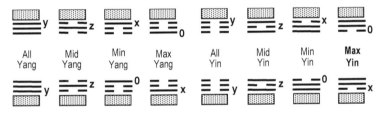

Figure 2: The top row shows the eight trigrams in the host position. Min-Yang and Min-Yin are in strong contact with the guest (x), All-Yang and All-Yin moderate contact (y), Mid-Yang and Mid-Yin weak contact (z), Max-Yang and Max-Yin not in contact at all (0).

The bottom row shows the eight trigrams in the guest position. Max-Yang and Max-Yin are in strong contact with the host (x), All-Yang and All-Yin moderate contact (y), Mid-Yang and Mid-Yin weak contact (z), Min-Yang and Min-Yin not in contact at all (0).

Max-Yang and Max-Yin: The bottom line is the identity line.

Min-Yang and Min-Yin: The top line is the identity line.

Mid-Yang and Mid-Yin: The center line is the identity line.

All-Yang and All-Yin: Since all three lines are the same, they should all be considered identity lines. However, the sense of identity for each line is weaker than the other 6 trigrams.

We recall from the last chapter that the contact between a host trigram and a guest trigram is the mathematical equivalent of a real-life phenomenon. This contact is made between lines 3 and 4. This has extremely interesting implications on how differently males and females tend to deal with the same real-life situation. We will discuss this intriguing topic in detail in a future book dedicated to the Yin Yang theory. For the purposes at hand, it suffices to recognize that the identity line is mathematically the position taken by a trigram.

For the case of a host trigram:
-Min-Yang and Min-Yin, with the identity line at position 3, are in strong contact with the guest and therefore strongly impacted by their relationship with the guest.

Min-Yang lacks aggressiveness; therefore he is at the mercy of the guest.

Min-Yin is aggressive; therefore she will try to react to the guest. This does not necessarily mean that her reaction will be beneficial for her.

-For the special case of All-Yang and All-Yin, line 3 must be considered as a partial identity of the trigram. This line is also in direct contact with the guest; therefore All-Yang and All-Yin are also impacted by the relationship with the guest, but only moderately.

-Mid-Yang and Mid-Yin, with the identity line at position 2, only feel an indirect impact from the guest. This impact is therefore weak.

-Max-Yang and Max-Yin, with the identity line at position 1, are far away from the guest and will not feel any impact at all.

For the case of a guest trigram:
-Min-Yang and Min-Yin, with the identity line at position 6, are completely removed from the host.

Min-Yang lacks aggressiveness; therefore the host cannot count on him. On the other hand, it also means that the host will try to help Min-Yang improve his situation.

Min-Yin is aggressive, therefore her behavior is considered as a deviation from the ordinary. Each host will deal with such a situation differently.

-For the special case of All-Yang and All-Yin, line 4 must be considered as a partial identity of the trigram. This line is also in direct contact with the host; therefore All-Yang and All-Yin have influence on the host, but only moderately.

-Mid-Yang and Mid-Yin, with the identity line at position 5, only have indirect influence on the host. This influence is weak and should only be considered when the main line of the host is at position 3, which corresponds to Min-Yang and Min-Yin.

-Max-Yang and Max-Yin, with the identity line at position 4, are in strong contact with the host, and have significant influence on him or her.

The special cases of hostess Max-Yin and host Mid-Yang

When Max-Yin serves as the hostess, we have a peculiar case that requires special attention.

Of the 8 trigrams, Max-Yin is the only trigram with three Yin properties:

Identity: Feminine (Yin)
Activity: Most tentative (strongly Yin)
Ability: Most common (strongly Yin)

Since Max-Yin has no Yang property, she is not qualified to be a hostess. By Yin Yang logic, it is impossible to have a trigram interaction without a host or hostess trigram, and it is impossible to have an event without a trigram interaction. Thus, not having Max-Yin as the hostess is not a practical option.

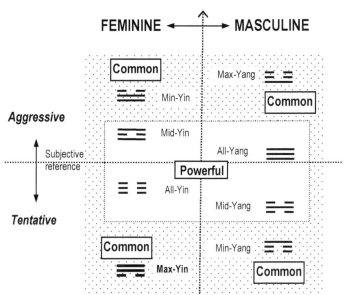

Figure 3: Because the host position is Yang, the reference horizontal line will be subjectively raised to a level higher than it should be. This skews the picture and creates (apparent) inequality. Specifically it makes Mid-Yang the weakest of the 4 powerful trigrams (farthest from reference line), and Max-Yin the most common trigram.

The only solution is that Max-Yin somehow transforms herself so that she becomes qualified for the hostess position. But what logic would allow the happening of this extraordinary event? To answer the question, we recall that extreme Yin will transform to Yang, and extreme Yang will transform to Yin. Objectively speaking, Max-Yin should not qualify as being extreme Yin, because if she were extreme Yin, then by a symmetry argument Max-Yang would be extreme Yang. The reason is that Max-Yin and Max-Yang are exact Yin Yang opposites of each other. Note, however, that we are not dealing with objectivity. We instead are dealing with a subjective viewpoint that considers the host position (i.e., based "subjective reference" in figure 3) as the reference point. This makes Max-Yin, who is the most Yin trigram under all circumstances, appear as the most extreme deviation from the center of power.

The subjective view, then, allows Max-Yin to modify herself to fit the hostess position. Since the main characteristic of Max-Yin is flexible, she will conform to the situation created by the guest in such a way that things do not come to a dead end. We will see more detail of her peculiar behavior later.

The situation of the powerful host Mid-Yang is no less peculiar. Because of the subjective view, he appears as the power trigram furthest away from the reference line (see figure 3). This means he is doomed into being considered the weakest of the four power trigrams. In order to compensate for weakness, one needs aggressiveness. The problem is, Mid-Yang is a tentative trigram. For these reasons, Mid-Yang is highly vulnerable when he serves as a host. But if Mid-Yang is stuck in this quandary, how could he be considered as a power trigram? Again, for the same reason as the case of hostess Max-Yin, when host Mid-Yang is reduced to a position of helplessness, he is also blessed with the choice to overcome his tentativeness and achieve great results. We will see his peculiar behavior in several cases later.

The law of Yin Yang reversal

The quite unexpected transformations of Max-Yin and Mid-Yang are manifestations of the more general "Law of Yin Yang reversal." This law is seen quite often in a field of future prediction known as Chinese Astrology.

Roles of the three trigram properties in trigram relationships

So far we know that the host position is a Yang position, therefore it prefers Yang over Yin (e.g., powerful over common, aggressive over tentative, masculine over feminine). Since each relationship involves two trigrams, we define the "net property" of a hexagram as the combined property of the host trigram minus that of the guest trigram. The general rule is that if the "net property" of the hexagram is Yang the hexagram will have favorable meaning; but if the "net property" is Yin the hexagram will have unfavorable meaning.

A qualification must be made at this point. Since the "net property" varies from one hexagram to the next, if we examine two arbitrarily chosen "favorable" hexagrams, we will find that they are not equally favorable. For example, we could find that the first hexagram is overwhelmingly favorable, while the second one only marginally so. The same is true with "unfavorable" hexagrams. Thus, the general rule only gives us a general picture, and more information is needed to establish the total meaning of a hexagram.

Since each trigram has three properties, we must know which property is the most important, which one is second, which one is third. It turns out the best way to do this is to divide the problem into cases and examine each case separately. We have the following six cases:

1. Max-Yin serves as hostess (8 trigrams): As we have learned from last chapter, because of the law of Yin-Yang reversal, Max-Yin is an exception to the general rule when she serves as the hostess.

2. Identity hexagrams (7 trigrams): There are eight hexagrams with identical host and guest. These are the identity hexagrams. However we will only cover 7 identity hexagrams, as Double Max-Yin belongs to case 1.

3. Power group interaction (12 hexagrams): These are the various interactions among the four power trigrams: All-Yang, All-Yin, Mid-Yang, and Mid-Yin. *(Except identity trigrams, which belong to case 2).*

4. Common group interaction (9 hexagrams): These are interactions among the four common trigrams: Max-Yang, Max-Yin, Min-Yang, and Min-Yin. *(Except Max-Yin serving as hostess, which belongs to case 1, and identity trigrams, which belong to case 2.)*

5. Power trigram hosting common trigram (16 hexagrams): A trigram in the power group hosting a trigram in the common group.

6. Common trigram hosting power trigram (12 hexagrams): A trigram in the common group hosting a trigram in the power group. *(Except Max-Yin serving as hostess, which belongs to case 1.)*

For easy reference, each hexagram is connected with the order that it appears in the I-Ching, and the English name that best approximates the original Chinese name. For example, when we say hexagram 10 "Stepping Cautiously," we mean this hexagram is listed as hexagram number 10 in the I-Ching, and the original Chinese name has approximate meaning "Stepping Cautiously."

Case 1: Max-Yin as hostess (8 hexagrams)

As we have established earlier, the law of Yin Yang reversal allows hostess Max-Yin to turn the table on her guest, giving the following 8 hexagrams:

-All-Yang as guest: Instead of playing the role of the timid girl at the mercy of this most powerful aggressive masculine guest, Max-Yin will try to match him with her own aggressiveness. This definitely shocks the aggressive guest, and we have hexagram 44 "Flirting," whose meaning is (morally) negative.

-All-Yin as guest: Instead of playing the role of a timid subordinate of this most powerful tentative feminine guest, Max-Yin will try to raise her level to match All-Yin's queen-like status, and we have hexagram 46 "Ascending."

-Mid-Yang as guest: Instead of letting this powerful tentative masculine guest dictate the relationship, Max-Yin absorbs his water-like strength, and we have hexagram 48 "The Well."

-Mid-Yin as guest: Instead of letting this powerful aggressive feminine guest be the leader, Max-Yin absorbs her fire-like energy, and we have hexagram 50 "The Cauldron."

-Max-Yang as guest: Instead of letting this common but most aggressive masculine guest drag her around with an uncertain future (as he expects to do with his strong influence on her at line 4) Max-Yin ties him up in a permanent relationship, and we have hexagram 32 "Permanence."

-Max-Yin as guest: Instead of staying helpless as the weakest hostess, Max-Yin will utilize the guest's flexible nature to achieve progress, and we have hexagram 57 "The Flexible."

-Min-Yang as guest: The lack of aggressiveness and commitment of this common tentative masculine trigram (who is also completely disconnected from Max-Yin) leads to

93

deterioration. Max-Yin will resolve to correct the situation, and we have hexagram 18 "Deterioration."

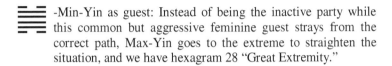-Min-Yin as guest: Instead of being the inactive party while this common but aggressive feminine guest strays from the correct path, Max-Yin goes to the extreme to straighten the situation, and we have hexagram 28 "Great Extremity."

Case 2: Identity hexagrams (7, without Double Max-Yin)

In identity hexagrams, the host and the guest are identical. The meaning for an identity hexagram, then, is very much the same as that of the individual trigram. Modifications have to be made to account for the fact that hexagram meaning reflects the situation of the host trigram, and the host position favors masculine over feminine, aggressiveness over tentativeness, and powerful over common.

-Double All-Yang (most powerful aggressive masculine): With all three properties fitting the host position, this is a hexagram of great promise. It represents the proper time for action, giving hexagram 1 "The Active."

-Double All-Yin (most powerful tentative feminine): All-Yin's ability property fits perfectly in the hostess position. However, since she is tentative feminine, this identity hexagram says that the proper course of action is to seek a leader instead of being one, giving hexagram 2 "The Receptive."

-Double Mid-Yang (powerful tentative masculine): In the power game if you are not the most powerful, you must compensate by being aggressive. The host's downfall is that he is tentative. This puts him in danger, giving hexagram 29 "Danger." This is a case where the law of Yin Yang reversal applies; and "Danger" is a great opportunity for the special few who are able and dare to take chances.

-Double Mid-Yin (powerful aggressive feminine): Hostess Mid-Yin compensates for her weaknesses by being the most aggressive trigram of the power group. This makes her the most active, like a bright sun, giving hexagram 30 "Brightness."

-Double Max-Yang (common most aggressive masculine): Being most aggressive masculine is favorable, but being common is a severe limit to what can be achieved by Max-Yang. He is like the strength of thunder, with startling impact, but of minor consequence, giving hexagram 51 "Thunder."

-Double Max-Yin (common most tentative feminine): This was covered in case 1.

-Double Min-Yang (common tentative masculine): Being masculine is the only positive aspect of the host. In his very weak position, he should not attempt anything at all. Hexagram 52 is therefore "Inactivity."

-Double Min-Yin (common aggressive feminine): Being aggressive is the only positive aspect of the hostess. In her very weak position, her aggressiveness is as inconsequential as child play, giving hexagram 58 "The Playful."

Case 3: Power group interactions (12 hexagrams)

The power group consists of All-Yang, All-Yin, Mid-Yang, and Mid-Yin. It is obvious that power is the key property here, but since the power property is related to the activity property, these two properties will have to be considered together. There are two approaches to achieve power: The aggressive approach and the tentative approach. These two approaches are clearly in conflict. Thus, when both trigrams are aggressive or both trigrams are tentative, we have a power agreement; but when one trigram is aggressive and the other tentative, we have a power conflict.

Power agreement is good, therefore a hexagram formed by two aggressive power trigrams or two tentative power trigrams will have favorable meaning.

Power conflict is good for the winner, bad for the loser. The factor that decides winner and loser is of course the power level. Thus, if the host is more powerful than the guest, however slightly, the hexagram has favorable meaning. On the other hand, if the host is less powerful than the guest, however slightly, the hexagram has unfavorable meaning.

The modifying factor is the identity property. Since I-Ching logic favors Yang, a favorable hexagram is even more favorable with a masculine host and a feminine guest, less favorable the other way around. An unfavorable hexagram has redeeming value with a masculine host and a feminine guest, and is even more unfavorable the other way around.

First we present the four hexagrams formed by two aggressive or two tentative power trigrams.

-Mid-Yin (aggressive) hosting All-Yang (aggressive) is a favorable but less-than-perfect interaction because it is feminine hosting masculine. It represents cooperation where weakness is overcome by willingness and activity, giving hexagram 13 "Alliance."

-All-Yang (aggressive) hosting Mid-Yin (aggressive) is a very favorable interaction because it is masculine hosting feminine, giving hexagram 14 "Great Possession."

-Mid-Yang (tentative) hosting All-Yin (tentative) is a very favorable interaction because it is masculine hosting feminine, giving hexagram 7 "The Army."

-All-Yin (tentative) hosting Mid-Yang (tentative). The favorable meaning of the hexagram is compromised by the fact that this is feminine hosting masculine. The situation is described in hexagram 8 "Union."

If one trigram is aggressive and the other tentative, there is a conflict of approach. Power is then the deciding factor. Thus, if the host is more powerful than the guest, even slightly, the outcome is favorable. However, there is a difference in degree. Since I-Ching logic favors Yang over Yin, masculine hosting feminine has more strength, while feminine hosting masculine has undesirable side effects.

-All-Yang (most powerful) hosting All-Yin (most powerful). The subjective view makes All-Yang appear slightly more powerful than All-Yin (see figure 1), giving hexagram 11 "Great Harmony." This is a highly favorable hexagram. One reason is that it is masculine hosting feminine.

-All-Yang (most powerful) hosting Mid-Yang (powerful). Obviously All-Yang is more powerful than Mid-Yang, giving the relatively favorable hexagram 5 "Waiting."

☷ -All-Yin (most powerful) hosting Mid-Yin (powerful). Obviously All-Yin is more powerful than Mid-Yin, giving hexagram 35 "Advance."

☵ -Mid-Yin (powerful feminine) hosting Mid-Yang (powerful masculine). The subjective view makes Mid-Yin appear slightly more powerful than Mid-Yang (see figure 1), giving hexagram 63 "Completion." Note that this particular case has undesirable side effect because it is feminine hosting masculine.

Understandably, also in the case of conflict, if the host is less powerful than the guest, even slightly, the outcome in unfavorable. However, there is a difference in degree. Since I-Ching logic favors Yang over Yin, masculine hosting feminine still has good potential.

☷ -All-Yin (most powerful) hosting All-Yang (most powerful). The subjective view makes All-Yin appear slightly less powerful than All-Yang, giving hexagram 12 "Stagnation." This hexagram is highly unfavorable because it is feminine hosting masculine.

☵ -Mid-Yang (powerful) hosting All-Yang (most powerful). Obviously Mid-Yang is less powerful than All-Yang, giving the trying situation of hexagram 6 "Contention."

☶ -Mid-Yin (powerful) hosting All-Yin (most powerful). Obviously Mid-Yin is less powerful than All-Yin, giving hexagram 36 "Brightness Dimmed."

☶ -Mid-Yang (powerful masculine) hosting Mid-Yin (powerful feminine). The subjective view makes Mid-Yang appear slightly less powerful than Mid-Yin, giving hexagram 64 "Incompletion." Note that, despite its unfavorable status, this particular hexagram does have redeeming value, as it is masculine hosting feminine.

Case 4: Common group interaction (9 hexagrams)

The picture in the world of the common group is entirely different from that of the power group. Here we do not have power agreement or power conflict; we only have the have-nots trying to survive with their limited capabilities. Understandably, power has no meaning in the common group. In the brutal fight for survival, identity is the deciding factor, and aggressiveness the modifying factor. Therefore the order of preference for the host is: Aggressive masculine is best, followed by tentative masculine, aggressive feminine; and tentative feminine is in last place. This order corresponds to Max-Yang, Min-Yang, Min-Yin, and Max-Yin.

Thus, Max-Yang will enjoy a favorable situation when he hosts any of the other three common hexagrams. Min-Yang's situation is not favorable when he hosts Max-Yang, but he will do well with the two feminine guests Min-Yin and Max-Yin. Min-Yin will be in deep trouble when she hosts Max-Yang, lesser trouble with Min-Yang, and she enjoy the company of Max-Yin.

Max-Yin's situation seems hopeless, but this is why she is rescued by the law of Yin Yang reversal (see case 1).

MAX-YANG AS HOST

-Min-Yang as guest: Although both trigrams are masculine, the situation is somewhat favorable because the host is aggressive while the guest is tentative, giving hexagram 27 "Feeding."

-Min-Yin as guest: The situation is favorable because, while both trigrams are aggressive, the host is masculine and the guest is feminine, giving hexagram 17 "Pursuing."

-Max-Yin as guest: The situation is very favorable, because the host is aggressive masculine while the guest is tentative feminine, giving hexagram 42 "Increase."

MIN-YANG AS HOST

-Max-Yang as guest: Although both trigrams are masculine, the situation is somewhat unfavorable because the host is tentative while the guest is aggressive, giving hexagram 62 "Small Extremity."

-Min-Yin as guest: The situation is somewhat favorable because, despite the fact that the host is tentative while the guest is aggressive, he has the upper hand being a masculine trigram hosting a feminine trigram, giving hexagram 31 "E-motions."

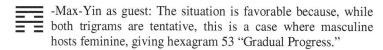 -Max-Yin as guest: The situation is favorable because, while both trigrams are tentative, this is a case where masculine hosts feminine, giving hexagram 53 "Gradual Progress."

MIN-YIN AS HOSTESS

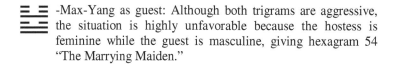 -Max-Yang as guest: Although both trigrams are aggressive, the situation is highly unfavorable because the hostess is feminine while the guest is masculine, giving hexagram 54 "The Marrying Maiden."

-Min-Yang as guest: Although this is an unfavorable situation of feminine hosting masculine, the hostess is not in such a bad shape, thanks to the fact that she is aggressive while the guest is tentative, giving hexagram 41 "Decrease."

-Max-Yin as guest: Since both trigrams are feminine, the situation is favorable because the hostess is aggressive while the guest is tentative, giving hexagram 61 "Central Harmony."

MAX-YIN AS HOSTESS: *Already covered in case 1.*

Case 5: Power group hosting common group (16 hexagrams)

When a power trigram hosts a common trigram, the action of the host is to either correct a guest who is out of line, or improve the situation of the guest if the guest is too weak, or simply interact with the guest. In this case, the hexagram meaning reflects the effectiveness of the host or hostess in carrying out his or her actions.

Actions are directly related to the activity property. Activity is therefore the top criterion in determining whether a hexagram is favorable. Power is the secondary factor because, as far as the common guests are concerned, all hosts are powerful. However, power could still be the tie breaker in marginal cases. This makes Mid-Yin, who is the most aggressive of all power trigrams, the most favorable hostess. She is followed by All-Yang (aggressive most powerful), All-Yin (tentative most powerful). Last in the list is Mid-Yang (tentative powerful).

Because of the disparity in power, the host or hostess is most effective when he or she deals with a guest of the same identity. That is because two entities with the same identity (both masculine or both feminine) will think along the same line, and therefore the risk of misunderstanding can be minimized.

Since the identity line of the guest is important, we will list the hexagram in groups of 4, each group with the same guest, hosted in order by Mid-Yin, All-Yang, All-Yin, and Mid-Yang.

MAX-YANG AS GUEST (most aggressive, strong influence on host)
Since Max-Yang's main line is on line 4, which is in contact with the host, Max-Yang will influence the host with his extreme aggressiveness.

-Mid-Yin as hostess: The extreme aggressiveness of Max-Yang creates a most favorable situation for the hostess (who identity is "brightness"). However, since the two trigrams do not share the same identity (feminine hosting masculine), there is a down side. This most favorable situation cannot last long. We have hexagram 55 "Abundance."

-All-Yang as host: The extreme aggressiveness of Max-Yang excites the already aggressive All-Yang, creating a tendency for the host to be very aggressive. While the situation should be highly favorable (both host and guest are masculine), All-Yang must be careful of the risk of becoming too aggressive, which would reduce his ability. This corresponds to hexagram 34 "Great Energy."

-All-Yin as host: The extreme aggressiveness of Max-Yang helps eliminate some of the tentativeness of All-Yin, and instills a sense of enthusiasm uncharacteristic of her. This is favorable because an increase in activity may not decrease her power, and in fact may increase it. However, since this is feminine hosting masculine, the impact may not lead to anything substantial. We have hexagram 16 "Exuberance."

-Mid-Yang as host: The extreme aggressiveness of Max-Yang helps Mid-Yang to wake up from his tentative state, which has been blocking his development as a power trigram. Therefore this is a favorable hexagram. There is no down side as both trigrams are masculine. We have hexagram 40 "Relief."

MAX-YIN AS GUEST (most tentative, strong influence on host)
Since Max-Yin's main line is on line 4, which is in contact with the host, she will be able to get the powerful host or hostess to pay attention to her extremely weak position and possibly offer help.

100

-Mid-Yin as hostess: Being the most aggressive power trigram, Mid-Yin has no problem helping Max-Yin. Since both trigrams are feminine, the situation is like a strong sister helping a weak sister, giving hexagram 37 "Family Members."

-All-Yang as host: Being the most powerful aggressive trigram, All-Yang has the ability to help Max-Yin. The problem is that he is masculine while Max-Yin is feminine. The outcome is expected to be modest, giving hexagram 9 "Small Cultivation."

-All-Yin as host: All-Yin is feminine like Max-Yin. The problem is: being tentative limits All-Yin's ability to help. She can only set examples for Max-Yin to follow. This is described in hexagram 20 "Observation."

-Mid-Yang as host: Mid-Yang has two problems. First, he is masculine while the guest is feminine. Second, he is tentative, which spells trouble. This is another case where the law of Yin Yang reversal applies. Mid-Yang has a choice. He could either play safe and fail miserably, or exceed all expectations by performing a great sacrifice to save Max-Yin in spectacular fashion. This is described in hexagram 59 "Dispersion" (Sacrifice).

MIN-YANG AS GUEST (tentative, far away from host)
Being common tentative, Min-Yang also needs help. Since his main line is on line 6, far away from the host, Min-Yang is like someone who does not know his way, and does not know how to ask for help.

-Mid-Yin as hostess: Having nothing in common with the guest, the only reason that makes Mid-Yin's situation favorable is that she is the most aggressive of all power trigrams. Her action will have very limited result, like decorating Min-Yin, making him more presentable (without improvement in substance), giving hexagram 22 "Decoration."

-All-Yang as host: Being the most powerful masculine trigram, All-Yang can help the masculine guest Min-Yin in a big way, giving hexagram 26 "Great Cultivation."

-All-Yin as host: All-Yin has three problems. First, she is feminine while the guest in need is masculine. Second, she is

101

SCIENTIFIC CODE OF THE I-CHING

tentative, which spells trouble. Third, I-Ching logic favors masculine; therefore it will not come to her rescue. Being a most powerful trigram, the situation of All-Yin is like one who is destroying instead of helping Min-Yin, giving hexagram 23 "Destruction."

-Mid-Yang as host: Being masculine like Min-Yang, Mid-Yang can help his weaker brother in need. Although being tentative is a negative asset, the good thing is that the guest is even more tentative. Mid-Yang can therefore help Min-Yang, but he will do so reluctantly, with much less result than "Great Cultivation." We have hexagram 4 "Teaching the ignorant" or simply "Ignorance."

MIN-YIN AS GUEST (aggressive, far away from host)
Since her main line is on line 6, far away from the host, Min-Yin's aggressiveness is considered as unwanted behavior that needs to be corrected.

-Mid-Yin as hostess: Being feminine like the guest, the aggressiveness of Mid-Yin is her great asset. She will be able to force Min-Yin to change her course of action, giving hexagram 49 "Revolution."

-All-Yang as host: Being the most powerful masculine trigram, All-Yang should be able to correct Min-Yin's behavior. The problem is: he is masculine while Min-Yin is feminine. So while his aggressiveness allows him to proceed, he will not be able to achieve anything substantial immediately. This is the situation of hexagram 43 "Correction."

-All-Yin as host: Being feminine like the guest is a great asset, but being tentative keeps All-Yin from taking dramatic steps against Min-Yin. She will instead show her strength as the most powerful of all feminine trigrams, which should be a sufficient warning that persuades Min-Yin to change her course of action. This is the situation of hexagram 45 "Gathering."

-Mid-Yang as host: Mid-Yang has two problems. First, he and the guest have opposite identities. Second, he is tentative, which spells trouble. The situation is like Mid-Yang becoming exhausted without getting any result, giving hexagram 47 "Exhaustion."

This is another case where the law of Yin Yang reversal could come to Mid-Yang rescue. For this reason, this hexagram is the downfall of ordinary people, but great opportunity for those who are capable.

Case 6: Common group hosting power group (12 hexagrams)

Common host trigrams are at the mercy of the powerful guests, and therefore need their sympathy. This makes proximity the best asset as a common host who is close to a powerful guest is more likely to win the guest's sympathy. The next factor is activity, as an aggressive host is more likely to react on time. The order therefore is: Min-Yin (close and aggressive), Min-Yang (close but tentative), Max-Yang (far but aggressive), Max-Yin (far and tentative).

When a common trigram deals with a power trigram, he or she has a much better chance if the identities of the two sides are complementary. This is in contrary to case 4, where same identity is preferred. (The reader can verify for him or herself that this is perfectly true in life.)

Since the identity line of the host is important, we will list the hexagrams in groups of 4, each with the same host in order cited (Min-Yin, Min-Yang, Max-Yang, Max-Yin), and the guests in order All-Yang, Mid-Yang, All-Yin, Mid-Yin.

MIN-YIN AS HOSTESS (aggressive feminine, good contact with guest)

-All-Yang as guest: With complementary identity, and good contact with the most powerful aggressive guest, Min-Yin will survive this close encounter by translating her aggressiveness to appropriate actions, giving hexagram 10 "Stepping Cautiously."

-Mid-Yang as guest: With complementary identity and good contact with the powerful but tentative guest, Min-Yin will be wise by restraining her aggressiveness, so that the tentative guest knows that she has come with good will, giving hexagram 60 "Self-Restraint."

-All-Yin as guest: Being feminine like this most powerful guest puts Min-Yin in potential trouble. The wise action for her is to rely on her aggressiveness. She would approach the tentative guest and demonstrate her good will. Since the situation is precarious, she must follow up with actions, as words alone will not be good enough. This is described in hexagram 19 "Approaching."

 -Mid-Yin as guest: Being feminine like this powerful guest puts Min-Yin in potential trouble. Since both trigrams are aggressive, Min-Yin aggressiveness will certainly be considered inappropriate by the guest. Min-Yin's saving grace is that she is in close contact with the guest and realizes the difference between them, as well as the potential problem that this difference may cause. This is described in hexagram 38 "Differences."

MIN-YANG AS HOST (tentative masculine, good contact with host)

 -All-Yang as guest: Having the same identity as this most powerful masculine guest, Min-Yang does not hope that the guest will have any sympathy on him. Being in direct contact, Min-Yang is scared by the guest's aggressiveness and therefore will try to back away to a safe distance. This is described by hexagram 33 "Retreating."

 -Mid-Yang as guest: Having the same identity as this powerful masculine guest, Min-Yang does not hope for any understanding. Being in direct contact, he perceives the tentative but powerful guest as an obstruction on his path. This is described in hexagram 39 "Obstruction."

 -All-Yin as guest: Having complementary identity, Min-Yang trusts the guest, who is the most powerful tentative feminine trigram All-Yin. Understanding the power disparity between him and the guest, Min-Yang will be humble to the guest, with good result at the end. This is described in hexagram 15 "Humility."

 -Mid-Yin as guest: Having complementary identity, Min-Yang will be treated fairly by the powerful guest Mid-Yin and may get something positive out of the interaction. However, since the guest is aggressive, the close contact will affects Min-Yin's behavior, and he himself will be somewhat aggressive. Since being aggressive is not suitable for his character, Min-

Yang behavior is not well defined, more like a wanderer. The situation is described in hexagram 56 "The Wanderer."

MAX-YANG AS HOST (most aggressive masculine, no contact with guest)

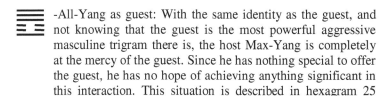

-All-Yang as guest: With the same identity as the guest, and not knowing that the guest is the most powerful aggressive masculine trigram there is, the host Max-Yang is completely at the mercy of the guest. Since he has nothing special to offer the guest, he has no hope of achieving anything significant in this interaction. This situation is described in hexagram 25 "Non-Expectation."

-Mid-Yang as guest: With the same identity as the guest, and not knowing that the guest is tentative, Max-Yang will not achieve any immediate result, but he may plan for the future on the strength of his aggressiveness, which can complement the guest's tentativeness. This is the situation of hexagram 3 "Difficulties."

-All-Yin as the guest: With the most powerful feminine guest sympathizing his cause, Max-Yang can make plans; but this is more like a revival than a great success. The situation is described in hexagram 24 "Revival."

-Mid-Yin as the guest: Although the powerful feminine guest considers his complementary identity favorably, Max-Yang will not win her sympathy because both trigrams are aggressive. The guest will not fail to notice that Max-Yang is too aggressive. He will get help from her, but in the form of punishment, like an inmate in a corrective institution. The situation is described in hexagram 21 "Biting (in pain)."

MAX-YIN AS HOSTESS: *Already covered in case 1.*

A special note on All-Yin

All-Yin is the most powerful feminine trigram, but the subjective view makes it inappropriate for her to dominate in her interaction with a masculine trigram. She is at her best when cooperation is feasible.

We have seen this in hexagram 7 "The Army" where All-Yin is the guest of Mid-Yang, hexagram 8 "Union" where she hosts Mid-Yang, hexagram 11 "Great Harmony" when she is the guest of All-Yang, hexagram 15 "Humility" when she is the guest of Min-Yang, hexagram 16 "Exuberance" when she hosts Max-Yang, hexagram 24 "Revival" when she is the guest of Max-Yang. When it is unlikely that cooperation can take place, the tremendous power of All-Yin only leads to disaster. This is seen in hexagram 12 "Stagnation" where she hosts All-Yang; and in hexagram 23 "Destruction" when she hosts Min-Yang.

Double checking the logic behind the 64 hexagrams

As the readers have seen in this chapter, the meanings of the hexagrams can be deduced in a systematic way without having to refer to I-Ching texts.

A more detailed account of all 64 hexagrams is presented in the second part of the book (in traditional order) so that the reader can confirm for him or herself that the Yin Yang logic derived in this work is in perfect agreement with the traditional meanings of the 64 hexagrams!

Since the materials in this chapter are quite involved, we will present them again in the next chapter in such a way that they can be memorized quickly. This will be our "lazy person's approach" to master the meanings of the 64 hexagrams.

First written April 2002
Completed July 2002
©T. Tran

Chapter 10
The 64 hexagrams III
The lazy person's approach to hexagram meanings

The lazy person's approach to Yin Yang and the 64 hexagrams

By definition, an expert is a person who has in-depth knowledge in his or her field of specialty. The goal of this chapter is to establish the reader as an expert on the meanings of the hexagrams. By default he or she should also be a Yin Yang expert.

REVIEW OF FUNDAMENTALS

Just in case you have forgotten, following is a review of fundamental concepts that you should master by now.

From Yin and Yang to the eight trigrams *(chapters 2 and 3)*

Yin and Yang are deviations from a reference state. They account for two dimensions: Time and one dimension of space.

Yin is represented as a broken line, Yang a solid line.

To represent any existence in space and time, the other two (equivalent) dimensions of space must be included. This leads to the result that all entities in the universe can be represented by the eight trigrams.

Each trigram consists of three Yin or Yang elements, traditionally presented as three lines (see the next section).

Naming system for the trigrams *(chapter 1)*

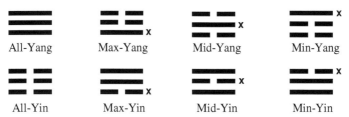

Fig 1: The proposed naming system for the 8 trigrams

The naming rules are:
1. Trigrams with odd number of solid lines are named Yang, with odd number of broken lines are named Yin.
2. The trigram with three solid lines is "All-Yang."
3. The trigram with three broken lines is "All-Yin."

4. The other six trigrams are differentiated by the order of the odd line. Starting from the bottom, the order is: Max, Mid, Min.

The trigrams are listed in figure 1. By noticing the position of the "identity line" (marked with an "x") and with the help of rule number 4, the average reader should be able to remember the names of all eight trigrams in 5 minutes. This feat should not be underestimated, considering that differentiating the eight trigrams has always been a very difficult task for Yin Yang beginners and even to some intermediate Yin Yang students.

The three trigram properties *(chapters 4 and 5)*

Each trigram has three Yin Yang properties, as shown in table 1.

TABLE 1: Detailed properties of the trigrams

Trigram	Activity	Ability	Identity
All-Yang	Aggressive	Most Powerful	Masculine
Mid-Yang	Tentative	Powerful	Masculine
Min-Yang	Tentative	Common	Masculine
Max-Yang	Aggressive	Most Common	Masculine
All-Yin	Tentative	Most Powerful	Feminine
Mid-Yin	Aggressive	Powerful	Feminine
Min-Yin	Aggressive	Common	Feminine
Max-Yin	Tentative	Most Common	Feminine

Good memory tricks:

1. *Identity (key word = odd):* If the number of Yin lines is odd, the trigram is Feminine. If the number of Yang lines is odd, the trigram is Masculine.
2. *Activity (key word = bottom line):* If the bottom line is Yang, the trigram is aggressive. If the bottom line is Yin, the trigram is tentative.
3. *Ability (key word = symmetry):* The power trigrams (most powerful and powerful) are symmetrical, the common trigrams are not.
4. *More trick:* "All" sounds more powerful than "Mid"; therefore All-Yang and All-Yang are most powerful, while Mid-Yang and Mid-Yin are powerful.

Impact of the subjective view on the ability property *(chapter 8)*

The only view that matters in the world is the subjective view. The subjective view distorts the balance of the 8 trigrams in favor of aggressiveness. As a result:

All-Yang (aggressive) appears slightly more powerful than *All-Yin*

Mid-Yin (aggressive) appears slightly more powerful than *Mid-Yang*

Min-Yin (aggressive) appears slightly more powerful than *Min-Yang*

Max-Yang (aggressive) appears slightly more powerful than *Max-Yin*

The 64 hexagram of the I-Ching *(chapter 8)*

There are 64 hexagrams in the I-Ching; each is formed by placing two trigrams on top of each other. Since there are 8 trigrams, there are 8×8=64 hexagrams.

The bottom trigram is also called "inner trigram;" our preferred name for it is "host trigram." The top trigram is also called "outer trigram;" our preferred name for it is "guest trigram."

Hexagram meaning *(chapter 8)*

Hexagram meaning is a description of the situation of the host trigram in its interaction with the guest trigram.

The Yang bias rule in hexagram meaning *(chapter 8)*

Since the host position is associated with Yang (and the guest position with Yin), hexagram meaning is biased toward masculine, aggressive, powerful (at the expense of feminine, tentative, common).

However, the actual application of this rule varies from case to case, which we will cover in detail.

The law of Yin Yang reversal in hexagram meaning *(chapter 9)*

Max-Yin, with three Yin properties, is not fit to be the hostess at all. The fact is, she is still the hostess in 8 hexagrams. Since the I-Ching describes states of existence, not of extinction, Max-Yin must have somehow modified herself to survive. Since the key word that describes Max-Yin is Flexibility, she changes herself to fit the character of the guest, obtaining good results most of the time.

Mid-Yang, falling victim to the subjective view, is the weakest of all power trigram. In addition, he is tentative. There is nothing more dangerous than being hesitant when you are playing the power game from the bottom of the group. This reflects in several situations where Mid-Yang serves as the host. Again, since the I-Ching describes states of existence, not of extinction, Mid-Yang could exceed himself in these particular situations and achieve great results against all odds.

The peculiar behavior of Max-Yin and Mid-Yang at the edge of catastrophe is called the "Law of Yin Yang Reversal."

MEANINGS OF THE 64 HEXAGRAMS *(chapter 9)*

Hexagrams with hostess Max-Yin (8)
MEMORY TRICK: Max-Yang modifies herself to fit the character of the host (thanks to the law of Yin Yang reversal). She does well with all guests except All-Yang (Yin Yang gap too big).

Identity hexagrams (7)
MEMORY TRICK: Guest is the same as host; therefore host retains very much the original trigram meaning.

Power trigram hosting power trigram (12)

MEMORY TRICK: Use the analogy of real life. There are two sides to every power struggle. Two persons on the same side get along; two persons on opposite sides are in conflict. In conflicts, the more powerful side wins. Within this larger picture of power conflicts, males (masculine) are preferred over females (feminine).

Rules: Power (agreement or conflict) is key, identity secondary (masculine preferred).

When two trigrams are not in conflict, the meaning of the hexagram is favorable. When two trigrams are in conflict, if the host or hostess is more powerful, he or she will win and the meaning of the hexagram is favorable. If the host or hostess is less powerful, he or she will lose and the meaning of the hexagram is unfavorable.

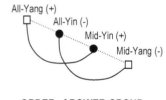

ORDER of POWER GROUP

Figure 2: Relationship in the power group is decided by the power scale (All-Yang highest, Mid-Yang lowest). The additional rule is that aggressive trigrams (+) are in agreement with each other, but in conflict with tentative trigrams (-). In case of conflict, the outcome is in favor of the more powerful trigram.

Hexagram meaning is enhanced with masculine host, degraded somewhat with feminine hostess. For example, All-Yang hosting Mid-Yin and Mid-Yin hosting All-Yang are both favorable (because these are aggressive trigrams), but the first hexagram is more favorable than the second.

Common trigram hosting common trigram (9)

MEMORY TRICK: Use the analogy of real life. In the world of common people, males (masculine) are unfairly preferred over females (feminine). Aggressiveness counts, but it is not as important as identity.

Rules: Identity is key (masculine preferred), activity secondary.

Order of preference for the host works out to be: Max-Yang (masculine aggressive), Min-Yang (masculine tentative), Min-Yin (feminine aggressive), Max-Yin (feminine tentative).

Favorable when guest is lower in order compared to host, unfavorable when higher. For example, Min-Yang's situation is somewhat unfavorable when the guest is Max-Yang, somewhat favorable when the guest is Min-Yin, favorable when the guest is Max-Yin, etc.

Max-Yang (+)
Min-Yang (-)
Min-Yin (+)
Max-Yin (-)

ORDER of COMMON GROUP

Figure 3: In the common group masculine is preferred over feminine, then aggressive over tentative; leading to the order on the left: Max-Yang (masculine aggressive), Min-Yang (masculine tentative), Min-Yin (feminine aggressive), Max-Yin (feminine tentative).

The logic spells serious trouble for Max-Yin. This is why she is saved by the law of Yin Yang reversal and becomes the exception to the rules. (For the record, Max-Yin's situation is good in all three cases, though her behavior is somewhat unnatural.)

Power trigram hosting common trigram (16)

MEMORY TRICK: Use the analogy of life. When a powerful person deals with a common person, it is his or her aggressiveness that counts the most. Power level comes in second because to the common person, there is not much difference in the power level (a king is not much more effective than a local feudal lord in the dealing with a peasant.) Also a powerful person feels more comfortable dealing with a common person of the same identity (this is why the protégé of a powerful man is usually another man, of a powerful woman is usually another woman.)

Rules: Activity is key, power secondary. More effective with same identity (both masculine or both feminine).

This makes Mid-Yin (most aggressive) the most favorable hostess, followed by All-Yang (aggressive most powerful), All-Yin (tentative most powerful). Last in the list is Mid-Yang (tentative powerful).

111

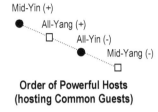

**Order of Powerful Hosts
(hosting Common Guests)**

Figure 4: When a powerful trigram hosts a common trigram, the most important factor is activity (the more aggressive the better). This makes Mid-Yin the most effective trigram in the hosting role, followed by All-Yang, All-Yin, and lastly Mid-Yang.

The logic spells serious trouble for Mid-Yang in his dealing with the two feminine guests Max-Yin and Min-Yin. Not surprisingly, he could be saved by the law of Yin Yang reversal in these two cases.

Common trigram hosting power trigram (12)

MEMORY TRICK: Use the analogy of real life. When a common person deals with a powerful person, the closer the contact the more fruitful the relationship. Aggressiveness definitely helps, but it is secondary to proximity. Also a common person has a much better chance when he or she deals with a powerful guest of opposite identity (Now we see why we usually get better service from government agents of opposite sex.)

Rules: Proximity to guest is key, activity secondary. Complementary identity receives preferential treatment.

The order is: Min-Yin (close and aggressive), Min-Yang (close and tentative), Max-Yang (far and aggressive), Max-Yin (far and tentative).

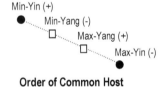

**Order of Common Host
(hosting Powerful Guests)**

Figure 5: When a common trigram hosts a powerful trigram, the best situation is to be close to the guest. Being aggressive is helpful. This leads to the order seen in the left: Min Yin (close and aggressive), Min-Yang (close but tentative), Max-Yang (far but aggressive), Max-Yin (far and tentative).

SUMMARY OF HEXAGRAM MEANINGS

A brief summary is given in the next 8 pages as a quick reference. The format is:

-Each page covers one host or hostess. The guest (in each page) follows the order: All-Yang, Mid-Yang, All-Yin, Mid-Yin, Max-Yang, Max-Yin, Min-Yang, and Min-Yin. In this order, the four powerful trigrams are listed first, followed by the four common trigrams.

-The same order is used for the host or hostess (one per page).

BRIEF LOGIC OF THE 64 HEXAGRAMS

TABLE 1: Host All-Yang (most powerful aggressive masculine)

Guest Trigram	Hexagram Name	Yin Yang Logic of Hexagram meaning
All-Yang (Heaven) MAP	The Active (I-Ching # 1)	This is an identity hexagram. Same meaning as trigram.
Mid-Yang (Water) MTP	Waiting (I-Ching # 5)	Power hosting power. There is conflict because of opposite activities. Host All-Yang is stronger and will win, but the tentative Mid-Yang will use delay tactics. Therefore All-Yang must wait.
All-Yin (Earth) FTP	Great Harmony (I-Ching # 11)	Power hosting power. Conflict -because of opposite activities- is smoothed out because the more powerful masculine host is in charge. Great result because both are most powerful.
Mid-Yin (Fire) FAP	Great Possession (I-Ching # 14)	Power hosting power. In agreement because both are aggressive. Very favorable because host is masculine.
Max-Yang (Thunder) MAC	Great Energy (I-Ching # 34)	Power hosting common with same identity. Extremely aggressive Max-Yang influences host, offsetting his balanced aggressiveness. Host becomes more aggressive than normal.
Min-Yang (Mountain) MTC	Great Cultivation (I-Ching # 26)	Power hosting common with same identity. Most powerful host helps weak guest with Yang potential. Great result.
Max-Yin (Wind) FTC	Small Cultivation (I-Ching # 9)	Power hosting common. Most powerful host helps weak guest, but guest is of opposite identity, therefore result is limited (compared to "Great Cultivation").
Min-Yin (Marsh) FAC	Correction (I-Ching # 43)	Power hosting common. Aggressive but weak feminine guest strays too far from host. Aggressive powerful host is determined to rectify situation. Result is limited because identities are opposite.

NOTATIONS:
M = Masculine   F = Feminine
A = Aggressive   T= Tentative
P = Powerful   C = Common

113

TABLE 2: Host Mid-Yang (powerful tentative masculine)

Guest Trigram	Hexagram Name	Yin Yang Logic of Hexagram Meaning
All-Yang (Heaven) MAP	**Contention** (I-Ching # 6)	Power hosting power. Conflict because of opposite activities. Host Mid-Yang is weaker than guest. He uses tentative tactics to get temporary results but eventually loses.
Mid-Yang (Water) MTP	**Danger** (I-Ching # 29)	This is an identity hexagram. Same meaning as trigram.
All-Yin (Earth) FTP	**The Army** (I-Ching # 7)	Power hosting power. Agreement because both are tentative. Host utilizes guest's power for his own agenda.
Mid-Yin (Fire) FAP	**Incompletion** (I-Ching # 64)	Power hosting power. Conflict because of opposite activities. Host is less powerful than guest, therefore unfavorable.
Max-Yang (Thunder) MAC	**Relief** (I-Ching # 40)	Power hosting common. Extremely aggressive Max-Yang (at line 4) influences host; helps host to overcome the tentative barrier that has been blocking his progress.
Min-Yang (Mountain) MTC	**Ignorance – Teaching the Ignorant** (I-Ching # 4)	Power hosting common. Powerful host helps weak guest. Some result, but not as conclusive as "Great Cultivation" because host is tentative.
Max-Yin (Wind) FTC	**Dispersion** (I-Ching # 59)	Power hosting common. Powerful host is supposed to help weakest guest. But because of host's tentative nature, goal can only be achieved with tremendous sacrifice (law of Yin Yang reversal).
Min-Yin (Marsh) FAC	**Exhaustion** (I-Ching # 47)	Power hosting common. Tentative host, despite being powerful, is not capable enough to rectify situation, becoming exhausted. Still can get result with tremendous effort (Yin Yang reversal).

NOTATIONS:
M = Masculine   F = Feminine
A = Aggressive   T = Tentative
P = Powerful   C = Common
Examples: All-Yang is Masculine Aggressive Powerful (MAP)
Min-Yin is Feminine Aggressive Common (FAC)

114

TABLE 3: Hostess All-Yin (most powerful tentative feminine)

	Guest	Name	Yin Yang logic
☰☷	All-Yang (Heaven) MAP	**Stagnation** (I-Ching # 12)	Power hosting power. Conflict because of opposite activities. Unfavorable because hostess is not as powerful as guest. Since both trigrams are most powerful, the conflict is very serious.
☵☷	Mid-Yang (Water) MTP	**Union** (I-Ching # 8)	Power hosting power. Agreement with same (tentative) activity. Hostess will help instead of giving orders to masculine guest.
☷☷	All-Yin (Earth) FTP	**The Receptive** (I-Ching # 2)	This is an identity hexagram. Same meaning as trigram.
☲☷	Mid-Yin (Fire) FAP	**Advance** (I-Ching # 35)	Power hosting power. Conflict because activities are opposite. Hostess All-Yin is most powerful; therefore she will overcome Mid-Yin's aggressiveness to advance.
☳☷	Max-Yang (Thunder) MAC	**Exuberance** (I-Ching # 16)	Power hosting common, opposite identities. Guest is most aggressive of all trigrams, creating a strongly positive first impression on host; but since identities are opposite, true impact is small.
☶☷	Min-Yang (Mountain) MTC	**Destruction** (I-Ching # 23)	Power hosting common, opposite identities. Guest is the weakest of all masculine trigrams. Identity mismatch adds to problem. Hostess' power is misguided and becomes destructive force.
☴☷	Max-Yin (Wind) FTC	**Observation** (I-Ching # 20)	Power hosting common, same identity. Although there is no conflict, the powerful but tentative hostess All-Yin only helps the weakest guest Max-Yin indirectly by setting examples for the guest to observe and follow.
☱☷	Min-Yin (Marsh) FAC	**Gathering** (I-Ching # 45	Power hosting common, same identity. The aggressive guest is straying (main line at position 6). The hostess, being tentative but most powerful, corrects the situation by "gathering" her power to persuade the guest to move back to the right place.

TABLE 4: Hostess Mid-Yin (powerful aggressive feminine)

Guest	Name	Yin Yang logic
All-Yang (Heaven) MAP	**Alliance** (I-Ching # 13)	Power hosting power. Agreement thanks to same activity. Hostess is weaker but more aggressive than guest. Has ability to convince guest to form alliance.
Mid-Yang (Water) MTP	**Completion** (I-Ching # 63)	Power hosting power. Conflict because of opposite activities. Hostess is more powerful than guest, therefore meaning is favorable. However, there are instabilities because hostess is feminine.
All-Yin (Earth) FTP	**Brightness dimmed** (I-Ching # 36)	Power hosting power. Conflict because of opposite activities. Hostess Mid-Yin is weaker than the guest All-Yin, therefore defeated. Her own aggressiveness is her downfall. She will suffer injury.
Mid-Yin (Fire) FAP	**Brightness** (I-Ching # 30)	This is an identity hexagram. Same meaning as trigram.
Max-Yang (Thunder) MAC	**Abundance** (I-Ching # 55)	Power hosting common, opposite identities. The influence of the guest's aggressiveness will help her maximize her potential as a power feminine trigram. But effect cannot last long.
Min-Yang (Mountain) MTC	**Decoration** (I-Ching # 22)	Power hosting common, opposite identities. Favorable because hostess is the most aggressive of all power trigrams. However, she can only achieve superficial results because of guest's tentativeness.
Max-Yin (Wind) FTC	**Family members** (I-Ching # 37)	Power hosting common, same identity. The powerful and aggressive hostess Mid-Yin will complement the tentative guest Max-Yin, like a capable sister helping a weaker sister.
Min-Yin (Marsh) FAC	**Revolution** (I-Ching # 49)	Power hosting common, same identity. Since the hostess is aggressive, she is successful in correcting the guest's aggressiveness, which she considers inappropriate.

116

TABLE 5: Host Max-Yang (common aggressive masculine)

	Guest	Name	Yin Yang logic
	All-Yang (Heaven) MAP	**Non-Expectation** (I-Ching # 25)	Common hosting power, same identity. Guest is better than host in every aspect. Host has nothing to offer and cannot expect that his activities will make a difference.
	Mid-Yang (Water) MTP	**Difficulties** (I-Ching # 3)	Common hosting power, same identity. Host is the most aggressive, but does not get the needed response from the guest, who is tentative and more powerful. Future greatness is possible, but present situation is difficult.
	All-Yin (Earth) FTP	**Revival** (I-Ching # 24)	Common hosting power. The opposite identities help the common host to tap into the vast power of the guest. This is a surprising opportunity for the extremely aggressive but ineffective host Max-Yang.
	Mid-Yin (Fire) FAP	**Biting in Pain** (I-Ching # 21)	Common hosting power. Opposite identities help, but host's extreme aggressiveness is superseded by guest, like an otherwise active person shackled and tortured during rehabilitation.
	Max-Yang (Thunder) MAC	**Thunder** (I-Ching # 51)	This is an identity hexagram. Same meaning as trigram.
	Min-Yang (Mountain) MTC	**Feeding** (I-Ching # 27)	Common hosting common, masculine host. The most aggressive host has to help out the tentative guest, but his ability is limited, therefore he can only feed the guest (lesser than "Great Cultivation")
	Max-Yin (Wind) FTC	**Increase** (I-Ching # 42)	Common hosting common. Favorable because host is masculine. Guest is in intimate contact with host. Host is like a man benefiting from his wife.
	Min-Yin (Marsh) FAC	**Pursuing** (I-Ching # 17)	Common hosting common. Favorable because host is masculine. Since two trigrams are disconnected from each other, guest is like a girl running away, host is like a man reacting to (and will catch) her.

117

TABLE 6: Host Min-Yang (common tentative masculine)

Guest	Name	Yin Yang logic
All-Yang (Heaven) MAP	**Retreating** (I-Ching #33)	Common hosting power of same identity. Host is close to guest but tentative. The guest's aggressiveness is scary to the tentative host. He has to retreat.
Mid-Yang (Water) MTP	**Obstruction** (I-Ching #39)	Common hosting power of same identity. Host Min-Yang is in contact with guest (at position 3) and feels inferior. The powerful guest's presence is perceived by Min-Yang as an obstruction.
All-Yin (Earth) FTP	**Humility** (I-Ching # 15)	Common hosting power of opposite identity. Host is in good contact with guest (at line 3). However, he is also aware that his capability is inferior to that of the guest.
Mid-Yin (Fire) FAP	**The Wanderer** (I-Ching # 56)	Common hosting power of opposite identity. Host is in contact with guest and receives influence; as if being pushed from (inactive) position. Moving with unclear destination.
Max-Yang (Thunder) MAC	**Small Extremity** (I-Ching # 62)	Common hosting common. Masculine host. Host is less aggressive than guest, but thanks to the proximity (host at position 3, guest at position 4) only causes small problems.
Min-Yang (Mountain) MTC	**Inactivity** (I-Ching # 52)	This is an identity trigram. Same meaning as trigram.
Max-Yin (Wind) FTC	**Gradual Progress** (I-Ching # 53)	Common hosting common. Host is masculine. Although both are tentative, host can proceed slowly.
Min-Yin (Marsh) FAC	**E-Motions** (I-Ching # 31)	Common hosting common. Perfect feminine / masculine opposites with masculine as host. These are movements induced by the natural vibrations between the two trigrams (contrasting the undirected motions of "The Wanderer")

NOTATIONS:
M = Masculine   F = Feminine
A = Aggressive   T= Tentative
P = Powerful   C = Common
Examples: All-Yang is Masculine Aggressive Powerful (MAP)
Min-Yin is Feminine Aggressive Common (FAC)

118

TABLE 7: Hostess Max-Yin (common tentative feminine, Yin Yang reversal)

	Guest	Name	Yin Yang logic
	All-Yang (Heaven) MAP	**Flirting** (I-Ching # 44)	Hostess Max-Yin tries to match the aggressiveness of the masculine guest. Her behavior is unfit for the interaction, because the guest is the most capable aggressive trigram and can tell the difference between true and fake aggressiveness.
	Mid-Yang (Water) MTP	**The Well** (I-Ching # 48)	Hostess Max-Yin tries to fit the situation. She is capable of utilizing the guest's potential (Water for nourishment) since the two trigrams have no conflict.
	All-Yin (Earth) FTP	**Ascending** (I-Ching # 46)	Hostess Max-Yin raises her own level to fit the most powerful feminine guest. This is possible because, being so low on the aggressiveness scale, she can go nowhere but up.
	Mid-Yin (Fire) FAP	**The Cauldron** (I-Ching # 50)	Hostess Max-Yin tries to fit the situation. She is capable of utilizing the guest's potential (Fire for cooking) since the two trigrams have no conflict.
	Max-Yang (Thunder) MAC	**Permanence** (I-Ching # 32)	Max-Yin modifies herself to turn the table on Max-Yang, forging the most aggressive (and changeable) guest to a permanent relationship.
	Min-Yang (Mountain) MTC	**Deterioration** (I-Ching # 18)	Hostess and guest are disconnected (main lines at positions 1 and 6). In addition, they are the two most tentative trigrams. The mutual lack of effort leads to deterioration. Then Max-Yin modifies herself to correct the situation.
	Max-Yin (Wind) FTC	**The Flexible** (I-Ching # 57)	This is an identity hexagram. Same meaning as trigram.
	Min-Yin (Marsh) FAC	**Great Extremity** (I-Ching # 28)	Hostess Max-Yin modifies herself to fit the situation. Since hostess and guest are disconnected, and guest is aggressive, hostess will try to be aggressive like guest. This is an extreme stand for the most tentative hostess.

119

TABLE 8: Hostess Min-Yin (common aggressive feminine)

	Guest	Name	Yin Yang logic
	All-Yang (Heaven) MAP	**Stepping cautiously** (I-Ching # 10)	Common hosting powerful of opposite identity. With close contact and being aggressive, the hostess will control her own aggressiveness so that she is not in trouble with the aggressive guest.
	Mid-Yang (Water) MTP	**Self-Restraint** (I-Ching # 60)	Common hosting powerful of opposite identity. With close contact, the hostess knows she has to limit her aggressiveness to get along with the tentative guest. This is an act of self-restraint.
	All-Yin (Earth) FTP	**Approaching** (I-Ching # 19)	Common hosting powerful of same identity. With close contact, the hostess can approach the powerful guest, but result is not ideal because both are feminine (not complementary).
	Mid-Yin (Fire) FAP	**Differences** (I-Ching # 38)	Common hosting powerful of same identity. Since both trigrams are aggressive, the weak hostess feels conflict with the guest in her proximity.
	Max-Yang (Thunder) MAC	**The Marrying Maiden** (I-Ching # 54)	Common hosting common. Trouble because host is feminine and less aggressive than masculine guest. Min-Yin is following the more aggressive and masculine Max-Yang (who has his way with her in "Pursuing").
	Min-Yang (Mountain) MTC	**Decrease** (I-Ching # 41)	Common hosting common. Slight trouble because guest is feminine, but more aggressive than guest. Since these are exact Yin Yang opposite, the picture is more like the hostess is willing to take a loss for the sake of the guest.
	Max-Yin (Wind) FTC	**Central Harmony** (I-Ching # 61)	Common hosting common, both feminine. Positions are proper because host is aggressive, guest tentative. This is like two girls who are in contact (at lines 3 and 4) and get along well.
	Min-Yin (Marsh) FAC	**The Playful** (I-Ching # 58)	This is an identity hexagram. Same meaning as trigram.

PART II

NEW LOGIC VS. HISTORICAL TEXTS

OF

THE 64 HEXAGRAMS

How to use this part

In this part the 64 hexagrams are presented in the order reportedly given by their originator, King Wen, more than three thousand years ago. The logic for this particular hexagram order is itself a mystery, which we will not discuss in this volume. (However, the writer plans to return to it in volume 2.)

Hexagram name

Each hexagram has a name. Best efforts have been made (with each hexagram) to choose an English name as close in meaning as possible to the original Chinese name. When this is not possible, an English name is chosen to best reflect the meaning of the hexagram. In cases of identity hexagrams, the alternative names are also given (e.g., Double All-Yang). There are also a few cases where an alternative name is given in addition to the English translation of the original Chinese name. This is done when it is believed that the alternative name conveys more direct meaning.

Guest/host and trigram properties

The guest and the host (or hostess) are identified for each hexagram, and their three properties (identity, activity, ability) are spelled out in table form. This table is intended to be a quick reference for the reader's convenience.

Yin Yang logic

Yin Yang logic is the logic developed in this book to arrive at the meaning of each hexagram. Since the logic is based completely on the host/guest relationship and the three trigram properties, the average reader can deduce the meaning of a given hexagram without having to memorize the texts given in I-Ching books (which are in archaic Chinese, whose meanings are at times unclear –even to native Chinese- and subjected to personal interpretation by the translator.)

Yin Yang logic is the main thesis of this book. It is recommended that the reader reads this part carefully to confirm that the conclusion that it reaches is scientific.

I-Ching reading

This is the English translation of the original text, believed to have been written by King Wen more than three thousand years ago. The writer has added his own comments *(in italic)* to help the reader grasp this part more easily.

The reader should compare I-Ching reading against the conclusion reached by Yin-Yang logic to confirm that the two are in agreement.

Elaboration on I-Ching reading

This part is believed by some scholars to have been written by Confucius about 2500 years ago. The more general consensus is that, while Confucius may have been the original influence that started the writing, the text itself was not the work of Confucius. In fact, it is now believed that the text was the work of multiple authors, possibly over many generations.

The theory of multiple authors is most likely to be correct, as the text lacks consistency. Sometimes one would see a brilliant and profound statement worthy of Confucius himself, sometimes one would see a statement that was possibly written by a novice.

However, the elaboration does bring out many interesting points that may have been intended (but not mentioned) in the original I-Ching reading.

Again the writer has added his own comments *(in italic)* to help the reader grasp this part more easily.

Symbolisms on I-Ching reading

This part is also credited to Confucius, but most likely it was the work of many authors, possibly with strong influence passed down orally from Confucius.

In contrast to the "elaboration of I-Ching reading" which only tries to clarify the meaning of the I-Ching reading, here we have for each hexagram a suggested course of actions for the superior man, and sometimes the great man (the accomplished superior man), or the benevolent king (referred to as "the ancient kings").

The writer found this part very intriguing. It seems that whoever wrote this part has realized that the Yin Yang world described by the I-Ching is imperfect, and the ideal person (superior man, great man, benevolent king, etc.) must rise above and beyond it. This part, then, gives us a glimpse of what (the Confucianists believe) we would have to do to approach the Middle Way.

For this reason, the writer recommends this part as a must-read. Again, comments *(in italic)* have been added to help the reader grasp the essence of the sayings more easily.

Miscellaneous

The symbolism of the Mass (a large group of people) is often used for All-Yin. This symbolism has not been mentioned in this book, but it fits All-Yin well (the Mass has tremendous power but lacks direction.)

The symbolism of Water is used once in a while for Min-Yin. This is quite unusual (because Water is more often associated with Mid-Yang) but not illogical, as a symbolism has to be understood as a part of a set of eight trigrams. The same symbolism may stand for 2 different trigrams in two different sets of symbolisms.

Important note by the author on sources and references

While translating the historical I-Ching texts from Chinese to English, I always consulted and compared my work against other I-Ching books published in English. I am certain that every book that I consulted had certain influence on my own work, but perhaps the greatest influence came from two books: the first by Wilhem/Bayes ("The I-Ching," English translation from German, 3rd edition, 27th printing, Princeton University Press, USA, 1997), the second by Z. D. Sung ("The Text of YiKing and its Appendixes," Cultural Books Company, China, 1935). I am indebted to these valuable references. Needless to say, all the mistakes are mine.

All-Yang
All-Yang

1. The Active
(Double All-Yang)

Role	Trigram	Identity	Activity	Ability
GUEST	*All-Yang*	Masculine	Aggressive	Most powerful
HOST	*All-Yang*	Masculine	Aggressive	Most powerful

YIN YANG LOGIC *(NEW)*

This is an identity hexagram. Recall that the meaning of a hexagram is the situation encountered by the host. All-Yang is the best qualified host because, from a Yin Yang standpoint, all three of his properties are Yang. For this reason All-Yang is a hexagram of great promise. Progress is almost guaranteed.

The guest is a cloned copy of the host. The 4th line may transfer some undesirable (aggressive) influence on the host, and may drive him toward being too aggressive for his own good. It is therefore important for the host to be firm in his resolve to stay on course.

In conclusion, this hexagram holds great potential. The key to success is to seize the initiative and act relentlessly.

I-CHING TEXTS AND COMMENTS
(For comparison)

I-Ching reading *(original text in Chinese)*

Translation: Great progress. It is advisable to stay firmly on course.

Comment: This reading is in agreement with Yin Yang logic. All-Yang is advised to stay firmly on course because he may be influenced by the guest and becomes too aggressive; which would diminish his ability.

Elaboration on I-Ching reading *(original text in Chinese)*

Translation: Great is the originating (power) of Double All-Yang. The beginning of all things. Comparable to the Heavens. The cloud moves and the rain disperses. All things settle into their developed forms.

Great understanding of the beginning and the end. The six positions form, then ride the six dragons through Heavens.

The Tao of The Active is transformation. Everything is in their correct cosmic order. Preserving union in harmony. Advisable to stay firmly on course.

The sage appears (in such a way that he is) higher than all things. All territories feel his influence of stability.

Comment: Double All-Yang is considered the originating power that creates all things because all of his lines are Yang, which represents pure aggressiveness or activity (without mixing with tentativeness or passivity.)

All-Yang is compared with Heaven for reasons that we have established in the chapter on symbolisms.

The dragon is a symbolism for Double All-Yang. (The reader should not be confused by the fact that the dragon is also used as a symbolism for Max-Yang somewhere in the jungle of Yin Yang books. In trigram symbolism construction, the key is the relationship among all eight trigrams. Thus, the same symbolism may represent different trigrams in different sets of symbolisms.)

Because the only essence that is present in Double All-Yang is Yang, and Yang represents activities, changes tend to happen quite quickly under the influence of Double All-Yang. That is why it was said "the Tao of the Active is transformation."

The sages were mentioned because their wisdom is worthy of the originating power of Double All-Yang.

Symbolisms of I-Ching reading *(original text in Chinese)*

Translation: Double All-Yang means "active." The superior man challenges himself with nonstop activities.

Comment: The superior man must be fully aware that the time of this hexagram is the proper time to carry out important tasks. He must therefore seize the opportunity and act continuously so that he can achieve the goals that he has set for himself.

All-Yin
All-Yin

2. The Receptive
(Double All-Yin)

Role	Trigram	Identity	Activity	Ability
GUEST	*All-Yin*	Feminine	Tentative	Most powerful
HOSTESS	*All-Yin*	Feminine	Tentative	Most powerful

YIN YANG LOGIC *(NEW!)*

This is an identity hexagram. Despite being feminine tentative, All-Yin will do well in the hostess position because she is one of the two most powerful trigrams (the other is All-Yang.)

However, since all of her lines are Yin, and the influence from the identical guest (from line 4) is also Yin, All-Yin should follow the instructions given to her instead of taking the initiative.

In conclusion, the time of The Receptive holds great potential, but the key to success is to follow, not to lead.

I-CHING TEXTS AND COMMENTS
(For comparison)

I-Ching reading *(original text in Chinese)*

Translation: Great progress. Advisable to stay firmly on the course of a mare. The superior man has places to go. Going first loses his way, (following) behind achieves result. Advisable to go in the southwest direction to gain friend. The northeast direction will lose friend. Staying peacefully but firmly on course. Good.

Comment: This reading emphasizes that Double All-Yin has great potential, but should follow, not lead. These are in agreement with Yin Yang logic.

As for the two mysterious directions southwest and northeast, they come from the so-called "Later Heaven trigram order" which we do not cover in this book (but will, in a future book dedicated to the Yin Yang theory.) It suffices to say that southwest corresponds to All-Yin and northeast to Min-Yang. "Going in the southwest direction" means behaving in the manner suggested by All-Yin. Should "gain friend" because this is the direction where the guest (All-Yin) is. "The northeast direction will lose friend" because this is the direction of Min-Yang. We will see the detrimental effect on All-Yin when Min-Yang is the guest in hexagram 23 "Destruction."

Elaboration on I-Ching reading *(original text in Chinese)*
Translation: So complete is the originating (quality) of the Receptive. The beginning of all things. Yielding to Heaven.

The depth of the Receptive can carry things. (Its) virtue can contain without limit. Comprehensive and brilliant. Things progress because of its influence.

The mare is an earthly animal. Its range (i.e., the area that it can cover) on earth is without limit. It is gentle, yielding and it stays firmly on course. This is the path the superior man should take.

(Going) first loses his way. (Following) behind gains the regular (course). Southwest direction gains friend, because he goes with his own kind. Northeast direction loses friend, yet at the end there is (reason for) celebration.

"Staying firmly on course with a peaceful mind" corresponds with the limitless expanse of Earth.

Comment: The originating quality of Double All-Yin is best understood with the analogy of a mother. It is she who gives birth to the children. And while the father (image of Heaven) initiates the process of procreation, the mother is the yielding party in the process.

The depth of the Receptive has its analogy in the womb of the mother. This is where all the sages develop their human forms and finally cry their way to the world, hence the Receptive "contains without limit. Comprehensive and brilliant. Things progress because of its influence."

In Double All-Yin, in addition to "staying firmly on course" like Double All-Yang, we see the additional requirement "with a peaceful mind," that is because All-Yin's power is best expressed in a coordinating role, not a leading role. Without a peaceful mind one can still be a great leader, but cannot be a great coordinator.

Symbolisms of I-Ching reading *(original text in Chinese)*
Translation: The nature of Earth is (the essence of) All-Yin. The superior man employs his deep virtue to carry things.

Comment: Since the essence of Double All-Yin is to carry out great things without being the leader, the virtue that requires of her is great. That is why the superior man needs to employ his "deep virtue," not just "virtue."

Mid-Yang
Max-Yang

3. Difficulties

Role	Trigram	Identity	Activity	Ability
GUEST	*Mid-Yang*	Masculine	Very tentative	Powerful
HOST	*Max-Yang*	Masculine	Most aggressive	Most common

YIN YANG LOGIC *(NEW!)*

Since this is an interaction between a common host (Max-Yang) and a powerful guest (Mid-Yang), the most important factor is proximity to the host, the second is aggressiveness, and the third is complementary identities. With his main line at position 1, too far from the guest, Max-Yang understandably has a problem; which is aggravated by the fact that both he and the guest are masculine (same identity). Max-Yang's extreme aggressiveness helps reduce the problem somewhat.

Max-Yang is like a risk taking entrepreneur whose time has not come (activity = most aggressive, ability = most common) trying to get a loan from the well financed but suspicious bank officer Mid-Yang (ability = powerful, activity = very tentative). Since there is a complementary relationship between the two men (aggressive vs. tentative and common vs. powerful), this meeting may set the stage for a loan approval in the future. However, since the position of Max-Yang's main line is far removed (line 1, too far from the guest trigram), he should not expect any immediate result.

In conclusion, this hexagram holds good promise for the future, but the present is filled with difficulties. No ambitious plan should be attempted right away, but the preparation for them should be set in motion.

I-CHING TEXTS AND COMMENTS
(For comparison)

I-Ching reading *(original text in Chinese)*

Translation: Progress is certain. Advisable to stay firmly on course. No place to go. Advisable to cultivate feudal lords.

Comment: There is no conflict between "Progress is certain" and "No place to go," that is because this hexagram corresponds to the correct time for preparation, and the wrong time for execution. "To stay firmly on course" therefore does not mean to execute one's plan at all cost. Rather it means one should not give up the planning, despite present difficulties. "Advisable to cultivate feudal lords" is a way to say that the potential for the future is very great.

128

All of the above are in excellent agreement with Yin Yang logic.

Elaboration on I-Ching reading *(original text in Chinese)*
Translation: In "Difficulties," the firm and the soft start their interactions, but production is difficult.

Movements in the midst of Danger. Great progress. It is advisable to stay firmly on course.

(With) the movements of thunder and rain, heaven creates the early forms of vegetables amid obscurity. It is good to prepare to be future feudal lords, but the situation is yet stabilized.

Comment: "The firm" means solid lines; "the soft" means broken lines in the hexagram. Metaphorically the relationship between the solid lines and the broken lines in this hexagram can be compared to a man and a woman starting to "feel out" each other. It is too much to ask for positive result immediately, but this is a promising beginning.

"Movements" is a symbolism for Max-Yang; "Danger" is a well known symbolism for Mid-Yang.

"Heaven creates the early forms of vegetables amid obscurity" signifies that this is the time to sow the seed for future success. This elaboration states clearly that the time of this hexagram is still too unstable for successful execution.

Symbolisms of I-Ching reading *(original text in Chinese)*
Translation: Cloud and Thunder: Difficulties. The superior man cultivates his skills.

Comment: "Cloud" is a symbolism for Mid-Yang, "Thunder" a well known symbolism for Max-Yang. "Difficulties" is not the proper time to take action, but it has great promise for the future. Since the superior man is supposed to be above the laws of Yin and Yang, he should not let the difficult situation bother him, but instead use it as a constructive opportunity to sharpen his skills.

Min-Yang

Mid-Yang

4. Ignorance
(teaching the ignorant)

Role	Trigram	Identity	Activity	Ability
GUEST	*Min-Yang*	Masculine	Highly tentative	Common
HOST	*Mid-Yang*	Masculine	Very tentative	Powerful

YIN YANG LOGIC *(NEW!)*

In this hexagram we have a power trigram hosting a common trigram. The most important criterion for success is aggressiveness; the second is power. Third, same identity is preferred over complementary identities. Host Mid-Yang does not do well with the first two, but meets the third criterion.

This hexagram can be compared to the relationship between two tentative men, with the host being more capable than the guest (ability = powerful vs. common.) Although both trigrams are tentative, the host Mid-Yang is less tentative than the guest ("very" is less than "highly"). One way to look at this is that both host and guest are involved in slow moving activities, in which the host plays the leading role (less tentative and more powerful).

However, since Mid-Yang is not the most capable of all trigrams (that honor belongs to All-Yang and All-Yin), the disconnect with Min-Yang (main line at position 6, too far removed from the host) may turn out to be too much of a communication challenge for the host.

Mid-Yang's situation is like that of a qualified but somewhat reluctant teacher (i.e., of reasonable ability but does not have sufficient aggressiveness and patience) having to teach a very slow student (Min-Yang). Some result can be expected, but there will be frustrating moments for both sides.

In conclusion, this hexagram implies that the subject will be in a position to assist the weak, but he or she is somewhat reluctant. There will be positive results because the subject is qualified for his or her task. However there will also be difficulties and frustrations. The obvious advice is to stay firmly on course.

I-CHING TEXTS AND COMMENTS
(For comparison)

I-Ching reading *(original text in Chinese)*

Translation: Ignorance. Progress. I am not seeking the ignorant youth. The ignorant youth seeks me. The first divination reading, I will tell him. The third time would be annoying (therefore) I would not tell him. It is advisable to stay firmly on course.

Comment: Starting with the "ignorance" of the guest, and the ability of the powerful host, progress is naturally expected. However, we do see a somewhat unwilling attitude by the host in his rather long statement: "I am not seeking the ignorant youth. The ignorant youth seeks me. The first divination reading, I will tell him. The third time would be annoying (therefore) I would not tell him." The advice for him "to stay firmly on course" is then necessary.

Needless to say, this reading is again in perfect agreement with Yin Yang logic.

Elaboration on I-Ching reading *(original text in Chinese)*

Translation: Ignorance. Danger at the foot of Mountain. Danger and Stopping: Ignorance.

"Ignorance" implies progress. Within progress there exists proper timing for action. "I am not seeking the ignorant youth. The ignorant youth seeks me," because there the minds of (the two sides) are in resonance. "The first divination reading, I will tell him," because the firm (line) is at the center. "The third time would be annoying (therefore) I would not tell him," (this is when) ignorance has become annoying.

"Teaching the ignorance" nourishes correctness. This undertaking is worthy of the sages.

Comment: "Danger" is one symbolism for Mid-Yang; "Mountain" is the symbolism for Min-Yang in the Nature set of symbolisms. "The minds of the two sides are in resonance" because they are both tentative masculine. "The firm (line) is at the center" meaning that line 2, which is the center line of the host trigram, is Yang. "The third time would be annoying (therefore) I would not tell him," shows a lack of patience; that is because Mid-Yang is not the right teacher for Min-Yang. The right teacher for Min-Yang is All-Yang (hexagram 26 "Great Cultivation").

Symbolisms of I-Ching reading *(original text in Chinese)*

Translation: At the foot of the Mountain emerges a Water Stream: Ignorance. The superior man acts carefully and increases his virtue.

Comment: "Mountain" is the symbolism for Min-Yang. "Water Stream" implies the host Mid-Yang, whose well known symbolism is water. The superior man should "act carefully and increase his virtue" because the time of ignorance is challenging not only for the ignorant student, who needs help, but also for the teacher, who may or may not be up to the task. The goal of the superior man is to rise above the laws of Yin and Yang; therefore he should try to be a better teacher than Mid-Yang.

Mid-Yang

All-Yang

5. Waiting (Hsu)

Role	Trigram	Identity	Activity	Ability
GUEST	*Mid-Yang*	Masculine	Very tentative	Powerful
HOST	*All-Yang*	Masculine	Aggressive	Most powerful

YIN YANG LOGIC *(NEW!)*

In this hexagram we have a power trigram hosting another power trigram. There is power conflict because host All-Yang is aggressive but guest Mid-Yang is tentative. In power conflicts, the meaning is favorable if the host is more powerful than the guest.

The host is in winning position (most powerful over powerful). However, we can predict from the tentative style of the guest that he will use delay tactics to create difficulties for the host. Since the opposition is also powerful, All-Yang will not win right away. His best strategy is to wait until his adversary gives up. Thus, the fitting hexagram name is "Waiting."

In conclusion, this is a very favorable hexagram. Success is guaranteed, even for great plans. However, it is necessary to wait patiently for the right time to act.

I-CHING TEXTS AND COMMENTS

(For comparison)

I-Ching reading *(original text in Chinese)*

Translation: "Hsu" (i.e., Chinese name of the hexagram). Having faith. Brilliant progress. Staying firmly on course will bring good fortune. Advantageous to cross the great stream.

Comment: "Having faith" because the host is a power trigram, therefore tends to be confident when it comes to competition. "Brilliant progress" because the host will be victorious over a very worthy opponent, who is also a power trigram. Since this struggle will not come to a quick end, but victory is all but certain for the host "Staying firmly on course will bring good fortune. It is advantageous to cross the great stream." Crossing the great stream is a metaphor meaning executing a major task.

Elaboration on I-Ching reading *(original text in Chinese)*

Translation: "Hsu" (i.e., Chinese name of the hexagram) means "waiting." Danger in front. Firm but resilient, therefore will not be trapped. Its meaning is not desperation.

132

"Hsu." Have faith. Brilliant progress. Staying firmly on course will bring good result. Position is that of Heaven, "Correct and Center." Advisable to cross the great stream. Action is fruitful.

Comment: "Danger in front" implies the opposing force, namely Mid-Yang, because "Danger" is one of Mid-Yang's symbolisms. "Firm but resilient, therefore will not be trapped" is the quality of All-Yang. "Firm" means being aggressive, "resilient" because All-Yang is closest to the Middle Way. "Its meaning is not desperation" confirms that this is a winning position, not a losing position.

"Position is that of Heaven" reminds us that the center of attention of this hexagram is the host All-Yang, who represents Heaven.

Symbolisms of I-Ching reading *(original text in Chinese)*

Translation: Above the Cloud is Heaven: Waiting. The superior man drinks, eats, and enjoys himself.

Comment: "The superior man drinks, eats, and enjoys himself" because he knows that the waiting is only temporary and victory will be his at the end.

All-Yang
Mid-Yang

6. Contention

Role	Trigram	Identity	Activity	Ability
GUEST	*All-Yang*	Masculine	Aggressive	Most powerful
HOST	*Mid-Yang*	Masculine	Very tentative	Powerful

YIN YANG LOGIC *(NEW!)*

Here the situation is reverse that of hexagram 5. Even with the advantage of being the host, Mid-Yang will not be able to overcome the superior ability of All-Yang. Being tentative, his strategy will be delay tactics, hoping that if the confrontation drags on long enough All-Yang's weakness will be exposed. Being a power trigram, Mid-Yang should be able to carry out this tactic effectively and create some difficulty for his opponent. However, in the long run he will lose to All-Yang.

In conclusion, this is not a favorable hexagram. The mandate, if any, belongs to the opposition. While the situation may appear favorable at times, the end will certainly be bad. One should self-examine him or herself seriously. It is advisable to seek the opinion of a qualified consultant. Definitely not the right time to attempt any important project.

I-CHING TEXTS AND COMMENTS
(For comparison)

I-Ching reading *(original text in Chinese)*

Translation: Contention. Having faith (still) encountering (unfriendly) obstruction. If being apprehensive, good at mid course. Bad at the end. Advisable to see the great man. Not advisable to cross the great stream.

Comment: "Having faith" because the host Mid-Yang is a power trigram and tends to be confident. "Still encountering unfriendly obstruction" because the guest All-Yang is Mid-Yang's nemesis. "If being apprehensive, good at mid course" because Mid-Yang is capable enough to utilize the host position to his advantage, provided that he understands that All-Yang is a formidable force. "Bad at the end" because at the end of the day, the host is no match for All-Yang. "Advisable to see the great man" because a second opinion may help Mid-Yang to know when to stop, and possibly minimize his loss. "Not advisable to cross the great stream" because Mid-Yang is in losing position.

134

Elaboration on I-Ching reading *(original text in Chinese)*
Translation: Contention. Firm above Danger below. Danger with Strength. Contention.

Contention. Having faith still encountering obstruction. If being apprehensive, good at mid course. The firm comes and gains center. Harmful at the end. Contention cannot be fruitful. Advisable to see the great man. At "center and correct" position. Not advisable to cross the great stream. Falls into an abyss.

Comment: "Firm above Danger below" implies All-Yang is above of Mid-Yang, as all of All-Yang's lines are Yang (firm) and one of Mid-Yang's symbolisms is Danger. "Danger with Strength" because strength is known as one basic character of All-Yang. "Good at mid course. The firm comes and claims center" means the main line of Mid-Yang is Yang, and it occupies the second line, which is the center of the host trigram. Mid-Yang may have some successes at mid course because center is the power position in the Yin Yang theory.

"Advisable to see the great man. At 'center and correct' position" implies that Mid-Yang should consult with line 5, which is the center line of the guest trigram. We will see in volume II that lines 1, 3, and 5 are Yang positions. Since line 5 is Yang, it is considered correct (Yang line at Yang position). Basically the advice is that the host should discuss the matter with his adversary! While this sounds paradoxical in a contention, it exemplifies the greatness of the ancient sage King Wen. The most serious error by the weaker party in a contention is that he or she refuses to discuss the matter with the adversary!

The reason why it is "not advisable to cross the great stream" is spelled out clearly. Because the host will "fall into an abyss."

Symbolisms of I-Ching reading *(original text in Chinese)*
Translation: Heaven and Water move far away: Contention. The superior man, in his undertaking, plans the first step carefully.

Comment: "Heaven" is a symbolism of All-Yang. "Water" is a symbolism of Mid-Yang. "Move far away" because they are in contention. The advice for the superior man is very meaningful. If the weaker party in a contention plans the first step carefully, he or she will understand the consequences, and therefore may be able to minimize detrimental effects or even avoid contention altogether.

All-Yin

Mid-Yang

7. The Army

Role	Trigram	Identity	Activity	Ability
GUEST	*All-Yin*	Feminine	Tentative	Most powerful
HOST	*Mid-Yang*	Masculine	Very tentative	Powerful

YIN YANG LOGIC *(NEW!)*

In this hexagram we have a power trigram hosting another power trigram. When two powers are in agreement the outcome is favorable. In addition, masculine is preferred as host.

Since Mid-Yang and All-Yin are both tentative, they are in agreement. All-Yin is a great power, but she will obey the host, who is masculine. In this particular case we can compare All-Yin to the Mass (a big crowd) without a clear agenda, waiting for instructions from Mid-Yang.

Theoretically, the Mass has the potential to achieve great constructive wonders. However, great constructive projects require superior leadership skills. Mid-Yang is a capable leader, but he is by no means a superior leader (that honor belongs to All-Yang). Being a masculine power trigram without a great vision, Mid-Yang will use the Mass for his own purpose. The great power of All-Yin will therefore be mobilized by Mid-Yang to destroy and conquer. All the factors add up to one of the most fearsome destructive forces: An army.

In conclusion, The Army is not a peaceful hexagram. There is no easy way out except confrontation, and damages will be unavoidable. However, the subject will be able to gather powerful support and emerge victorious.

I-CHING TEXTS AND COMMENTS
(For comparison)

I-Ching reading *(original text in Chinese)*

Translation: Advisable to stay firmly on course. Good fortune for a mature person. No error.

Comment: "The Army" corresponds to a time of confrontation at a massive scale. In military operation, obviously it is "advisable to stay firmly on course." Although this is a favorable hexagram, the confrontational nature that it implies does require that the party involved is mature, as immaturity is unacceptable when one has to deal with life and death, as in the case of "the Army." Since the hexagram has favorable meaning, even if a mistake is committed, recovery is possible. Therefore "No error."

Elaboration on I-Ching reading *(original text in Chinese)*
Translation: The Army: The Mass. Stay firmly on course, because (the cause is) just. Able to utilize the Mass for a just cause, can become king or feudal lord. The firm (line) is at center and in resonance. Walk in Danger but (the situation) is Yielding. This is harmful to (territories) under Heaven, but the Mass still follows. Favorable. How could there be error?

Comment: The Army describes the power to conquer obstacles by a large group of individuals (i.e., the Mass, represented by the powerful guest All-Yin) under a competent leadership, which is the powerful host trigram Mid-Yang. "The cause is just" because otherwise the Mass would not allow itself to be in the guest position and receive orders from the less powerful host. Mid-Yang can utilize the immense power of the Mass to conquer barriers (including opposing forces) and establish himself as the next ruler, therefore "can become king or feudal lord."

By having the only solid line of the hexagram, the situation of Mid-Yang is like a person surrounded by danger (broken lines), but because he is strong (main line is solid and occupies center), danger has to yield to him.

When the immense power of the Army is unleashed, destruction is unavoidable, but destruction is exactly what an army is set out to achieve, therefore "This is harmful to (territories) under Heaven, but the Mass follows. Favorable. How could there be error?"

Symbolisms of I-Ching reading *(original text in Chinese)*
Translation: In the middle of Earth there is Water: The Army. The superior man offers opportunity to the people and cultivates the mass.

Comment: "Earth" and "Water" are symbolisms for All-Yin and Mid-Yang respectively. It is interesting to note that the advice for the superior man is not to use the strength of the Mass for his conquest, but "offers opportunity to the people and cultivates the mass." That is because the superior man is supposed to rise above the law of Yin and Yang. He is certainly ready for war but would rather see the soldiers return to their everyday's life (in the original meaning of the Mass) with ample opportunities.

Mid-Yang
All-Yin

8. Union

Role	Trigram	Identity	Activity	Ability
GUEST	*Mid-Yang*	Masculine	Very tentative	Powerful
HOSTESS	*All-Yin*	Feminine	Tentative	Most powerful

YIN YANG LOGIC *(NEW!)*
In this hexagram we have a power trigram hosting another power trigram. Favorable because there is power agreement, but relatively weaker than hexagram 7 "The Army" because here we have a feminine trigram in the hostess position.

All-Yin is a great power. In fact, she is more powerful than Mid-Yang. In this particular case, we can compare her to a visionary queen who has just found a capable leader (Mid-Yang) in her "queendom." Although the activity level of All-Yin is "tentative," on a relative scale she is still more active than Mid-Yang, who is "very tentative." Combining all of these, we get the picture of a great queen approaching a somewhat suspecting regional leader and demonstrating her willingness to work closely with him. Thus, the fitting hexagram name is "Union."

In conclusion, Union suggests the spirit of cooperation from the hostess, who is in a strong position but prefers to be a coordinator, not a leader. This spirit leads to a positive outcome.

I-CHING TEXTS AND COMMENTS
(For comparison)
I-Ching reading *(original text in Chinese)*
Translation: Union. If self-examination shows great long-term determination to stay firmly on course, no error. The unstable will come (to seek union). Being late has harmful consequences.

Comment: Union is difficult to achieve, because this is the case where the most powerful (All-Yin) is yielding to the less powerful (Mid-Yang). This is why good intention alone is not sufficient. One needs to go one step further by self examining him or herself to confirm that a long-term commitment exists. By offering services instead of giving out orders, the leader sends out a positive message, which will be reciprocated, and people will seek him or her for their own stability. All these are in agreement with Yin Yang logic.

The only additional information in the reading is "Being late has harmful consequences." This information can be deduced from the

138

essence of the hexagram. Union only has value when it is offered early. Late offers for Union will be considered as a sign of weakness (by the powerful guest, who may overestimate himself) and will have reverse effect, with possible harmful consequences.

Elaboration on I-Ching reading *(original text in Chinese)*

Translation: Union is auspicious. Union is helping. The low (lines) yield and follow. If self-examination shows great long-term determination to stay firmly on course, no error; because the firm (line) is centered. The unstable will come (to seek union), because the high and the low are "in resonance." Being late has harmful consequences: The Tao (of "Union") has reached its end.

Comment: This hexagram suggests that the hostess, who is in a stronger position than the guest, is lending the guest a helping hand, therefore "Union is helping. The low (lines) yield and follow." The reason for "no error" is because "the firm (line) is center," which means that the guest is capable and therefore worthy of receiving help. The hostess is more stable than the guest, but both are powerful tentative, therefore "The unstable will come (to seek union), because the high and the low are 'in resonance.'" Offering Union late may be mistaken as a sign of weakness, which defeats the purpose of Union, therefore "Being late has harmful consequences: The Tao (of "Union") has reached its end."

Symbolisms of I-Ching reading *(original text in Chinese)*

Translation: Above the Earth there is Water, giving Union. The ancient kings help the various territories and maintain good relationships with the regional feudal lords.

Comment: "Earth" and "Water" are symbolisms for All-Yin and Mid-Yang respectively. Since Union means help offered from a position of highest power to another position of power, it would be arrogant to say that this is the way of the superior man. Therefore image of "the ancient kings" was used instead.

Max-Yin
All-Yang

9. Small Cultivation

Role	Trigram	Identity	Activity	Ability
GUEST	*Max-Yin*	Feminine	Most tentative	Most common
HOST	*All-Yang*	Masculine	Aggressive	Most powerful

YIN YANG LOGIC *(NEW!)*

In this hexagram we have a power trigram hosting a common trigram. The top criterion is aggressiveness; the second is power level; the third is identity (identical identity preferred).

All-Yang is a favorable host (most powerful aggressive), while Max-Yin, with her main line at position 4, is in direct contact with him. All-Yang is like a powerful king who, in an excursion, meets a plain looking country girl (Max-Yin), and is deeply touched by her simplicity and vulnerability.

The natural outcome of this encounter is that All-Yang, acting like a fatherly figure, will help Max-Yin to improve her situation. Being the most resourceful person, All-Yang's help could be very significant. However, since the identities of the two trigrams are not identical (All-Yang is masculine, Max-Yin is feminine), the result will be more modest than All-Yang has come to expect; thus the fitting hexagram name is "Small Cultivation."

In conclusion, Small Cultivation describes an attempt of the most powerful to help the weakest. Progress is guaranteed by the ability of the most powerful host, but the weakness of the guest and the incompatibility of the two sides are too much to overcome; and only limited result can be expected.

NOTE:

There is a real risk in the time of Small Cultivation, as the weak Max-Yin may not understand her limitations and becomes arrogant after being cultivated by her mentor All-Yang.

I-CHING TEXTS AND COMMENTS
(For comparison)

I-Ching reading *(original text in Chinese)*

Translation: Small Cultivation. Progress. Dense clouds but no rain coming from our western border.

Comment: "Dense clouds but no rain coming from our western border" is a cryptic way to say that while the progress is positive, no significant result can be expected from the interaction implied in Small Cultivation. Cryptic explanations are common in the I-Ching. The writer's theory is that King Wen wrote the meanings of the 64 hexagrams when he was in prison. The possibility of getting executed any time might have forced him to be very careful with words.

The images "clouds" and "rain" are used because they are two symbolisms for Min-Yin, and if we take lines 2, 3, and 4 as the so-called "lower nuclear trigram," then this trigram is Min-Yin for the case of Small Cultivation. "Western border" is mentioned because Min-Yin is located in the West according to the "Later Heaven" order of the trigrams. (The reason for this particular trigram order will be explained in another book.)

Elaboration on I-Ching reading *(original text in Chinese)*

<u>Translation</u>: Small Cultivation. Because the soft (line) is in the right position, and the high and the low are in resonance, say "Small Cultivation."

Strength and Flexibility. The firm is centered; (therefore) the will can be realized, leading to progress.

Dense clouds but no rain: Still moving. From our western border: Still cannot be realized.

<u>Comment</u>: "The soft (line) is in the right position" means line 4, which is the main line of the guest trigram. At position 4, it has a strong influence on the host trigram. "The high and the low" refers to the two trigrams. The host is the most powerful trigram, the guest is the weakest, and the host is aware of this fact; therefore "the high and the low are in resonance."

"Strength" and "Flexibility" refer to All-Yang and Max-Yin respectively. "The firm is centered, (therefore) the will can be realized, leading to progress" refers to line 2, which is Yang (firm) and occupies the center position of the host hexagram.

"Dense cloud but no rain. Still moving" is an ambiguous explanation. It makes more sense to explain that, since Max-Yin's ability is limited, even with the help offered by All-Yang she is like a dense cloud that cannot culminate into rain.

Symbolisms of I-Ching reading *(original text in Chinese)*

<u>Translation</u>: Wind blows above Heaven: Small Cultivation. The superior man enhances the beauty of his virtue.

<u>Comment</u>: "Wind" and "Heaven" are symbolisms for Max-Yin and All-Yang respectively. "The superior man enhances the beauty of his virtue" because he understands that the result of Small Cultivation is limited, and cannot be used for any important purpose.

All-Yang
Min-Yin

10. Stepping Cautiously

Role	Trigram	Identity	Activity	Ability
GUEST	*All-Yang*	Masculine	Aggressive	Most powerful
HOSTESS	*Min-Yin*	Feminine	Highly aggressive	Common

YIN YANG LOGIC *(NEW!)*

In this hexagram we have a common trigram hosting a power trigram. The top criterion for favorable meaning is proximity; the second is aggressiveness; the third is (complementary) identities. All three are met by this hexagram.

Being a feminine but active trigram, Min-Yin's situation is like that of an active young girl who is playing too loudly, then suddenly realizes that she may have waken up her stern father from his sleep.

The saving grace for Min-Yin is that her main line (in position 3) is in contact with the guest. This proximity effect helps her to know exactly how precarious her situation is so that she could adjust her behavior accordingly. In addition, there exists a natural affinity between the two sides (the hostess is feminine, the guest is masculine) which helps minimize misunderstanding.

For these reasons, we anticipate that, after realizing that her father may have waken up, the young girl Min-Yin will wisely reduce her noise level and escape the incident without reproach.

The I-Ching's symbolism is that of a person stepping cautiously on the tail of a tiger. This is a great symbolism because the tiger is an excellent fit for the all-powerful All-Yang, a person stepping cautiously on the tiger's tail fits the image of Min-Yin (aggressive feminine) with the main line in contact with All-Yang. The proximity with All-Yang makes the situation scary, but it also helps Min-Yin to react correctly and escape danger. Thus, the fitting hexagram name is "Stepping cautiously."

In conclusion, Stepping Carefully is a dangerous situation that will come to pass, provided that one understands his or her weak position and respects the formidable force he or she is facing.

I-CHING TEXTS AND COMMENTS

(For comparison)

I-Ching reading *(original text in Chinese)*

Translation: Stepping cautiously on the tail of the tiger. (Tiger) does not bite. Progress

Comment: The tiger is a fitting symbolism for the guest All-Yang in this particular situation, because in it we immediately see the danger that the hostess is facing. The image of "Stepping cautiously on the tail of the tiger" is also very fitting because Min-Yin's main line is line 3, which is (geometrically) right behind All-Yang. "Tiger does not bite. Progress" is in perfect agreement with Yin Yang logic.

Elaboration on I-Ching reading *(original text in Chinese)*
Translation: Stepping Cautiously. The soft is stepping carefully on the firm. "The Playful" in resonance with "Heaven." That is stepping cautiously on the tiger's tail. Tiger does not bite. Progress.

The firm possesses "Center and Correctness." Stepping cautiously on the position of Heaven, yet not harmed. Brilliant.

Comment: "The soft" is the only Yin line in the hexagram, which is line 3, the main line of the hostess Min-Yin. "The firm" means the guest All-Yang. "The soft is stepping carefully on the firm" because the main line of the hostess is in direct contact with the guest. "The Playful" is a symbolism for Min-Yin, a young and playful girl. "Heaven" is the best known symbolism for All-Yang. "The playful in resonance with Heaven" because Min-Yin is in direct contact with All-Yang and therefore fully understands the dangerous situation she is facing.

"The firm possesses center and correctness" because All-Yang possesses symmetry, therefore well centered, and represents correctness. Min-Yin is praised: "Stepping cautiously on the position of Heaven, yet not harm. Brilliant!" This is possible because Min-Yin is herself aggressive; therefore she has the ability to react to the aggressiveness of the guest. We will see a much less glorious situation in hexagram 33 "Retreating," where the host trigram also has the main line in contact with All-Yang, but lacks the aggressiveness of Min-Yin. Therefore he has to retreat to seek safety.

Symbolisms of I-Ching reading *(original text in Chinese)*
Translation: Heaven above, the Marsh below: "Stepping cautiously." The superior man differentiates high from low, and assesses the will of the people.

Comment: "Heaven" and "Marsh" are well known symbolisms for All-Yang and Min-Yin. Min-Yin's brilliance lies in her ability to recognize that, although she and the guest are both aggressive, she is in a much weaker position than the guest. The lesson to learn is that there exists a social hierarchy (caused by the imperfections of Yin and Yang), and the wise must develop the ability to recognize this hierarchy in all people so that he or she can act correctly.

11. Great Harmony

Role	Trigram	Identity	Activity	Ability
GUEST	*All-Yin*	Feminine	Tentative	Most powerful
HOST	*All-Yang*	Masculine	Aggressive	Most powerful

YIN YANG LOGIC *(NEW!)*

In this hexagram we have a power trigram hosting another power trigram. Since the two sides have opposite activities (aggressive vs. tentative), the meaning is favorable if the host is more powerful than the guest; and further enhanced if the host is masculine. Both criteria are met by this hexagram.

Being the most powerful masculine trigram with reasonable aggressiveness, All-Yang is very comfortable in his leading role as the host. Similar to hexagram 7 (The Army), we can compare All-Yin to the Mass (a big crowd) waiting for instructions from All-Yang.

The Mass has the ability to accomplish great constructive wonders. Great constructive projects require superior leadership skills. Being the most powerful and most stable of all masculine trigrams, All-Yang exactly fits this leadership role. We therefore expect constructive accomplishments of the highest order from this interaction.

The situation is like that of a superior king (All-Yang), who has the ability and integrity to motivate his people (All-Yin). Working together, they bring the country to unheard of levels of harmony and prosperity. The most fitting name for the hexagram is therefore "Great Harmony."

In conclusion, Great Harmony marks a time of great potential. Not only that success is very much certain, but also that the general atmosphere is one of happiness and relaxation.

NOTE:

In this imperfect Yin Yang universe, it is impossible to achieve the Middle Way. One can only get close to it. "Great Harmony" is the only hexagram that best approximates the Middle-Way for two reasons. First, it is the interaction of the two most powerful trigrams; therefore the outcome is more significant than that of any other combinations. Second the identity and activity properties both fit their positions perfectly (Yang at host position and Yin at guest position).

I-CHING TEXTS AND COMMENTS
(For comparison)

I-Ching reading *(original text in Chinese)*

Translation: Great Harmony. The small has left, the great has arrived. Good fortune and progress.

Comment: "The small" implies the Yin essence; "the great" implies the Yang essence. Since All-Yin is in the guest position, which is an outsider's role, "the small has left." Since All-Yang is in the host position, which is an insider's role, "the great has arrived."

Elaboration on I-Ching reading *(original text in Chinese)*

Translation: Great Harmony. The small has left, the great has arrived. Good fortune and progress. That is because the interaction between Heaven and Earth makes it possible for all things to interchange smoothly with one another. The high and the low interact with the same will. Inside Yang, outside Yin. Inside strong, outside yielding. Inside the superior man, outside the small man. The Tao of the superior man is developing. The Tao of the small man is disintegrating.

Comment: Since both All-Yin and All-Yang are most powerful, it is their identities and activities that decide whether they are in appropriate positions. In "Great Harmony" the positions are ideal for both, because All-Yang, whose masculine and aggressive properties are both Yang, is in the host position, while All-Yin, whose feminine and tentative properties are both Yin, is in the guest position. Since both trigrams are happy where they are at, there will be no resistance or jealousy, and good communication is achieved naturally. Therefore it is said "the interaction between Heaven and Earth makes it possible for all things to interchange smoothly with one another. The high and the low interact with the same will."

The differentiation between "the small man" and "the superior man" needs clarification. From an objective viewpoint, All-Yang and All-Yin deviate equally from the Middle Way. However, from the subjective viewpoint of I-Ching logic, which is biased toward Yang, All-Yang is closer to the Middle Way. Since the goal of the superior man is to approximate the Middle Way, he is best represented by All-Yang. Relatively speaking, All-Yin becomes the way of the small man. The small man, then, does not mean a person without ability. Rather he is limited by his tentative nature, which makes it difficult for him to achieve the Middle Way.

Symbolisms of I-Ching reading *(original text in Chinese)*

Translation: Heaven and Earth in contact: Great Harmony. To complete the Tao of Heaven and Earth, their underlying principles should be applied to help the people.

Comment: "Heaven" and "Earth" are well known symbolisms for All-Yang and All-Yin. The lesson from Great Harmony is that the superior man should play the leading role, and the small man the supporting role.

All-Yang
All-Yin

12. Stagnation

Role	Trigram	Identity	Activity	Ability
GUEST	*All-Yang*	Masculine	Aggressive	Most powerful
HOSTESS	*All-Yin*	Feminine	Tentative	Most powerful

YIN YANG LOGIC *(NEW!)*

In this hexagram we have a power trigram hosting another power trigram. Since the two sides have opposite activities (aggressive vs. tentative), the meaning is unfavorable if the hosting trigram is weaker than the guest; and worse if the hosting trigram is feminine. Both are true with this hexagram.

We can visualize the tentative hostess All-Yin waiting for the guest All-Yang to make the first move instead of expressing her desire to follow his lead (This is in contrast to trigram 8 "Union," where All-Yin plays a relatively more active role.) On the other hand, since being a guest is a passive position, there is no guarantee that All-Yang will make the first move that All-Yin is hoping for.

For the powerful trigram All-Yin, this uncertain situation is extremely frustrating. In fact, it could even be dangerous for All-Yin, as All-Yang may mistake her as a threat to his power, or worse, a powerful enemy that he needs to get rid of. The name of the hexagram is therefore "Stagnation."

In conclusion, in Stagnation the relative positions of the two trigrams are such that harmonious communication is impossible. Since both trigrams are most powerful, the consequence of this stalemate will be very serious. Plans cannot be carried out successfully.

I-CHING TEXTS AND COMMENTS
(For comparison)
I-Ching reading *(original text in Chinese)*

Translation: Stagnation does not fit (the situation of) man. Not favorable for the superior man's commitment to stay firmly on course. The great has left, the small has arrived.

Comment: Here we have the reverse of hexagram 11. Since All-Yang is in the guest position, which is an outsider's role, "the great has left." Since All-Yin is in the hostess position, which is an insider's role, "the small has arrived."

Elaboration on I-Ching reading *(original text in Chinese)*

Translation: Stagnation does not fit (the situation of) man. Not favorable for the superior man's commitment to stay firmly on course. The great left, the small arrived. That is because Heaven and Earth do not interact, making it impossible for things to interchange smoothly with one another. The high and the low do not interact; therefore there exists no (territory) under Heaven. Inside Yin, outside Yang. Inside soft, outside firm. Inside the small man, outside the superior man. The Tao of the small man is developing. The Tao of the superior man is disintegrating.

Comment: With the situation in reverse of hexagram 11 "Great Harmony," the masculine aggressive All-Yang is now in the wrong role as the guest, and the feminine tentative All-Yin in the wrong role as the hostess. The role of a guest is frustrating for All-Yang; the role of a hostess makes it impossible for All-Yin to play the supporting role. The two trigrams are cursed with a distant relationship, and effective communication is impossible.

Symbolisms of I-Ching reading *(original text in Chinese)*

Translation: Heaven and Earth not in contact: Stagnation. The superior man nourishes his virtue and avoids possible harm. He cannot plan for fame or wealth.

Comment: In the time of Stagnation, being capable is a liability instead of an asset because capability will be the target of jealousy. Since the superior man understands this well, he will keep himself out of the center of attention. He will continue to nourish this virtue with no expectation for fame or wealth.

All-Yang
Mid-Yin

13. Alliance

Role	Trigram	Identity	Activity	Ability
GUEST	*All-Yang*	Masculine	Aggressive	Most powerful
HOSTESS	*Mid-Yin*	Feminine	Very aggressive	Powerful

YIN YANG LOGIC *(NEW!)*

In this hexagram we have a power trigram hosting another power trigram. Since both trigrams are of the same activity (aggressive), there is power agreement. However, since Mid-Yin is feminine, her position as the hostess is relatively weak.

Being a power trigram, Mid-Yin of course knows how to play the power game. Being more aggressive than the guest, she does what every smart hostess in her position should do: Forging an alliance with the more powerful All-Yang to enhance her own position. Thus, the name of the hexagram is "Alliance."

Since Alliance is a positive combination of two power trigrams, it has great promise for achievement and success.

NOTES:
1. Mid-Yin and All-Yin are both feminine, and Mid-Yin is not as powerful as All-Yin. Yet Mid-Yin is enjoying "Alliance" with the powerful guest All-Yang, while All-Yin had to suffer through "Stagnation" in the company of the same guest. Why? The answer is: Mid-Yin is aggressive like the guest, while All-Yin is tentative. This is a clear example that power agreement is the key to success when the hostess is weaker than her masculine guest.
2. "Alliance" is the perfect Yin Yang opposite of "The Army" (hexagram 7). In "The Army" the masculine host utilizes the power of the guest to conquer his adversaries. In "Alliance" the feminine hostess forms alliance with the powerful guest. Since most males are masculine and most females are feminine, the I-Ching brings out a very interesting contrast between men and women: Men like to conquer, women prefer collaboration. No wonder why most wars have been initiated by men.

I-CHING TEXTS AND COMMENTS
(For comparison)
I-Ching reading *(original text in Chinese)*
Translation: Alliance in remote district. Progress. Favorable to cross the great stream. Favorable for the superior man's commitment to stay firmly on course.

Comment: Alliance happens when a powerful party cannot manage a situation on its own and decides to seek the cooperation of a guest party. The party that seeks Alliance obviously wants to improve its position. We can compare it to a person in a remote district looking for a way to get to the center of the city, where the power lies. This is possibly why the first statement in the I-Ching reading is "Alliance in remote district."

With Alliance, the powerful hostess becomes even more powerful, and can certainly achieve great successes, therefore "Favorable to cross the great stream." With success everything becomes feasible, including the commitment to stay firmly on course.

Elaboration on I-Ching reading *(original text in Chinese)*

Translation: Alliance. The soft in proper position and well centered, therefore in resonance with All-Yang, say "Alliance."

"Alliance" says:

Alliance in remote district. Progress. Favorable to cross the great stream: It is the motion of All-Yang. Civilization and Strength. "Center and Correctness" allows (communication) in resonance. The correctness of the superior man. Only the superior man can comprehend the will under Heaven.

Comment: In Alliance, the main line of the hostess is the only Yin line of the hexagram. It is at position 2, which is the center position of the hostess trigram. Further, we will find out in volume II that position 2 is a Yin position. Thus, the position is also compatible with the identity of the hostess. We say that the Yin line is in proper position. By combining these two factors, we have "The soft in proper position and well centered."

Civilization is a symbolism of Mid-Yin, because by definition the word "civilization" has the meaning of "brilliance," and brilliance is a character of Mid-Yin. "Strength" refers to All-Yang. With "center and correctness" the main line of Mid-Yin (line 2) can communicate with All-Yang. "The correctness of the superior man. Only the superior man can comprehend the will under Heavens" are praises for the wisdom of Mid-Yin in seeking Alliance with the most powerful All-Yang.

Symbolisms of I-Ching reading *(original text in Chinese)*

Translation: Heaven above Fire: Alliance. The superior man treats matters according to their classes.

Comment: "Heaven" and "Fire" are symbolisms for All-Yang and Mid-Yin respectively.

Since nobody would want a weak ally, the act of Alliance requires the ability to classify the various parties according to their strengths and weaknesses. The more general advice for the superior man, then, is to treat matters according to their classes.

Mid-Yin

All-Yang

14. Great Possession

Role	Trigram	Identity	Activity	Ability
GUEST	*Mid-Yin*	Feminine	Very aggressive	Powerful
HOST	*All-Yang*	Masculine	Aggressive	Most powerful

YIN YANG LOGIC *(NEW!)*

In this hexagram we have a power trigram hosting another power trigram. Since both trigrams are of the same activity (aggressive), there is power agreement. In addition, since All-Yang is masculine, his position is very favorable.

Being the most powerful masculine trigram, All-Yang is clearly in control in the host position. In this interaction, All-Yang's "aggressive" activity is reciprocated by Mid-Yin's "very aggressive" activity. The relationship is therefore very favorable.

All-Yang is like a powerful king who searched aggressively and found a very capable leader who was more than willing to serve as his minister. The new minister becomes a great asset to the king's government. Thus, the very fitting hexagram name is "Great Possession."

Needless to say, Great Possession will lead to great progresses.

NOTES:

1. Mid-Yin and All-Yin are both feminine, but Mid-Yin is aggressive while All-Yin is tentative. The aggressiveness of Mid-Yin makes it possible for her to act has All-Yang's right-hand person, creating the proactive atmosphere of "Great Possession." The tentativeness of All-Yin, on the other hand, allows an atmosphere of total efficiency in the time of "Great Harmony" (hexagram 11).

2. "Great Possession" is the perfect Yin Yang opposite of "Union" (hexagram 8). In "Union," the masculine guest is more reluctant than the hostess, but in "Great Possession," the feminine guest is even more aggressive than the host in their favorable relationship. The contrast reminds us of the mental barrier that inflict most men when they deal with powerful women. This barrier does not exist in most women (they would have no problem dealing with powerful men.)

3. Another interesting prediction by the I-Ching: To achieve power positions, women's tendency is to form alliance and

union (hexagrams 13 "Alliance," and 8 "Union"), men's tendency is to conquer and possess (Hexagrams 7 "The Army" and 14 "Great Possession").

I-CHING TEXTS AND COMMENTS
(For comparison)
I-Ching reading *(original text in Chinese)*
Translation: Great Possession. Great Progress.
Comment: The I-Ching reading is in perfect agreement with Yin Yang logic. There is no need for further comment.

Elaboration on I-Ching reading *(original text in Chinese)*
Translation: Great Possession. The soft gains the high position at the great center, allowing the high and the low to be in resonance; say "Great Possession."

Its virtue consists of Civilization and Strength. Being in resonance with Heaven, it is proper time to act. Therefore great progress.

Comment: In Great Possession, the only Yin line of the hexagram is at position 5. We will see in volume II that position 5 is a Yang position, and is the best position of the 6 lines, partly because it is the center position of the guest trigram. These explain the statement "The soft gains the high position at the great center." Although the host trigram is the most powerful, it must respect the Yin line at position 5, therefore "the high (trigram) and the low (trigram) in resonance."

"Civilization" and "Strength" refer to Mid-Yin and All-Yang respectively. All-Yang is the trigram of effective activity. Since it is in the host position with great support by the guest trigram, this is definitely the proper time to act.

Symbolisms of I-Ching reading *(original text in Chinese)*
Translation: Fire on top of Heaven: Great Possession. The superior man represses the bad and promotes the good, in accordance to the will of Heaven and Destiny.

Comment: "Fire" and "Heaven" are symbolisms for Mid-Yin and All-Yang respectively. For All-Yang, who is the best approximation of the superior man, the time of Great Possession allows him the luxury of choosing the good and suppressing the bad without having to fear that he will be the only (good) person left in the world. This explains the statement "The superior man represses the bad and promotes the good, in accordance to the will of Heaven and Destiny."

151

All-Yin

Min-Yang

15. Humility

Role	Trigram	Identity	Activity	Ability
GUEST	*All-Yin*	Feminine	Tentative	Most powerful
HOST	*Min-Yang*	Masculine	Highly tentative	Common

YIN YANG LOGIC *(NEW!)*

In this hexagram we have a common trigram hosting a power trigram. The top criterion for favorable hexagram meaning is proximity with the guest; the second is aggressiveness; the third is (complementary) identity. Min-Yang meets the most important criterion and also the third, but weak in the second criterion.

Understandably, Min-Yang is overwhelmed by the power of All-Yin. Fortunately, his main line (at position 3) is in direct contact with All-Yin. This proximity helps him to realize that, despite her immense power, All-Yin is looking for a leader. In addition, the natural Masculine/Feminine affinity assures Min-Yang that the relationship will be friendly.

Being a very weak trigram in alliance with the most powerful trigram, the natural tendency of Min-Yang is to stay humble and try to learn as much as he can from the guest. Thus, the fitting hexagram name is "Humility."

Genuine humility is the sober realization of one's weakness. This realization leads naturally to the desire to improve, and hence the ability to improve. Genuine humility, then, guarantees progress. However, it is necessary to differentiate genuine humility from "acting with humility," which is a learned behavior. A very proud person may act as if he or she is humble (and does not mean it.) This act is not genuine, and though it may be a successful social strategy, it promises no improvement of the self.

A weak leader will have difficulties, but with genuine humility he will improve and become successful eventually.

ADDITIONAL COMMENTS:

"Humility" is the exact Yin Yang opposite of hexagram 10 "Stepping cautiously." Both are valuable lessons to learn in the dealing with an authority of the opposite sex. The lesson for a weak woman dealing with a male authority is "careful conduct" (Stepping carefully), for a weak man dealing with a female authority is "humility."

I-CHING TEXTS AND COMMENTS
(For comparison)
I-Ching reading *(original text in Chinese)*

Translation: Humility. Progress. The superior man has good end.

Comment: We have seen why genuine Humility leads to progress in Yin Yang logic. Paradoxically, genuine Humility can only be realized by the so-called superior man because it takes incredible courage and determination to realize and accept one's own weaknesses, and to improve on them. Most of us would either lie to ourselves that our weaknesses do not exist, or console ourselves that "That's the way I am. I can't help it!" The latter is an act of defeatism. The superior man does not believe in defeatism. He believes that man has the infinite potential to improve on his weaknesses. This is why, in the time of Humility, "the superior man has good end."

Elaboration on I-Ching reading *(original text in Chinese)*

Translation: Humility (leads to) progress. The Tao of Heaven moves downward yet is brilliant. The Tao of Earth is low, yet is moving up.

The Tao of Heaven decreases the full and increases the humble. The Tao of Earth transforms the full and distributes the humble. The spirits harm the full and bless the humble. The Tao of Man hates the full and likes the humble. Humility is noble and brilliant. Low yet cannot be surpassed. That is the result of (the work) of the superior man.

Comment: Recall that both Yin and Yang are states of deviation from the Middle Way. This elaboration explains how the so-call "Law of Average" works to reduce both Yin and Yang. Humility is a Yin state representing deficiencies. The Law of Average tends to work in favor of the deficient to bring everything toward the Middle Way. Since the superior man pursues the Middle Way, (genuine) Humility is one of his essential practices.

Symbolisms of I-Ching reading *(original text in Chinese)*

Translation: Within Earth there is Mountain: Humility. The superior man reduces the excessive and improves the deficient, to bring about equality in all things.

Comment: "Earth" and "Mountain" are symbolisms for All-Yin and Min-Yang respectively. The superior man starts with the assumption that he may have deviated from the Middle Way. This assumption helps him to calmly identify the excessive as well as the deficient, so that he can reduce the first and enhance the second to approach the Middle Way.

 Max-Yang

All-Yin

16. Exuberance

Role	Trigram	Identity	Activity	Ability
GUEST	*Max-Yang*	Masculine	Most aggressive	Most common
HOSTESS	*All-Yin*	Feminine	Tentative	Most powerful

YIN YANG LOGIC *(NEW!)*

In this hexagram we have a power trigram hosting a common trigram. The first criterion for favorable hexagram meaning is aggressiveness; the second is power; the third is (identical) identity. Although All-Yin fails the first criterion, the proximity of the extremely aggressive guest (at line 4) does transfer some aggressiveness to her. The second criterion helps. The third criterion weakens the situation as the hostess and her guest are of opposite identities.

In this interaction, Max-Yang's main line (at position 4) is in direct contact with All-Yin. This allows him to have a strong influence on her. Since Max-Yang is the most aggressive trigram there is, his unusual aggressiveness gives All-Yin the impression that he could be an extraordinary leader. Thus, the outcome of this interaction is the extreme joy of All-Yin when she meets Max-Yang, giving the hexagram name "Exuberance."

Exuberance is more an exaggerated feeling than an active engagement. We should keep in mind, however, that exaggerated feeling does play a very important role in people's life. It could in fact motivate them to the extreme. Since All-Yin represents a large group of people (i.e., the Mass), the impact of Exuberance could be very great, although it should not last long (because the two trigrams are of opposite identities.)

NOTES:

"Exuberance" is the exact Yin Yang opposite of hexagram 9 "Small Cultivation." In "Small Cultivation," the great effort by All-Yang translates to small result with Max-Yin. Likewise, the extreme joy of All-Yin when she encounters Max-Yang in "Exuberance" is not expected to lead to anything substantial. One reason is that Max-Yang, being the most common trigram, is not the capable leader that he first appears to be.

I-CHING TEXTS AND COMMENTS
(For comparison)
I-Ching reading *(original text in Chinese)*

Translation: Exuberance. Favorable for the establishment of feudal lords and military operation.

Comment: Exuberance will temporarily unite the Mass (represented by All-Yin) and make them fit for projects that are short-term but require massive man power. This is why this hexagram is "Favorable for the establishment of feudal lords and military operation."

Elaboration on I-Ching reading *(original text in Chinese)*

Translation: Exuberance. The firm (line) in resonance, therefore the will can be realized. Yielding and Aggressive. Exuberance.

Exuberance is yielding and aggressive; like Heaven and Earth. Need we say more about establishment of feudal lords and military operation?

Heaven and Earth yielding and aggressive, therefore the sun and the moon are not in error, and the four seasons do not deviate. The sages yielding and aggressive, therefore their (rules on) punishments and penalties are just and respected by the people. So great is the meaning of the time of Exuberance!

Comment: "The firm (line) in resonance" meaning that line 4 is in the right position to influence the hostess. "Yielding" is the character of All-Yin, "Aggressive" is the (only significant) character of Max-Yang.

Heaven, normally associated with All-Yang, is mentioned in this elaboration, possibly to emphasize the importance of aggressiveness, which is also a characteristic off All-Yang. However, the writer is afraid that the examples on the sun and the moon, punishments and penalties have missed the point of this hexagram. Both examples fit better with hexagram 11 "Great Harmony," because it takes the well controlled aggressiveness of All-Yang, not the extreme aggressiveness of Max-Yang to explain the smooth flow of the four seasons and the correctness of the rules and regulations. Is it possible that a part of the original text was lost, and the second and third paragraphs (of the elaboration) were mistakenly added later?

Symbolisms of I-Ching reading *(original text in Chinese)*

Translation: Thunder occurs, the Earth is excited: Exuberance. The ancient kings composed music to promote virtue; then offered (this music) to the King of Heaven, ancestors and past father.

Comment: "Thunder" and "Earth" are symbolisms of Max-Yang and All-Yin. The first sentence explains clearly that Exuberance is a state of the hostess hexagram All-Yin.

Music is one common means to express happiness. Exuberance is an extreme state of happiness, therefore the music that comes from it will be worthy of the gods. Being very wise and non-violent, the ancient kings realize that this is the best application of Exuberance (not the establishment of feudal lords or the engagement in military battles, although these are also favorable in the time of Exuberance.)

155

Min-Yin

Max-Yang

17. Pursuing

Role	Trigram	Identity	Activity	Ability
GUEST	*Min-Yin*	Feminine	Highly aggressive	Common
HOST	*Max-Yang*	Masculine	Most aggressive	Most common

YIN YANG LOGIC *(NEW!)*

In this hexagram we have a common trigram hosting another common trigram. Recall from chapter 10 that in this case the hexagram quality depends strictly on the relative ranking of the host and the guest: 1. Max-Yang, 2. Min-Yang, 3. Min-Yin, 4. Max-Yin. Since host Max-Yang has higher ranking than the guest, the hexagram has favorable meaning.

Since Max-Yang's main line is at position 1 and Min-Yin's main line is at position 6, these two trigrams are completely disconnected from each other. Their relationship comes from the Feminine/Masculine affinity and the fact that both are aggressive trigrams.

Since both trigrams are common, this hexagram corresponds to an interaction of two ordinary persons, with no earth shaking consequences. We can visualize Min-Yin as an active girl who appears to play hard-to-catch (activity = highly aggressive, with identity line far away from host), and Max-Yang as a man who is after her (activity = most aggressive). Thus, the name of the hexagram is "Pursuing," which should be understood as acting according to the changes of the situation.

The distance between the two trigrams makes Pursuing a challenging game for Max-Yang. However, in addition to being the host, Max-Yang also enjoys the advantage of being relatively more aggressive than Min-Yin. We can therefore expect that Max-Yang will somehow react correctly to Min-Yin's unpredictable movements and even win her heart eventually.

Pursuing, then, is a favorable hexagram; but it requires considerable effort by the host, with continuous attention to the action of the guest.

I-CHING TEXTS AND COMMENTS
(For comparison)

I-Ching reading *(original text in Chinese)*

Translation: Pursuing. Great progress. Advisable to stay firmly on course. No error.

Comment: Although Pursuing is a favorable hexagram, the situation will be unpredictable most of the time. It is therefore important for the host to stay firmly on course. This way he can be sure that no error is committed.

Elaboration on I-Ching reading *(original text in Chinese)*
Translation: Pursuing. The firm comes and is below the soft. Aggressive yet Playful. Pursuing.

Great progress. Staying firmly on course leads to no error. (This applies to) All under Heaven in the time of Pursuing.

Great is the meaning of the time of Pursuing.

Comment: "The firm comes and is below the soft" points to the first line, which is the main line of the host Max-Yang. In this hexagram, Max-Yang is placed below Min-Yin, which corresponds to "the soft."

"Aggressive" and "Playful" correspond to Max-Yang and Min-Yin respectively. The rest of the elaboration is a repeat of the I-Ching reading.

Symbolisms of I-Ching reading *(original text in Chinese)*
Translation: Within the Marsh there is Thunder: Pursuing. When it is getting dark, the superior man starts feasting and resting.

Comment: "Marsh" and "Thunder" are symbolisms for Min-Yin and Max-Yang respectively. The suggested action of the superior man in the time of Pursuing shows that the ancient sage had a good sense of humor. (Since Pursuing has no earth shattering consequences) When it is getting dark, the most appropriate action that fits the time of Pursuing is, naturally, to feast and rest.

Min-Yang

Max-Yin

18. Deterioration

Role	Trigram	Identity	Activity	Ability
GUEST	*Min-Yang*	Masculine	Highly tentative	Common
HOSTESS	*Max-Yin*	Feminine	Most tentative	Most common

YIN YANG LOGIC *(NEW!)*

In this hexagram we have Max-Yin serving as the hostess, which is a case of Yin-Yang reversal.

Since Max-Yin's main line is at position 1 and Min-Yang's main line is at position 6, these two trigrams are completely disconnected from each other.

Adding to the problem, as far as Yin Yang logic is concerned, Max-Yin is the worst hostess. Not only that all three of her properties are Yin, but they are the most Yin possible (activity = most tentative, ability = most common). There is no way that Max-Yin will initiate anything in this relationship. Since Min-Yang is himself a weak trigram and highly tentative, in the passive role of a guest he is not qualified to initiate anything either. Adding the disconnection of the main lines (1 and 6), there will be no effort by either party, and things must get worse and worse, giving the fitting hexagram name "Deterioration."

However, recall that when Max-Yin serves as the hostess, she will somehow get things under control. Thus, after deterioration has set in, the process of correction will start and the situation will improve dramatically.

"Deterioration" therefore consists of two stages: The deterioration stage and the recovery stage, with good result at the end.

ADDITIONAL COMMENTS:

"Deterioration" is the exact Yin Yang opposite of hexagram 17 "Pursuing." In "Pursuing" the host responded to aggressiveness with aggressiveness, whereas in "Deterioration" the hostess responded to tentativeness by tentativeness (and then tries to correct the situation when it deteriorates).

I-CHING TEXTS AND COMMENTS
(For comparison)
I-Ching reading *(original text in Chinese)*

Translation: Deterioration. Great progress. Advantageous to cross the great stream. Three days before *Ya*. Three days after *Ya*.

Comment: *Once deterioration has taken place, the (unexpected) action by Max-Yin will force a dramatic improvement, therefore "Great progress." Paradoxically, as seen often in real life, the deterioration of an existing situation usually allows a greater and better situation to develop; therefore "Advantageous to cross the great stream." Ya is the first of the 10 Heavenly roots, which are an integral part of Chinese day counting system (with repeating cycles of 60 days). "Three days before Ya. Three days after Ya" is one way to say that Deterioration is not a one-shot event, but a development over time (that includes Deterioration and Recovery.)*

Elaboration on I-Ching reading *(original text in Chinese)*
Translation: Deterioration. The firm above the soft below. Flexible and Stopping. Deterioration.

Deterioration. Great progress, therefore all under Heaven will be in order. Favorable to cross the great stream. Activities lead to the tasks (to be achieved). Three day before Ya, three days after Ya. The end must have a beginning. That is the activity of Heaven.

Comment: *"The firm above" refers to the masculine guest trigram Min-Yang, "the soft below" the feminine hostess trigram Max-Yin. "Flexible" and "Stopping" are symbolisms for Max-Yin and Min-Yang respectively.*

"Great progress, therefore all under Heaven will be in order" refers to the corrections made by Max-Yin after deterioration has taken its toll. "The end must have a beginning" refers to the fact that Deterioration is not a one-shot situation, but rather a development over time.

Symbolisms of I-Ching reading *(original text in Chinese)*
Translation: At the foot of the Mountain there is Wind: Deterioration. The superior man improves the (situation of) the people and promotes virtue.

Comment: *"Mountain" and "Wind" are symbolisms for Min-Yang and Max-Yin respectively. Deterioration would have adverse effects on the welfare of people as well as their sense of virtue. This is why in the time of Deterioration "The superior man improves the (situation of) the people and promotes virtue."*

All-Yin

Min-Yin

19. Approaching

Role	Trigram	Identity	Activity	Ability
GUEST	*All-Yin*	Feminine	Tentative	Most powerful
HOSTESS	*Min-Yin*	Feminine	Highly aggressive	Common

YIN YANG LOGIC *(NEW!)*

In this hexagram we have a common trigram hosting a power trigram. The most important criterion for favorable hexagram meaning is to have the host or hostess in proximity of the guest (main line at line 3); the second is to have an aggressive host or hostess; the third is to have two trigrams with opposite identities. For this hexagram the first two are met, but not the third.

Although the guest All-Yin is the most powerful of all Yin trigrams, Min-Yin has nothing to fear as she is not competing for power. Being highly aggressive and having her main line (at position 3) in direct contact with the most powerful feminine guest, Min-Yin is like a girl who approaches her mother and actively seeks a dialog. Thus, the fitting name of the hexagram is "Approaching."

Note that the only thing that the hostess has to offer the guest is her aggressiveness. This makes sense in real life, where the best strategy to approach a tentative person in power is to demonstrate the willingness to deal from a weak position.

Since both trigrams are feminine, their identities are not complementary. There is a risk that instabilities will set in eventually.

NOTE:

The above example of an active girl seeking a dialog with her mother may give the false impression that the guest is more respectable than the person that approaches her. The academically inclined reader may find this image unsatisfactory.

For a more general understanding of this hexagram, imagine the guest as a formidable force, which may or may not be friendly but is in a wait-and-see mode. The host (or hostess) is aggressive, but lacks either power or credibility. The task of the host is to approach the formidable force mentioned, and try to initiate a constructive relationship.

The bottom line in Approaching is this: The host (or hostess) is in a weaker position than the guest, but has an opportunity to improve his or her standing.

I-CHING TEXTS AND COMMENTS
(For comparison)

I-Ching reading *(original text in Chinese)*

Translation: Approaching. Great progress. Advisable to stay firmly on course. There is evil in the eighth month.

Comment: "Great progress" is achieved with Approaching, because the guest is a powerful trigram. The interaction with her will benefit the common hostess trigram. Approaching the powerful is a difficult task, therefore "Advisable to stay firmly on course."

Approaching only brings one close to the guest, and follow-up will be necessary. Otherwise the powerful guest will run out of patience. This is described in "There is evil in the eight month."

Elaboration on I-Ching reading *(original text in Chinese)*

Translation: Approaching. The firm invades and stays long. Playful and Yielding. The firm at the center, yet in resonance. Great progress along with correctness. That is the Tao of Heaven.

There is evil in the eighth month. Decay in a short time.

Comment: "The firm invades and stays long" refers to the aggressiveness of Min-Yin, which came from the two Yang lines 1 and 2. "Playful" and "Yielding" correspond to Min-Yin and All-Yin respectively. "The firm at the center, yet in resonance" refers to line 2, which occupies the center position of the hostess trigram. This reminds us that the aggressiveness of the hostess is not due to her main line at position 3, but to the (auxiliary) Yang lines at positions 1 and 2. These Yang lines help Min-Yin to be "in resonance" with the guest.

This elaboration explains clearly that "There is evil in the eight month" because the time of Approaching does not last long.

Symbolisms of I-Ching reading *(original text in Chinese)*

Translation: Above the Marsh there is Earth: Approaching. The superior man is unlimited in his intention to transfer knowledge (to others), and in his willingness to offer opportunities to the people.

Comment: "Marsh" and "Earth" are symbolisms for Min-Yin and All-Yin respectively. Since Approaching only brings the host close to the guest, the superior man has to go beyond Approaching to make a meaningful interaction out of it. "Transferring knowledge" and "offering opportunities to the people" are two meaningful follow ups that he should perform.

Max-Yin

All-Yin

20. Observation

Role	Trigram	Identity	Activity	Ability
GUEST	*Max-Yin*	Feminine	Most tentative	Most common
HOSTESS	*All-Yin*	Feminine	Tentative	Most powerful

YIN YANG LOGIC *(NEW!)*

In this hexagram we have a power trigram hosting a common trigram. The first criterion for favorable hexagram meaning is aggressiveness, the second is power, the third is (identical) identity.

Although hostess All-Yin lacks aggressiveness, she is clearly in control as she is the most powerful feminine trigram while her guest Max-Yin is the weakest, and the two trigrams have identical identity.

On the other hand, since both trigrams are feminine and tentative, All-Yin will not try to use her power to complement Max-Yin weakness; but the two cannot ignore each other, as Max-Yin's main line (at position 4) is in direct contact with the hostess All-Yin; and the hostess herself is in direct contact with Max-Yin (through line 3, because all three lines of All-Yin are Yin.)

Putting all the factors together, we have All-Yin performing the most passive interaction of all: Setting examples (of proper actions and behavior) for Max-Yin to observe and follow, and observing Max-Yin to assess her progress, giving the fitting hexagram name "Observation."

As far as host-guest interaction is concerned, "Observation" is the most inactive of all 64 hexagrams.

I-CHING TEXTS AND COMMENTS
(For comparison)
I-Ching reading *(original text in Chinese)*

Translation: Observation. Washes hands but not offering. Having faith. Noble appearance.

Comment: "Washes hands but not offering" describes an action by the most powerful (feminine) hostess All-Yin, who knows that she is with the weakest feminine trigram, and therefore has to act as a role model. All-Yin is setting an example in the 'dos and don'ts' of worshipping, by washing her hands (a must before a ceremony). Since this is only an example, she need not and does not have the choice of performing the actual offering.

"Having faith" refers to the fact that the hostess is acting with the utmost sincerity or with the belief that she is setting a good example for

162

the guest. *"Noble appearance" emphasizes that All-Yin is the most noble of all feminine trigrams, a good example for others to observe and imitate.*

Elaboration on I-Ching reading *(original text in Chinese)*

Translation: Great observation at the high position. Yielding and Flexible. "Center and Correct" watches (things) under Heaven.

Observation. Washes hands but not offering. Having faith. Noble appearance. The low observes and transforms.

The Tao of the saints, based on the observation of Heaven, will reveal that the four seasons do not deviate. The sages follow the Tao of the saints to establish their teaching; therefore (their teaching) is revered by all under Heaven.

Comment: "Great observation at the high position" refers to the act of observation by the powerful hostess All-Yin. "Yielding" and "Flexible" refer to All-Yin and Max-Yin respectively. "'Center and correct' watches (things) under Heaven" refers to line 2, which is the major line of the hostess trigram. This line is not only the center line of the hostess trigram, but also compatible with the (Yin) position of the line; hence "center and correct."

"The low observes and transforms." In this case it does not make sense for "the low" to mean the lower trigram (i.e., hostess trigram). Most likely it means people in lower positions, which would apply to the guest trigram Max-Yin. The statement then means that by simply observing All-Yin's actions, Max-Yin's life can be transformed. (Which is often the case in real life. An ordinary person's life may be transformed by the action of his or her role model.)

"The Tao of the saints, based on the observation of Heaven, will reveal that the four seasons do not deviate" is a praise of the accuracy of the early scientific method in calendar calculations, which started with the observation of the movements of the Heavenly bodies. Observations are also the necessary steps that led to the teaching of the sages (i.e., early scientists and philosophers).

It is reassuring to know that the ancient sages also stressed the importance of observation as a part of the scientific method, just like we do today.

Symbolisms of I-Ching reading *(original text in Chinese)*

Translation: Wind blows over Earth: Observation. The ancient kings examine the different regions, observe the people, and put in place (necessary) educational programs.

Comment: "Wind" and "Earth" are symbolisms for Max-Yin and All-Yin respectively. The ancient kings, who are known for their wisdom, must have gone beyond the implications of Observation. That is why they followed up the act of observation and "put in place (necessary) educational programs."

Mid-Yin

Max-Yang

21. Biting (in pain)

Role	Trigram	Identity	Activity	Ability
GUEST	Mid-Yin	Feminine	Very aggressive	Powerful
HOST	Max-Yang	Masculine	Most aggressive	Most common

YIN YANG LOGIC *(NEW!)*

In this hexagram we have a common trigram hosting a feminine power trigram. The first criterion for favorable hexagram meaning is to have the host close to the guest; the second is to have an aggressive host; the third is to have a masculine host (to complement the feminine power guest). Max-Yang meets the second and third criteria, but not the most important one, giving a mixed hexagram meaning.

Max-Yang's strength as the most aggressive masculine trigram is over-extended when he interacts with the guest Mid-Yin who, despite her feminine identity, has her own aggressiveness. The main difference is that Mid-Yin's aggressiveness is more controlled than the aggressiveness of Max-Yang. This makes Mid-Yin a power figure who considers Max-Yang's extreme aggressiveness unacceptable.

Whether Max-Yang's extreme aggressiveness is that of a hooligan or of a moral activist, it doesn't matter. As far as Mid-Yin is concerned, he has abused the Masculine/Feminine affinity. Unfortunately, Max-Yang's main line (at position 1) is too far from the guest. This causes him to be ignorant of Mid-Yin's opinion and to keep on with his extreme aggressiveness. Punishment (by the powerful guest) is the price that he has to pay for this ignorance.

The six lines of this hexagram give the image of a mouth biting on something (i.e., Line 1 gives the image of the lower lip, line 6 upper lip, lines 2 and 3 lower teeth, line 5 upper teeth, line 4 "something"), like the mouth of a tortured prisoner who is clenching his teeth in pain. Thus the fitting hexagram name is "Biting."

"Biting" is, paradoxically, a good thing for the host, who is extremely aggressive. That is because, from the standpoint of law and order (represented by the guest Mid-Yin), extreme aggressiveness must be constrained early so that it does not develop into lawless behavior.

NOTES:

1. The same extreme aggressive behavior that works for Max-Yang in hexagram 17 "Pursuing" now gets him into trouble in "Biting," although in both cases he is dealing with an aggressive feminine guest. The different being that in "Pursuing" the guest Min-Yin is a common trigram like Max-Yang, but

in "Biting" the guest Mid-Yin is a power trigram. The lesson is not new: Extreme aggressiveness without substance leads one into trouble in an environment of power, especially when that power is law and order.

2. In hexagram 3 "Difficulties," Max-Yang has a difficult time to achieve immediate result with the guest; here he is punished by the guest. In both cases the guest is powerful. The difference is that in Difficulties the guest is tentative; here in Biting the guest is aggressive.

I-CHING TEXTS AND COMMENTS
(For comparison)
I-Ching reading *(original text in Chinese)*

Translation: Biting. Progress. Favorable to enforce legal constraints (on criminals).

Comment: Paradoxically, legal constraints are beneficial for the host as it helps him to know when and where to limit his extreme activity, therefore "progress." Since the guest is more powerful than the extremely active host, she can constrain him, therefore "Favorable to enforce legal constraints."

Elaboration on I-Ching reading *(original text in Chinese)*

Translation: There is something inside the mouth, say "Biting."

Biting yet making progress. The firm and the soft are separated. Active and Bright. Lightning uniting yet Brilliant. The soft gaining center moving upward. Although not in proper position, can enforce legal constraints.

Comment: "There is something inside the mouth" refers to the image formed by the 6 lines of the hexagram "Biting."

"Biting yet making progress" refers to the act of legal constraint, which is beneficial for the host (under constraint). "The firm and the soft are separated" refers to the fact that the masculine host (firm) is not aware of the reaction of the powerful feminine guest (soft).

"Active and Bright" refers to the host Max-Yang and the guest Mid-Yin respectively. "Lightning uniting yet Brilliant" again refers to the same two trigrams. "The soft gaining center moving upward" refers to the main line of Mid-Yin, which occupies the center (line 5) of the guest trigram. "Although not in proper position, can enforce legal constraints" refers to the fact that position 5 is a Yang position, which is improper for the Yin line. The guest "can enforce legal constraints" because she is aggressive, and more powerful than the most aggressive guest.

Symbolisms of I-Ching reading *(original text in Chinese)*

Translation: Thunder and Lightning: Biting. The ancient kings clarify regulations and punishments.

Comment: "Thunder" and "Lightning" are symbolisms for Max-Yang and Mid-Yin respectively. The actions by the wise ancient kings are fitting for this hexagram, which is about legal constraints.

Min-Yang
Mid-Yin

22. Decoration

Role	Trigram	Identity	Activity	Ability
GUEST	Min-Yang	Masculine	Highly tentative	Common
HOSTESS	Mid-Yin	Feminine	Very aggressive	Powerful

YIN YANG LOGIC *(NEW!)*

In this hexagram we have a power trigram hosting a common trigram. The first criterion for favorable hexagram meaning is to have an aggressive host or hostess; the second is to have a masculine host; the third is to have both trigrams of the same identity. This hexagram meets the most important criterion, but fails the other two. We expect favorable meaning, but not of significant consequence.

Being a powerful and aggressive trigram, hostess Mid-Yin can complement her guest, Min-Yang, who is a common and tentative trigram. Note that the guest's role is highly passive, as his main line (at position 6) is too far from the hostess. This gives Mid-Yin complete freedom.

Mid-Yin gives Min-Yang the most meaningful gift that she has. Being a balanced feminine aggressive trigram, she is the expert of (feminine) beauty. She will concentrate her efforts in making the (rather dull) Min-Yang more artistically beautiful. Thus, the fitting hexagram name is "Decoration."

While hexagram 16 "Exuberance" is the hexagram of the audio arts (e.g., music), "Decoration" is the hexagram of the visual arts, where the artist transfers beauty to passive media, and gives them life.

Visual art adds quality to our lives; therefore this is a hexagram of progress. As in the case of arts, the immediate impact of Decoration will be limited.

NOTE:

Max-Yin is the other tentative common trigrams (in addition to Min-Yang), but Mid-Yin hosting Max-Yin does not correspond to visual art because the main line of Max-Yin is at position 4, in active communication with the hostess, and therefore does not give her the freedom to express her creativity.

I-CHING TEXTS AND COMMENTS
(For comparison)
I-Ching reading *(original text in Chinese)*

Translation: Decoration. Progress. Small advantage in moving forward.

Comment: Decoration definitely leads to progress. However, its immediate value is not expected to be great. Therefore only small advantage is implied by the hexagram.

Elaboration on I-Ching reading *(original text in Chinese)*

Translation: Decoration. Progress.

The soft arrives and decorates the firm; therefore there is progress. The firm separates upward, decorating the soft; therefore small advantage in moving forward. That is the decoration of the Heaven. Civilizing and Stopping. That is the decoration of humanity.

The observation of Heavenly decoration confirms the changes of time. The observation of the decoration of humanity transforms to all things under Heaven.

Comment: "The soft arrives and decorates the firm" refers to the action of Mid-Yin (the soft), who decorates Min-Yang (the firm). "Civilization and Stopping. That is the decoration of humanity." Civilization and Stopping correspond to Mid-Yin and Min-Yang respectively. These two symbolisms also bring out the fact that, in visual arts, beauty is captured and kept for a long time (as if time has been stopped).

"The observation of Heavenly decoration confirms the changes of time" refers to the correspondence between the great work of natural art, e.g., the slowly changing appearance of the sky, and the changes of time. "The observation of the decoration of humanity transforms to all things under Heaven" refers to the pervasive impact of (man-made) visual arts on life.

Symbolisms of I-Ching reading *(original text in Chinese)*

Translation: At the foot of the Mountain there is Fire: Decoration. The superior man beautifies (the process of) government, but dares not apply the same to regulations and legal constraints.

Comment: Mountain and Fire are symbolisms for Min-Yang and Mid-Yin respectively. Since Decoration corresponds to visual art, the superior man must know where visual art is applicable. Beautifying the process of government makes sense, but not the process of regulations and legal constraints (e.g., there is no point in beautifying the prison.)

Min-Yang

All-Yin

23. Destruction

Role	Trigram	Identity	Activity	Ability
GUEST	Min-Yang	Masculine	Highly tentative	Common
HOSTESS	All-Yin	Feminine	Tentative	Most powerful

YIN YANG LOGIC *(NEW!)*

In this hexagram we have a power trigram hosting a common trigram. The most important criterion for favorable hexagram meaning is aggressiveness; the second is power; the third is to have two trigrams with the same identity. All-Yin fails the first criterion. Moreover, since the guest is also tentative, he will not be able to transfer any aggressiveness to her. All-Yin also fails the third criterion, because she is feminine while the guest is masculine.

Despite her immense power, hostess All-Yin lacks direction. The masculine guest Min-Yang is not only too weak to assume leadership, but also disconnected from the hostess (his main line is at position 6). Without clear direction, the immense power of All-Yin becomes a potent destructive force. Thus, the fitting hexagram name is "Destruction."

All plans will fail in the time of Destruction.

NOTE:

The reason that Destruction follows hexagram 22 "Decoration" is philosophically significant. In Decoration the aggressive powerful feminine hostess creates beauty, in Destruction the even more powerful hostess destroys. This is a great lesson to learn: When power is coupled with the lack of beautiful energy (i.e., being tentative instead of aggressive) there can be no art, just destruction. We have seen this in attempts by dictators to exploit arts to further their political agenda.

I-CHING TEXTS AND COMMENTS
(For comparison)

I-Ching reading *(original text in Chinese)*

Translation: Destruction. There is no advantage in making any movement.

Comment: In the time of Destruction, all plans will be met with opposition. It is best not to attempt anything significant.

Elaboration of I-Ching reading *(original text in Chinese)*

<u>Translation</u>: Destruction is Stripping Away. The soft transforms the firm.

No advantage in making any movement. The small man has developed. Yielding and Stopping. (By) observing the symbolisms, the superior man (comprehends the) decrease and increase, fullness and emptiness. That is the activity of Heaven.

Comment: "Destruction is Stripping Away" brings out the difference between Decoration (hexagram 22) and Destruction. In Decoration the guest is beautified by hostess Mid-Yin, in Destruction he is stripped away by hostess All-Yin. "The small man has developed" refers to the status of All-Yin, powerful and in control, without direction and leadership.

Symbolisms of I-Ching reading *(original text in Chinese)*

<u>Translation</u>: Mountain next to Earth: Destruction. Superiors go all out to help those below them, so that their own position can be stabilized.

Comment: "Mountain" and "Earth" are symbolisms for Min-Yang and All-Yin. Anticipating the detrimental effects of Destruction, wise superiors understand that they cannot be inactive (like Min-Yang); otherwise people below them (like All-Yin) will destroy them. They therefore have to go all out to help the people.

169

All-Yin

Max-Yang

24. Revival

Role	Trigram	Identity	Activity	Ability
GUEST	All-Yin	Feminine	Tentative	Most powerful
HOST	Max-Yang	Masculine	Most aggressive	Most common

YIN YANG LOGIC *(NEW!)*

In this hexagram we have a common trigram hosting a power trigram. The most important criterion is to have a host that stays close to the guest (main line at position 3). The second is to have an aggressive host. The third is to have two trigrams of opposite identities to serve as the host and the guest. Although this hexagram fails the first criterion, the consequence is not too great because the guest All-Yin is quite accommodating. Because criteria 2 and 3 are met, we expect that the meaning is somewhat favorable.

Being the most common of all trigrams, Max-Yang is definitely not a symbol of power or capability. However, being the most aggressive masculine trigram, he is like a sudden promise, a shock therapy that people tend to respond to in times of desperation.

With the guest All-Yin representing an immense power without direction (that may have caused havoc in the past), host Max-Yang's extreme aggressiveness finds its perfect niche. With the main line (in position 1) too far away from the guest, Max-Yang does not know enough to be fearful of All-Yin immense power. He will therefore carry out his extreme activities, which happen to fit this moment of extreme instability and make him the accidental hero. Max-Yang's appearance gives the feeling that order will soon be restored. Thus, the fitting hexagram name is "Revival."

Since Max-Yang's ability is limited, it is not likely that the enthusiasm of "Revival" will be substantiated with meaningful action. "Revival" is therefore a very unpredictable time; with the strong possibility that things may get worse, not better. Thus, this is the perfect moment for unusual plans or plans that have been hindered in the past, but not a good time for normal activities (that have been conducted smoothly in the past.)

In summary, in the time of Revival, progress is certain; but this is an unpredictable time, where only unusual actions are appropriate.

I-CHING TEXTS AND COMMENTS
(For comparison)
I-Ching reading *(original text in Chinese)*
Translation: Revival. Progress. Exiting and entering without distress. Friends come. No error. Returns to his Tao. Return in seven days. Advantageous to move forward.

Comment: The time of Revival will certainly lead to progress. "Exiting and entering without distress" marks the improvement from the difficult past. "Friends come" marks the change of time, where cooperation, which has been so rare before, suddenly happens. "No error" because the time of Revival marks the end of a terrible past, now everything is an improvement. "Returns to his Tao" reminds us that the time of Revival has come. "Return in seven days" because Revival is a chaotic time, not everything will turn around immediately. "Advantageous to move forward" should be understood as being applicable only to unusual plans that fit the chaotic time of Revival.

Elaboration on I-Ching reading *(original text in Chinese)*
Translation: Revival. Progress. (It is) the revival of the firm.

Aggressive and Yielding in movements. Therefore exiting and entering without distress. Friends come. No error.

Return to his Tao. Return in seven days. This is the activity of Heaven.

Advantageous to move forward. The firm has developed.

Don't we see in Revival the mind of Heaven and Earth?

Comment: "The revival of the firm" means the revival of the host trigram Max-Yang. "Aggressive and Yielding" correspond to Max-Yang and All-Yin respectively.

"Advantageous to move forward. The firm has developed" reminds us that the advantage is applicable to Max-Yang (the firm). Since Max-Yang is the trigram with the most extreme aggressiveness, only unusually aggressive plans fit the time of Revival.

Symbolisms of I-Ching reading *(original text in Chinese)*
Translation: Thunder in the middle of Earth: Revival. The ancient kings close the gates for the whole day. Businessmen do not travel. The princes do not inspect their respective regions.

Comment: "Thunder" and "Earth" are symbolisms for Max-Yang and All-Yin respectively. The wise ancient kings understand that the time of Revival is a chaotic time, that is why they "close the gates for the whole day." Other regular activities should also be suspended temporarily, therefore "Businessmen do not travel. The princes do not inspect their respective regions."

All-Yang

Max-Yang

25. Non-Expectation

Role	Trigram	Identity	Activity	Ability
GUEST	All-Yang	Masculine	Aggressive	Most powerful
HOST	Max-Yang	Masculine	Most aggressive	Most common

YIN YANG LOGIC *(NEW!)*

In this hexagram we have a common trigram hosting a power trigram. To have favorable meaning, the top criterion is to have a host that stays close to the guest. The second criterion is to have an aggressive host. The third criterion is to have host and guest of opposite identities. Since this hexagram fails the first and the third criteria, its meaning is unfavorable.

In hexagram 24 "Revival," because the guest was All-Yin, the extremely aggressive masculine Max-Yang was the perfect fit and became the accidental hero. In contrast, when the guest is All-Yang, the same Max-Yang will find himself in a very precarious situation.

There are several reasons for this. First, with the main line at position 1, the host is far removed from the guest and therefore not fully aware of his limitation. Second, Max-Yang's extreme aggressiveness is no match for the more controlled aggressiveness of All-Yang, who is the most capable of all masculine trigrams. The fact that All-Yang is the most powerful trigram and Max-Yang the most common does not help either. Third, both All-Yang and Max-Yang are masculine.

Try the best as he may, the outcome of Max-Yang activities is at the mercy of the powerful guest. Thus, the fitting trigram name is "Non-Expectation."

I-CHING TEXTS AND COMMENTS
(For comparison)

I-Ching reading *(original text in Chinese)*

Translation: Non-Expectation. Great progress. Advisable to stay firmly on course. If not correct, there will be error. Not advantageous to move forward.

Comment: "Great progress" should be understood as having a spiritual meaning. Max-Yang, despite his extreme aggressiveness, realizes in the time of Non-Expectation that all of his efforts may lead nowhere because the situation is completely out of his control. This helps him to look inward and correct his own conduct. He is advised to

172

stay firmly on course not because such action guarantees success, but because it minimizes the possibility of committing errors. Every single error is costly in the time of Non-Expectation.

In fact, the greatest risk in the time of Non-Expectation is to try to outsmart the all-powerful guest All-Yang. Such an ill-advised strategy would be a grave error and might lead to disastrous consequences.

All that said and done, Max-Yang should not expect any success in the time of Non-Expectation.

Elaboration on I-Ching reading *(original text in Chinese)*

Translation: Non-Expectation. The firm comes from the outside and takes control of the inside. Aggressiveness and Strength. The firm at the center, therefore in resonance. Great progress if correct. That is the (cosmic) order coming from Heaven. If not correct will commit error. Not advantageous to move forward. Movement with Non-Expectation leads to what? Without the help of the cosmic order, how can movement be made?

Comment: "The firm comes from the outside and takes control of the inside" refers to the fact that All-Yang, which is the (outer) guest trigram, has a strong effect on the (inner) host trigram. "The firm at the center" refers to line 5, which is occupied by the major Yang line of All-Yang. "Great progress is correct. That is the (cosmic) order coming from Heaven. If not correct will commit error." refers to the fact that the host Max-Yang has no control whatsoever of the situation, all depends on the guest All-Yang. "Not advantageous to move forward. Movement with Non-Expectation leads to what? Without the help of the cosmic order, how can movement be made?" describes the difficulty for the host in the time of Non-Expectation.

Symbolisms of I-Ching reading *(original text in Chinese)*

Translation: Under Heaven, Thunder makes movements, things are with Non-Expectation. The ancient king nourishes all things according to the seasons.

Comment: "Heaven" and "Thunder" are symbolisms for All-Yang and Max-Yang respectively. The wise ancient king "nourishes all things according to the seasons" because seasons are the only signs that the Heaven reveals to him, and in the time of Non-Expectation he should plan to give, not take.

 Min-Yang

All-Yang

26. Great Cultivation

Role	Trigram	Identity	Activity	Ability
GUEST	Min-Yang	Masculine	Highly tentative	Common
HOST	All-Yang	Masculine	Aggressive	Most powerful

YIN YANG LOGIC *(NEW!)*

In this hexagram we have a power trigram hosting a common trigram. The first criterion for favorable meaning is to have an aggressive host; the second is to have a host with high standing in the power scale; the third is to have matching identities. This hexagram meets all three criteria; therefore the meaning is clearly favorable.

Being the most powerful masculine trigram, host All-Yang is supposed to help cultivate the weakest masculine trigram Min-Yang. Although the present state of the guest is highly tentative, the agreement in identities (both masculine) qualifies Min-Yang as All-Yang's protégé. For this reason, All-Yang's efforts will lead to very positive outcome.

However, since the guest (with his main line at position 6) is disconnected from the host, the cultivation effort will be challenging and require patience.

NOTES:

1. Both hexagram 4 "Ignorance" and "Great Cultivation" give us the image of a powerful host cultivating Min-Yang; but while in Ignorance the host is quite hesitant, in Great Cultivation we have a very willing and determined host. That is because the host in Ignorance is Mid-Yang, who is tentative; while the host in Great Cultivation is All-Yang, who is aggressive and more capable than Mid-Yang.

2. In hexagram 22 "Decoration" and "Great Cultivation," the tentative common guest Min-Yang benefits from the aggressiveness of the host or hostess trigram. The difference is that Mid-Yin is not as powerful as All-Yang. Thus, the hostess Mid-Yin can only transform Min-Yang into a beautiful object of art, while the host All-Yang transforms Min-Yang into a capable man.

174

I-CHING TEXTS AND COMMENTS
(For comparison)

I-Ching reading *(original text in Chinese)*

Translation: Great Cultivation. Advisable to stay firmly on course. Not eating at home. Favorable. Advantageous to cross the great stream.

Comment: Great Cultivating is a challenging task for the host All-Yang, because the guest Min-Yang is highly tentative. It is necessary therefore that All-Yang stays firmly on course. "Not eating at home" since the great dedication that All-Yang must exercise will require him to temporarily abandon a normal life. "Advantageous to cross the great stream" because Great Cultivation is a great constructive project that fits the great ability of All-Yang; success is all but certain.

Elaboration on I-Ching reading *(original text in Chinese)*

Translation: Great Cultivation. The firm is strong. Emitting true brilliance. Revises his virtue daily. Firm yet constructive, can stop the strong. Great correctness.

Not eating at home. Favorable. Nourishing the constructive.

Advantageous to cross the great stream. In resonance with Heaven.

Comment: In Great Cultivation we have the most powerful and most common masculine trigrams dealing with each other, with the most powerful in the host position. In the very difficult process of cultivating the much weaker Min-Yang, the host All-Yang will see his own weaknesses exposed. Min-Yang then is not only a passive student, but also a barrier and an opportunity for All-Yang to improve himself. These lead to "Revises his virtue daily. Firm yet constructive, can stop the strong." Great Cultivation will improve the already great All-Yang, leading to great correctness.

"Not eating at home. Favorable. Nourishing the constructive" means that the task in Great Cultivation is to nourish the guest. This difficult task forces the host out of his normal routine, but it is a favorable sign, not a bad sign.

"Advantageous to cross the great stream. In resonance with Heaven" shows the great promise of Great Cultivation.

Symbolisms of I-Ching reading *(original text in Chinese)*

Translation: Heaven at the center of the Mountain. Great Cultivation. The superior man, with broad understanding of the words and activities of former (great) men, cultivates his virtue.

Comment: "Heaven" and "Mountain" are symbolisms for All-Yang and Min-Yang respectively. Great Cultivation allows the superior man to see all of the weaknesses that he has. He should actively try to improve on them.

 Min-Yang

Max-Yang

27. Feeding
(The Mouth)

Role	Trigram	Identity	Activity	Ability
GUEST	Min-Yang	Masculine	Highly tentative	Common
HOST	Max-Yang	Masculine	Most aggressive	Most common

YIN YANG LOGIC *(NEW!)*

In this hexagram we have a common trigram hosting another common trigram. Recall from chapter 10 that in this case the hexagram quality depends strictly on the relative ranking of the host and the guest: 1. Max-Yang, 2. Min-Yang, 3. Min-Yin, 4. Max-Yin. Since host Max-Yang has higher ranking than the guest, the hexagram has favorable meaning.

Both trigrams are common masculine. Since they are both common, there is no great outcome or consequence. The aggressive host is in the position to help cultivate the guest, who is the weakest masculine trigram. However, since the two trigrams are disconnected (host's main line at position 1, guest's main line at position 6) and since the host is a common trigram, the outcome will be modest compared to that of "Great Cultivation," despite the fact that the host is the most aggressive trigram. In "Great Cultivation," the powerful aggressive host All-Yang can offer the guest everything that he needs. Here we should expect much less from the common aggressive host Max-Yang. The most basic help that one can offer the other is food; therefore the fitting hexagram name is "Feeding."

It is interesting to note that Max-Yang is the most common masculine trigram, yet in Feeding he is helping Min-Yang. He is able to achieve this altruistic goal simply because he is extremely aggressive. This teaches us a lesson on giving and volunteerism. As long as there is a strong desire to help (extreme aggressiveness), the most common person can do a lot of good for others and for the society.

"Feeding" is the hexagram of giving and caring for other human beings.

NOTE:

It is very natural for Feeding to follow hexagram 26 "Great Cultivation." Here we still have the same guest, but a less powerful aggressive host. Max-Yang's ability is much more limited than All-Yang's, but his effort is still beneficial to the guest.

176

I-CHING TEXTS AND COMMENTS
(For comparison)

I-Ching reading *(original text in Chinese)*

Translation: The mouth. Favorable if staying firmly on course. Seeks the proper food for oneself.

Comment: While All-Yang gave Min-Yang total nourishment in Great Cultivation (hexagram 26), Max-Yang can only offer Min-Yang the most practical form of nourishment: Food. Understandably, the rule of success for this limited nourishment is still "to stay firmly on course." Obviously the food offered has to be proper; therefore the task is to "seek proper food."

Elaboration on I-Ching reading *(original text in Chinese)*

Translation: The mouth. Favorable if staying firmly on course. Nourishing correctness, therefore favorable. Observing the mouth is observing one's nourishment. Seeks the proper food for oneself: Observing one's own nourishment.

Heaven and Earth nourish all things. The sages nourish the constructive to provide to the people. So great is the time of the mouth.

Comment: This elaboration does not add anything new to the I-Ching reading.

Symbolisms of I-Ching reading *(original text in Chinese)*

Translation: There is Thunder at the foot of the Mountain. The mouth. The superior man is careful with his words and exercises self restraint in drinking and eating.

Comment: "Thunder" and "Mountain" are symbolisms for Max-Yang and Min-Yang respectively. The superior man, as usual, must outperform the Yin Yang meaning of the hexagram in his drive toward the Middle Way. Since nourishment is the key word in this case, he must exercise self-restraint in eating and drinking. Also realizing that the most basic nourishment also involves the use of language in communication, the superior man will also exercise self-restraint in his words.

Min-Yin
Max-Yin

28. Great Extremity

Role	Trigram	Identity	Activity	Ability
GUEST	Min-Yin	Feminine	Highly aggressive	Common
HOSTESS	Max-Yin	Feminine	Most tentative	Most common

YIN YANG LOGIC *(NEW!)*

In this hexagram we have Max-Yin serving as the hostess; which makes it a case of Yin-Yang reversal.

Both trigrams are feminine. In fact they are the exact Yin Yang reverses of the two masculine trigrams in hexagram 27 "Feeding." We expect no great outcome or consequence because both (trigrams) are common.

Max-Yin, who is most tentative, is not at all qualified to host the highly aggressive Min-Yin. To make matters worse, her main line is at position 1 while that of the guest is at position 6. Such extreme distance makes it impossible for the two sides to establish any kind of meaningful communication.

Necessity forces Max-Yin to the extreme. Like a normally patient person who is pushed over the edge, Max-Yin reverses her tendency to keep up with the aggressiveness of her guest. This sudden impulse has to be very forceful, as the two trigrams are completely disconnected from each other. Thus, the fitting hexagram name is "Great Extremity."

Good result is expected from "Great Extremity." However, since this is an artificial game that goes against the nature of the hostess, one should be prepared for unwanted side effects and consequences.

I-CHING TEXTS AND COMMENTS

(For comparison)

I-Ching reading *(original text in Chinese)*

Translation: Great Extremity. The wooden bar is bent. Advantageous to move forward. Progress.

Comment: The 6 lines of Great Extremity give us the image of a wooden bar that is bent at the two ends; hence "The wooden bar is bent." The time of Great Extremity will force success and progress, therefore "Advantageous to move forward. Progress."

Elaboration on I-Ching reading *(original text in Chinese)*

Translation: Great Extremity. The great is in its extremity. The wooden bar is bent. Its physical makeup is weak.

178

The firm is in error but possesses the center. Flexible and Playful go together. Advantageous to move forward. Therefore progress.

Great is the time of Great Extremity.

Comment: "The great is in its extremity" possibly refers to the situation of the 4 Yang lines. The writer begs to differ with this view, since lines 1 and 6 are main lines of the two trigrams, and they are Yin. "Extremity" here should refer to the situation of Max-Yin. Fortunately this difference in viewpoint is academic and has no effect on the meaning of the hexagram. "The wooden bar is bent. Its physical makeup is weak" refers to the fact that "Great Extremity" is a superficial phenomenon that masks the true weakness of the hostess Max-Yin. "The firm is in error but possesses the center" refers to line 2, which is the center line of the hostess trigram. This line is Yang, which is not compatible with its position.

"Flexible" and "Playful" correspond to Max-Yin and Min-Yin respectively. Great Extremity forces success, therefore "Advantageous to move forward."

Symbolisms of I-Ching reading *(original text in Chinese)*

Translation: The Marsh covers the Tree. Great Extremity. The superior man is not afraid of standing alone. He withdraws from the world without regret.

Comment: "Marsh" and "Tree" are symbolisms for Min-Yin and Max-Yin, respectively. The time of Great Extremity is the time of artificial success by those who are much weaker than they appear. To stay beyond and above the Yin and Yang of the hexagram the superior man will not take any part in this. Therefore "The superior man is not afraid of standing alone. He withdraws from the world without regret."

Mid-Yang

Mid-Yang

29. Danger
(Double Mid-Yang)

Role	Trigram	Identity	Activity	Ability
GUEST	Mid-Yang	Masculine	Very tentative	Powerful
HOST	Mid-Yang	Masculine	Very tentative	Powerful

YIN YANG LOGIC *(NEW!)*

This is an identity hexagram formed by one Mid-Yang trigram on top of the other. Mid-Yang is a powerful masculine trigram, but his power is compromised by his tentativeness. For this reason, Mid-Yang is not as powerful as All-Yang.

Recall that the meaning of a hexagram is the situation encountered by the host, and being tentative is not fitting for the host position. More specifically, Mid-Yang has a realistic possibility of becoming too tentative and therefore losing his strength as a power trigram. The possibility of losing power is extremely dangerous for the tentative Mid-Yang, because he may not be able to run away fast enough from his enemies. Thus, the fitting hexagram name is "Danger."

But because Mid-Yang must be a power trigram, this is a case where the law of Yin-Yang reversal applies; and the situation could be transformed into a great opportunity if the host deals with it appropriately.

When a person is confronted with a dangerous situation, he must take risk; and when he takes risk it is impossible for him to have everything under control. Thus, he must have either strong faith in himself or spiritual belief in the unknown. While this is not advisable in most cases, it may just work for Mid-Yang, because his (masculine) identity does fit the host position. He is therefore qualified for this unusual mode of operation and this is how he achieves his status as a power trigram despite being tentative.

In summary, Danger is a challenge for the weak, but a great opportunity for those who have confidence in themselves and in the (cosmic) order. They will make progress and achieve great things in the time of danger.

I-CHING TEXTS AND COMMENTS
(For comparison)

I-Ching reading *(original text in Chinese)*

Translation: Repeated Mid-Yang. Having faith. Being spiritual. Progress. Action has high value.

180

Comment: "Having faith" refers to the host Mid-Yang's confidence, that he is a powerful trigram. "Being spiritual" applies because the host is putting his trust in the unknown. "Progress. Action has high value" because the host is a powerful trigram with great potential, and action is the best way to deal with the time of Danger.

Elaboration on I-Ching reading *(original text in Chinese)*

Translation: Repeated Mid-Yang means Double Danger. Water flows but does not accumulate. Walking in the midst of Danger without losing one's faith. Being spiritual. Progress (because) firm (line) is at center. Action has high value. Undertaking is fruitful.

The Danger of Heaven makes it unreachable. The Danger of Earth is manifested in mountains, rivers, hills, and mounds. Kings and lords arrange Danger to keep their territories. So great is the proper use of the Time of Danger!

Comments: "Water flows but does not accumulate" describes the dynamic power of Mid-Yang. "Progress (because) firm (line) is at center" refers to line 2, which is Yang (firm) and occupies the center position of the host trigram.

Danger is not necessarily a bad thing. It is in fact needed in certain cases, as explained in the elaboration: "The Danger of Heaven makes it unreachable. The Danger of Earth is manifested in mountains, rivers, hills, and mounds. Kings and lords arrange Danger to keep their territories."

Symbolisms of I-Ching reading *(original text in Chinese)*

Translation: Water flowing continuously forms Repeated Mid-Yang. The superior man acts according to his everyday's virtue and practices education.

Comment: Water is the symbolism for Mid-Yang. The superior man has to rise beyond the meaning of Danger implied by the hexagram. He therefore calmly practices his daily virtue (because danger has no effect on his thinking). He also educates other about the advantage of danger.

Mid-Yin
Mid-Yin

30. Brightness
(Double Mid-Yin)

Role	Trigram	Identity	Activity	Ability
GUEST	Mid-Yin	Feminine	Very aggressive	Powerful
HOSTESS	Mid-Yin	Feminine	Very aggressive	Powerful

YIN YANG LOGIC *(NEW!)*

This is an identity hexagram formed by one Mid-Yin trigram on top of the other. Mid-Yin is a powerful feminine trigram, but her power is compromised by her aggressiveness, which is inconsistent with her feminine identity. For this reason, Mid-Yin is not as powerful as All-Yin. It should be noted, however, that the meaning of a hexagram is the situation encountered by the host or hostess, and being feminine is a disadvantage. Paradoxically then, Mid-Yin's aggressiveness, which fits the hostess position, is also the main source of her strength in this hexagram.

Being feminine aggressive and powerful, Mid-Yin gives us the image of an active woman who is so graceful that her presence radiates a commanding energy. The fitting hexagram name is therefore "Brightness."

Undoubtedly, Mid-Yin possesses great promise for progress; but there is a potential problem. Since there is internal conflict, Min-Yin must practice mindfulness to stay firmly on course and balance her aggressiveness with her femininity.

I-CHING TEXTS AND COMMENTS
(For comparison)

I-Ching reading *(original text in Chinese)*

Translation: Brightness. It is advisable to stay firmly on course. Progress. Cultivating cow-like virtue. Good.

Comment: Brightness is a symbolism for Mid-Yin. "Advisable to stay firmly on course" because there is a real possibility of becoming too aggressive at the sacrifice of effectiveness. Progress is very much guaranteed. "Cultivating cow-like virtue" is a meaningful advice, as the cow is not an aggressive animal. Good results are expected.

Elaboration on I-Ching reading *(original text in Chinese)*

Translation: Mid-Yin means brightening. The sun and the moon brighten the Heaven. The various grains, grass, and trees brighten the

182

Earth. Double Brightness brightens correctness. The world is formed from them.

The soft brightens "being central and correct," therefore "progress" (can be made). It is the cultivation the virtue of a cow that is good.

Comment: Many translators, most notably James Legge[1], used "being attached to" or "attaching itself to" for the meaning of Mid-Yin. In the writer's opinion, this translation is a good description for the feminine aggressiveness of Mid-Yin, but fails to include her most important character, that she represents radiant beauty. The more complete translation would be "attaching its brilliance to" or "attaching its brightness to," which the writer has simplified as "brightening." Thus, "the sun and the moon brighten the Heaven. The various grains, grass, and trees brighten the Earth. Double Brightness brightens correctness" describes the lovely value that Mid-Yin adds to all aspects of life.

"The soft brightens 'being central and correct'" refers to line 2, which is the main line of the hostess. This line is in the central position, and –being Yin- it is in agreement with the position. The Yin character of the line corresponds to the quality of a cow, yielding yet powerful. Progress is guaranteed.

Symbolisms of I-Ching reading *(original text in Chinese)*

Translation: Brightness, repeated, forms Mid-Yin. The great man continuously cultivates brightness and distributes it in all four directions.

Comment: "Brightness" is a symbolism for Mid-Yin. The great man (who is a superior man with superior ability) must rise above and beyond the meaning of the hexagram. He therefore not only cultivates his virtue until it becomes bright, but also distributes his bright virtue to all directions.

---

[1] "The I Ching – the Book of Changes," James Legge, reprinted by Dover Publications, New York, 1963.

Min-Yin

Min-Yang

31. E-Motions

Role	Trigram	Identity	Activity	Ability
GUEST	Min-Yin	Feminine	Highly aggressive	Common
HOST	Min-Yang	Masculine	Highly tentative	Common

YIN YANG LOGIC *(NEW!)*

In this hexagram we have a common trigram hosting another common trigram. Recall from chapter 10 that in this case the hexagram quality depends strictly on the relative ranking of the host and the guest: 1. Max-Yang, 2. Min-Yang, 3. Min-Yin, 4. Max-Yin. Since host Min-Yang has higher ranking than the guest Min-Yin, the hexagram has favorable meaning.

Since these two trigrams are exact Yin Yang opposites of each other, they have perfect feminine-masculine affinity. In addition, since both are common, neither trigram has the power to overwhelm the other. The masculine host Min-Yang is in direct contact (main line at position 3) with the guest and well aware of her presence. Min-Yin aggressiveness catches his attention, though she may not be aware of it (main line at position 6). Since his basic character is not aggressive, Min-Yang is not reacting to Min-Yin (as in hexagram 17 "Pursuing" with Max-Yang hosting Min-Yin). However, under the spell of the feminine aggressiveness of the guest Min-Yin, the highly tentative but masculine host Min-Yang feels a strong vibration that he has never felt before. It is difficult to describe this vibration, but it is the very kind of vibration that a boy would feel when he meets his special girl. This vibration is caused by the heart, by emotion. For lack of better words, we will choose to call the hexagram "E-motions" (Motions induced by emotion).

The proper symbolism for Min-Yang is a male teenager, and Min-Yin a female teenager. The vibration felt by Min-Yang is what most of us call "first love." This is therefore the hexagram of Love.

Love is the most appropriate motivation for marriage. Therefore this hexagram is very favorable for love and marriage.

I-CHING TEXTS AND COMMENTS
(For comparison)

I-Ching reading *(original text in Chinese)*

Translation: E-motions. Progress. Advisable to stay firmly on course. It is good to marry the girl.

Comment: "*Advisable to stay firmly on course*" *because E-motions is a state unfamiliar to Min-Yang, he must stays composed and does not over-react. For obvious reasons, the time of E-motions is very favorable for marriage.*

Elaboration on I-Ching reading *(original text in Chinese)*

Translation: E-motions correspond to feelings.

The soft above the firm below. The two *chi* feel each other in resonance and are therefore together. Stopping and Playful. Male below female, therefore enjoying progress. Advisable to stay firmly on course. It is good to marry the girl.

Heaven and Earth feel each other; therefore all things evolve in their existence. The sages feel the heart of humanity therefore (all territories) under Heaven are peaceful. Observing feelings can help us see the emotion of all things.

Comment: "The soft above the firm below" refers to Min-Yin (the soft) and Min-Yang (the firm). "Stopping and Playful" refers to Min-Yang and Min-Yin. "Male below female, therefore enjoying progress" means that the masculine trigram Min-Yang enjoys progress because he is in the proper position (the host position is below the guest position.)

"Heaven and Earth feel each other, therefore all things evolve in their existence. The sages feel the heart of humanity therefore (all territories) under Heaven are peaceful" states the importance of e-motions in this otherwise materialistic world.

Symbolisms of I-Ching reading *(original text in Chinese)*

Translation: Above the Mountain is the Marsh: E-motions. The superior man empties his mind so he can receive (the feelings of) others.

Comment: "Mountain" and "Marsh" are symbolisms for Min-Yang and Min-Yin respectively. If one's mind is occupied, it would be impossible for him or her to be receptive to emotion, which is controlled by the heart. Therefore in the time of E-motions, the superior man "empties his mind so he can receive others."

Max-Yang

Max-Yin

32. Permanence

Role	Trigram	Identity	Activity	Ability
GUEST	Max-Yang	Masculine	Most aggressive	Most common
HOSTESS	Max-Yin	Feminine	Most tentative	Most common

YIN YANG LOGIC *(NEW!)*

In this hexagram we have Max-Yin serving as the hostess; which makes it a case of Yin-Yang reversal.

Since these two trigrams are exact Yin Yang opposites of each other, they have perfect feminine-masculine affinity. In addition, since both are common, neither trigram has the power to overwhelm the other. The most aggressive masculine guest, with his main line at position 4, has a strong influence on the hostess, who is not qualified to be the hostess at all as she is the most tentative of all trigrams. By common wisdom we would guess that the influence of the guest will make the hostess highly changeable (which would be similar to the reaction of Min-Yang, see trigram 62 "Small Extremity.") Note, however, that Max-Yin will reverse her basic tendency when that is necessary to maintain her hostess position. By so doing, she turns the table on the guest, making the situation the reverse of changeability. Thus, the fitting hexagram name is "Permanence."

Here we have two trigrams that are perfect Yin Yang opposites, and a permanence relationship between them. It is a natural belief that the relationship between husband and wife should last a lifetime. For this reason, Permanence describes the *Tao of marriage*, which is very difficult to achieve, but is desired by everyone who is contemplating getting married.

Permanence, then, is the hexagram of (ideal) relationship between husband and wife.

I-CHING TEXTS AND COMMENTS
(For comparison)

I-Ching reading *(original text in Chinese)*

Translation: Permanence. Progress. No error. Advisable to stay firmly on course. Advantageous to move forward.

Comment: Thanks to the reversal in the behavior of Max-Yin, Permanence promises progress, with no error. Since it is difficult to maintain a long-term relationship, it is "advisable to stay firmly on

186

course." Permanence is a good situation; therefore it is "advantageous to move forward."

Elaboration on I-Ching reading *(original text in Chinese)*

Translation: Permanence means a long time. The firm above and the soft below. Thunder and Wind together. Flexible and Aggressive. Firm and soft in resonance. Permanence.

Permanence. Progress. No error. Advisable to stay firmly on course. Keep the Tao for a long time. The Tao of Heaven and Earth. Permanence without stopping.

Advantageous to move forward. The end must have a beginning.

Thanks to Heaven, the sun and the moon can shine for a long time. The four seasons keep transforming therefore they can keep forming for a long time. The sage prolongs his Tao therefore (all territories) under Heaven change to their forms. By observing permanence, we can see the emotion of all things.

Comment: "The firm above and the soft below. Thunder and Wind together. Flexible and Aggressive." refers to Max-Yang (the firm, Thunder, Aggressive) and Max-Yin (the soft, Wind, Flexible).

Permanence should not be mistaken as a static state. In fact, permanence can only be maintained by staying forever dynamic. This is explained in the elaboration: "The four seasons keep transforming therefore they can keep forming for a long time. The sage prolongs his Tao therefore (all territories) under Heaven change to their forms."

By observing closely, we will see that Permanence is maintained by a process of continuous re-invention, this is why the elaboration says "By observing permanence, we can see the emotion of all things."

Symbolisms of I-Ching reading *(original text in Chinese)*

Translation: Thunder and Wind: Permanence. The superior man stands without changing his position.

Comment: "Thunder" and "Wind" are symbolisms for Max-Yang and Max-Yin respectively. In the time of Permanence, the superior man must stay constant in his position, regardless of other factors.

All-Yang

Min-Yang

33. Retreating

Role	Trigram	Identity	Activity	Ability
GUEST	All-Yang	Masculine	Aggressive	Most powerful
HOST	Min-Yang	Masculine	Highly tentative	Common

YIN YANG LOGIC *(NEW!)*

In this hexagram we have a common trigram hosting a power trigram. Host Min-Yang, with his main line at position 3, has the benefit of being next to the guest. The problem is that he is tentative, which does not help. Furthermore, his and the guest's identities are identical instead of being complementary, which makes things worse.

Host Min-Yang, with his main line at position 3, is in direct contact with the most powerful guest All-Yang and therefore fully aware of the presence of the most powerful of all masculine trigrams. In contrast, Min-Yang is the weakest of all masculine trigrams. Understandably, this interaction is a trying experience for the host.

All-Yang is an aggressive trigram. His aggressiveness causes grave concerns for the highly tentative host Min-Yang. Naturally Min-Yang will try to keep a safe distance from the guest. In order to achieve this, he must move away from the aggressive guest. Thus, the fitting name of the hexagram is "Retreating."

NOTES:

With the same powerful guest All-Yang we have three different scenarios with the three masculine hosts:

Host Max-Yang, who is extremely aggressive, will continue trying. But he has no hope for success, giving hexagram 26 "Non-expectation"

Host Mid-Yang, who is also powerful, is not giving up his position right away, giving hexagram 6 "Contention."

Host Min-Yang, who is the weakest of all masculine trigrams, simply gives up, giving this hexagram "Retreating."

I-CHING TEXTS AND COMMENTS
(For comparison)

I-Ching reading *(original text in Chinese)*

Translation: Retreating. Progress. Advisable to stay firmly on course in small matters.

Comment: "Progress" in the time of Retreating has to be understood as having the meaning of "making progress by retreating."

188

The equivalent is a person who is going through a bad experience. There is a positive lesson even in this case, provided that the person involved is calm in his or her assessment of the situation.

In the time of Retreating, all great plans should be abandoned. However, one should not make the mistake of not paying attention to detail, that is why the advice is "to stay firmly on course in small matters."

Elaboration on I-Ching meaning *(original text in Chinese)*

Translation: Retreating. Progress. The retreat can take place. The firm in proper position and in resonance. Act according to time.

Advisable to stay on course in small matters. Encroaching and developing.

Great is the time of Retreating!

Comment: "Progress. The retreat can take place" clarifies the meaning of progress in the time of Retreating. "The firm in proper position and in resonance" refers to line 3, which is the main line of the host Min-Yang. This line is in contact with the guest, which helps the host to assess his situation correctly. In addition, it is Yang, which is compatible with position 3. "Act according to time" is the praise for the act of Retreating, because this is the correct action implied by the hexagram.

"Advisable to stay on course in small matters. Encroaching and developing" refers again to the position of the main line of the host. While the host is retreating, the proximity of his main line allows him to keep achieving smaller goals to get ready for a brighter future when the tide is turning in his favor.

Symbolisms of I-Ching reading *(original text in Chinese)*

Translation: Below Heaven is the Mountain. Retreating. The superior man keeps a distance from small men, not by hatred but by his gravity.

Comment: "Heaven" and "Mountain" are symbolisms for All-Yang and Min-Yang respectively. The superior man must outperform the meaning implied by Retreating. For this reason he anticipates trouble, and keeps a distance from small men. Of course he must do so in a way that does not feed hatred.

Max-Yang

All-Yang

34. Great Energy

Role	Trigram	Identity	Activity	Ability
GUEST	Max-Yang	Masculine	Most aggressive	Most common
HOST	All-Yang	Masculine	Aggressive	Most powerful

YIN YANG LOGIC *(NEW!)*

In this hexagram we have a power trigram hosting a common trigram. Since the host is aggressive and masculine, the meaning is expected to be favorable. The matching of identities (both host and guest are masculine) makes things even better.

Being the most powerful masculine trigram, host All-Yang plays the leader's role in the relationship with Max-Yang. However, since the main line of Max-Yang (at position 4) is in direct contact with All-Yang, All-Yang will also be influenced by the extreme aggressiveness of Max-Yang. All-Yang is an aggressive trigram, but his aggressiveness level is usually very well-controlled. With Max-Yang's influence, All-Yang's aggressiveness will be raised to a level unusually high for him. Thus, the fitting hexagram name is "Great Energy."

With All-Yang's ability, it is most likely that he will be able to manage this unusually high level of aggressiveness and produce positive results with it. However, he must be mindful of the risk of moving too far from the center, where his power lies.

NOTES:

With the same all powerful All-Yang as the host, we have three different situations with the three masculine guests:

All-Yang goes all out to cultivate the weakest guest Min-Yang, giving hexagram 26 "Great Cultivation"

All-Yang must wait until the powerful guest Mid-Yang gives up his challenge, giving hexagram 5 "Waiting."

All-Yang is influenced by the extremely aggressive guest Max-Yang, giving this hexagram "Great Energy."

I-CHING TEXTS AND COMMENTS
(For comparison)

I-Ching reading *(original text in Chinese)*

Translation: Great Energy. Advisable to stay firmly on course.

Comment: "Advisable to stay firmly on course" because in the time of Great Energy, there is a real risk that the host will be hyperactive, which will compromise his position as the most powerful trigram.

Elaboration on I-Ching reading *(original text in Chinese)*

Translation: Great Energy. The great is energetic. The firm is moving, therefore energetic.

Great Energy. Advisable to stay firmly on course. The Great is correct. With "correct and great" the emotion of Heaven and Earth can be seen.

Comment: "The great is energetic" refers to All-Yang, the greatest of all masculine trigrams. Here All-Yang is influenced by the extreme aggressiveness of Max-Yang, who corresponds to "The firm is moving."

"The Great is correct" is a warning for the host that he should stay within his correctness, instead of becoming hyperactive under the influence of Max-Yang.

"With 'correct and great' the emotion of Heaven and Earth can be seen" refers to the (cosmic) order, where a deviation in Great Energy can overextends the power of All-Yang, who represents Heaven. This would, in turn, upset the balance between Heaven and Earth.

Symbolisms of I-Ching reading *(original text in Chinese)*

Translation: Thunder above Heaven forms Great Energy. The superior man does not take any single step without propriety or caution.

Comment: "Thunder" and "Heaven" are symbolisms for Max-Yang and All-Yang respectively. Since the risk in the time of Great Energy is that All-Yang may become hyperactive, "the superior man does not take any single step without propriety or caution."

Mid-Yin

All-Yin

35. Advance

Role	Trigram	Identity	Activity	Ability
GUEST	Mid-Yin	Feminine	Very aggressive	Powerful
HOSTESS	All-Yin	Feminine	Tentative	Most powerful

YIN YANG LOGIC *(NEW!)*

In this hexagram we have one power trigram hosting another power trigram. Since their activities are opposite (All-Yin is tentative, Mid-Yin is aggressive), this is a power conflict. The winning side is the hostess All-Yin, because she is more powerful than the guest Mid-Yin.

Mid-Yin's aggressiveness, which works so well for her in so many cases, becomes a liability in this encounter because the tentative hostess All-Yin is the most powerful of all feminine trigrams. We have the image of the tentative hostess All-Yin winning the battle of the powerful, not by attacking but by waiting for her aggressive enemy to make mistakes. Thus, the fitting hexagram name is "Advance."

This hexagram is easy to remember as it has the image of the Sun (Mid-Yin) above the Earth (All-Yin), suggesting the idea of "Advancing." However, the reader is warned not to take these symbolisms as a valid account for the meaning of the hexagram, because the advance is made by the hostess All-Yin (the Earth), not by the guest Mid-Yin (the Sun).

NOTE:

All-Yin has the power of a large group of people without direction (in the ideal sense of a mandate from Heaven). An example is a powerful army of barbarians. Mid-Yin has the beautiful balance of a civilized people, still aggressive, but lacks unity. This hexagram explains why in the conflicts between barbarians and civilization, in most cases the barbarians grow strong, while civilization retreats backward (or weakens itself with internal conflicts). No wonder why most civilizations have been destroyed by barbarians!

I-CHING TEXTS AND COMMENTS
(For comparison)

I-Ching reading *(original text in Chinese)*

Translation: Advance. The feudal lord of a tranquil territory is given many horses and received 3 times a day.

Comment: *"The feudal lord of a tranquil territory is given many horses and receives 3 times a day" refers to the favorable position of the hostess All-Yin. "Many horses" and "3 times a day" are partial symbolisms that we do not get into in this book (but will explain in a future book dedicated to the Yin Yang theory.) It suffices to say that All-Yin is winning concessions from the guest Mid-Yin and gains brightness herself.*

Elaboration on I-Ching reading *(original text in Chinese)*

Translation: Advance means moving forward.

Brightness moves above Earth. Yielding and Brightening like the Great Brightness. The soft advances upward. Therefore (giving the image of) the feudal lord of a tranquil territory is given many horses and received 3 times a day.

Comment: *"Brightness" and "Earth" are symbolisms for Mid-Yin and All-Yin. "Yielding and Brightening" refers to All-Yin and Mid-Yin. "The soft advances upward" refers to the favorable position of All-Yin (the soft). The image of the feudal lords who are given horses and received three times have been explained in the part of I-Ching reading.*

Symbolisms of I-Ching reading *(original text in Chinese)*

Translation: Brightness moves above Earth: Advance. The superior man radiates his brilliant virtue.

Comment: *"Brightness" and "Earth" are symbolisms for Mid-Yin and All-Yin. The superior man takes advantages of his favorable situation, which brightens his virtue, to influence other people.*

All-Yin

Mid-Yin

36. Brightness Dimmed (injury)

Role	Trigram	Identity	Activity	Ability
GUEST	All-Yin	Feminine	Tentative	Most powerful
HOSTESS	Mid-Yin	Feminine	Very aggressive	Powerful

YIN YANG LOGIC (NEW!)

Here we again have the two trigrams that formed the preceding hexagram "Advance," but with Mid-Yin as the hostess and All-Yin as the guest. The aggressiveness of the powerful hostess proved to be a fatal tactical mistake because her guest All-Yin, despite being tentative, is the most powerful of all feminine trigrams. The consequence is that Mid-Yin (because of her very aggressiveness) will suffer heavy losses. Since a well known symbolism for Mid-Yin is brilliant light, the symbolism for this case is the dimming of the light. Thus, the fitting hexagram name is "Brightness Dimmed," or simply "Dimming."

This hexagram is easy to remember as it has the image of light (Mid-Yin) below the Earth (All-Yin), suggesting the idea of "Dimming."

Dimming is an unusual time, and requires unusual strategy. This is when brilliance can lead to calamity. A real-life example was the case of the intellects under the Khmer Rouge regime in Cambodia. Since the Khmer Rouge tried to eliminate civilization, it ordered execution of all intellects. This was a very clear case where one must keep his or her brilliance in obscurity.

NOTE:

This hexagram gives the same picture as the preceding picture, just from a different angle. The civilized lacks the unity in their conflict against the unruly force of the mob and usually ends up being the losing party.

I-CHING TEXTS AND COMMENTS
(For comparison)
I-Ching reading (*original text in Chinese*)
Translation: Brightness Dimmed. It is advised to stay firmly on course in difficulty.
Comment: The I-Ching reading is self explanatory. The advice "to stay firmly on course" will be explained in the elaboration, next.

Elaboration on I-Ching reading *(original text in Chinese)*

<u>Translation</u>: Brightness entering inside Earth. Dimming.

Inside Civilized, outside Soft and Yielding; leading to great calamity. This is the case of King Wen.

"It is advisable to stay firmly on course in difficulty" means dimming one's brightness. Facing inner difficulty, yet one still keeps his will on the correct path. This is the case of the feudal lord *Ki*.

<u>Comment</u>: "Civilized" refers to Mid-Yin; "Soft and Yielding" refers to All-Yin. King Wen was brilliant, but had to appear soft and yielding under the rule of the then malevolent emperor. This was an example of Dimming.

The case of the feudal lord Ki was used as the second example for Dimming. Here lord Ki was facing tremendous difficulties, yet he was able to keep his inner brilliance.

Since Dimming is a time where brilliance only leads to calamity, "to stay firmly on course" means the intentional dimming of one's brightness.

Symbolisms of I-Ching reading *(original text in Chinese)*

<u>Translation</u>: Brightness entering inside Earth. Dimming. The superior man, in conducting his management of men, keeps his brightness in obscurity.

<u>Comment</u>: "Brightness" and "Earth" are symbolisms for Mid-Yin and All-Yin respectively. The superior man knows that this is the time when his brilliance must be kept in obscurity.

195

Max-Yin

Mid-Yin

37. Family Members

Role	Trigram	Identity	Activity	Ability
GUEST	Max-Yin	Feminine	Most tentative	Most common
HOSTESS	Mid-Yin	Feminine	Very aggressive	Powerful

YIN YANG LOGIC *(NEW!)*

In this hexagram we have a power trigram hosting a common trigram. Mid-Yin is the most favorable power trigram in such a situation, because she is the most aggressive of the power group. The matching of identity (both are feminine) makes the situation even more favorable.

With her main line at position 4, the guest is in direct contact with the hostess. We have the image of two persons sharing a common identity (feminine), with the much weaker guest informing the hostess of her situation. Since there is no conflict, we expect the more capable and aggressive hostess to help out her guest. This is exactly how two family members should interact with each other. Thus, the fitting hexagram name is "Family Members."

NOTES:

The reader may want to compare "Family Members" against hexagram 20 "Observing," where All-Yin hosts Max-Yin. Although in both cases the hostess is a power trigram, the difference is that All-Yin is tentative while Mid-Yin is aggressive. This is why All-Yin only observes Max-Yin (like a mother watching her weak daughter) while Mid-Yin helps Max-Yin (like a capable girl looking after her weak sister.)

Hexagram 27 "Feeding" is also worth mentioning. In "Feeding" we also have two trigrams with a common identity (masculine), and the aggressive host helping the tentative guest. The difference is that the host Max-Yang in "Feeding" is a common trigram with limited capability, therefore his effort cannot be compared to the comprehensive help that Mid-Yin offers Max-Yin.

I-CHING TEXTS AND COMMENTS
(For comparison)
I-Ching reading *(original text in Chinese)*

Translation: Family Members. Advantageous for females to stay firmly on course.

Comment: "Advantageous for females to stay firmly on course" refers to the nature of this hexagram, which deals with matters between close members who are related to each other by a mutual bond that has nothing to do with masculine/feminine affinity. We call this kind of relationship "feminine" but it should not be taken to mean that it only applies to females. Rather, it has the meaning of spiritual support (as opposed to the case of materialistic support of hexagram 27 "Feeding" between two masculine trigrams.) To stay on course, then, means that the more capable person must pay attention to the feedback from the weaker person in the time of Family Members.

Elaboration on I-Ching reading *(original text in Chinese)*
Translation: Family Members. Correct position for female is inside, for male is outside. Male and female are both correct is the great meaning of Heaven and Earth.

In Family Members there is a stern ruler in the authority of the parents. Father acts properly as father. Son acts properly as son. Elder brother acts properly as elder brother. Younger brother acts properly as younger brother. Husband acts properly as husband. Wife acts properly as wife. Then the Tao of the family is correct. Correct families lead to stability under Heaven.

Comment: "Correct position for female is inside, for male is outside. Male and female are both correct is the great meaning of Heaven and Earth" possibly refers to lines 2 and line 5. Line 2 belongs to the inner trigram and is Yin, fitting position 2. Line 5 belongs to the outer trigram and is Yang, fitting position 5.

The relationships among family members do follow a hierarchy, with parents playing the role of an authority. However, in Family Members, the main line of the hostess is Yin, and there is feedback from the guest. These tell us that the Yin element (understanding and spiritual support) is more important than the Yang element (order and hierarchical power) in a happy family.

Symbolisms of I-Ching reading *(original text in Chinese)*
Translation: The Wind gets out from Fire: Family Members. The superior man speaks with substance, and acts with a sense of permanence.

Comment: "Wind" and "Fire" are symbolisms for Max-Yin and Mid-Yin respectively. The superior man must rise above the meaning of the hexagram. He must speak with substance because substance automatically guarantees understanding, making the exercise of hierarchical power unnecessary. He must act with a sense of permanence, because permanent relationships are the ideal for all family members.

Mid-Yin

Min-Yin

38. Difference

Role	Trigram	Identity	Activity	Ability
GUEST	Mid-Yin	Feminine	Very aggressive	Most powerful
HOSTESS	Min-Yin	Feminine	Highly aggressive	Common

YIN YANG LOGIC *(NEW!)*

In this hexagram we have a common trigram hosting a powerful trigram. Although hostess Min-Yin has the benefit of being close to the guest (via her main line at position 3) and is reacting aggressively, her situation is less than ideal because the identities of the two trigrams are not complementary (both are feminine instead of one masculine one feminine.)

With her main line at position 3, Min-Yin is in direct contact with her guest and fully aware that she is dealing with a powerful force. We have the image of hostess Min-Yin as an active girl dealing with another active girl, and knowing that her guest is more capable or more beautiful than she is. It is unlikely that there is no feeling of envy or jealousy; and we should not expect a completely harmonious relationship. Thus, the fitting hexagram name is "Difference."

Since Min-Yin (with her main line in contact with the guest) has a clear picture of the situation, "Difference" is not necessarily a bad hexagram. In fact, the aggressive Min-Yin may learn from her inferior position to make improvements. However, the situation cannot be labeled as "ideal."

I-CHING TEXTS AND COMMENTS

(For comparison)

I-Ching reading *(original text in Chinese)*

Translation: Difference. Favorable for small matters.

Comment: The time of Difference is favorable for the planning of small matters because the inferior position of the hostess forces her to be realistic. It is not favorable for great matters because the hostess may be jealous of the guest, and jealousy will cloud the clear judgment required for great plans.

Elaboration on I-Ching reading *(original text in Chinese)*

Translation: Difference. Fire moves above, Marsh moves below. Two females in the same place, but their minds move in different paths.

The Playful brightens Brightness. The soft advances upward, gains center and is in resonance with the firm. Therefore favorable for small matters.

Heaven and Earth are different, yet their things are the same. Male and female are different, yet their minds can be connected. All things are different, yet they can be classified. Great is the time of Difference!

Comment: "Fire" and "Marsh" are symbolisms for Mid-Yin and Min-Yin respectively. "Two females in the same place, but their minds move in different paths" refers to the clear difference between hostess Min-Yin and her guest Mid-Yin. The difference is painful for Min-Yin, because the only difference between her and the guest is that the guest is more powerful (which most likely means more beautiful and capable, in the case of two young girls.)

"The soft advances upward, gains center and is in resonance with the firm" refers to line 5, which is a Yin line (soft) occupying the center position in the guest trigram. "The firm" here refers to line 2, but we will not go into the reason for this statement, as it is –in the opinion of the writer- irrelevant to the meaning of the hexagram. The reason for the reading "favorable for small matter" is better explained by the hostess' main line at position 3, which is in direct contact with the guest. The proximity helps the hostess to fully understand her inferior position, so that she can change her plans accordingly. This allows her to achieve successes in small matters.

Being different is not necessarily the same as being incompatible, as explained in the elaboration: "Heaven and Earth are different, yet their things are the same. Male and female are different, yet their minds can be connected."

Symbolisms of I-Ching reading *(original text in Chinese)*

Translation: Fire above Marsh below: Difference! The superior man is the same and yet different (from ordinary men).

Comment: "Fire" and "Marsh" are symbolisms for Mid-Yin and Min-Yin respectively. The observation regarding the superior man is interesting. On the surface he is not any different from ordinary men, but –since he understands the Middle Way- he is fundamentally different from all of them.

Mid-Yang

Min-Yang

39. Obstruction

Role	Trigram	Identity	Activity	Ability
GUEST	Mid-Yang	Masculine	Very tentative	Most powerful
HOST	Min-Yang	Masculine	Highly tentative	Common

YIN YANG LOGIC *(NEW!)*

In this hexagram we have a common trigram hosting a powerful trigram. Although Min-Yang has the benefit of being in close proximity with the guest (via his main line at position 3), he is limited by his tentativeness. The fact that both trigrams are masculine (not of complementary identities) does not help either.

Note that this hexagram is the exact Yin Yang opposite of the preceding hexagram "Difference." The main difference is that now both trigrams are tentative. Just like Min-Yin in "Difference," the host Min-Yang is fully aware that he is inferior to the powerful guest (Mid-Yang). However, since he is tentative, he lacks the initiative to make proper corrections by himself. The guest Mid-Yang, then, is perceived as an obstruction to whatever plan Min-Yang has in mind. Thus, the fitting hexagram name is "Obstruction."

Since Min-Yang is fully aware of the difficult situation that he is in, most likely he will ask for help to overcome the obstruction and learn one thing or two in the process. For this reason, "Obstruction" is more like a meaningful challenge than a bad situation for the host Min-Yang.

I-CHING TEXTS AND COMMENTS

(For comparison)

I-Ching reading *(original text in Chinese)*

Translation: Obstruction. The southwest direction is favorable. The northeast direction not favorable. Advisable to see the great man. It is good to stay firmly on course.

Comment: The southwest and northeast directions have specific meanings in connection with the Later Heaven order of the 8 trigrams, which we do not cover in this book (and will cover in another book dedicated to the Yin Yang theory.) It suffices to state that the southwest direction is associated with All-Yin and the northeast direction with Min-Yang. The only difference between All-Yin and Min-Yang is the top line, which is Yin in All-Yin and Yang in Min-Yang.

The southwest direction is favorable because it corresponds to the case where All-Yin is the guest, giving hexagram 15 "Humility," with good ending for the host Min-Yang. The northeast direction in not favorable because the guest there is also Min-Yang, which does not help in the time of Obstruction.

Actually Min-Yang's situation is not all that bad; he just does not feel comfortable hosting a powerful masculine trigram. While Mid-Yang appears threatening, he is actually in a position of a helper (see hexagram 4 "Ignorance," where Mid-Yang hosts Min-Yang.) The main line of Mid-Yang is Yang and occupies the best position at line 5. This makes the line "centered and correct." Paradoxically, then, Mid-Yang is the great man that Min-Yang should consult, not the threat that he should be afraid of.

Min-Yang's quandary is self inflicting, and can be relieved if he is clear on what he is doing, the advice is therefore "to stay firmly on course."

Elaboration on I-Ching reading *(original text in Chinese)*
Translation: Obstruction means difficulty. Danger in front. Seeing Danger and being able to stop. Isn't this wise?

Obstruction. The southwest direction is favorable, because going (in this direction) will gain the center. The northeast direction is unfavorable. Its Tao has ended.

It is advisable to see the great man. This action is fruitful. The correct position leads to good result if staying firmly on course. To bring the territories to their correct state. Great is the time of Obstruction!

Comment: "Danger" is a symbolism for the guest Mid-Yang. The situation of the hexagram is like seeing Danger, therefore Stopping (note: Stopping is a symbolism for Min-Yang).

The southwest is associated with All-Yin, which has a center of symmetry, therefore "The southwest direction is favorable, because going (in this direction) will gain the center." The northeast direction is not favorable because Min-Yang would stay in his original self, whose meaning is Stopping, Ending; therefore the elaboration is "The northeast direction is unfavorable. Its Tao has ended."

"The correct position leads to good results if staying firmly on course" refers to the correct position of line 3, which is Yang and is in good contact with the guest.

Obstructions are natural at borders between countries. They are necessary to keep different territories under control; this is the meaning of "To bring the territories to their correct state."

Symbolisms of I-Ching reading *(original text in Chinese)*
Translation: Above the Mountain there is Water. Obstruction. The superior man turns around and cultivates his virtue.

Comment: "Mountain" and "Water" are symbolisms for Min-Yang and Mid-Yang respectively. The superior man understands that obstructions are a natural part of life. He would turn around, examine himself and seek improvement.

Max-Yang
Mid-Yang

40. Relief

Role	Trigram	Identity	Activity	Ability
GUEST	Max-Yang	Masculine	Most aggressive	Most common
HOST	Mid-Yang	Masculine	Very tentative	Powerful

YIN YANG LOGIC *(NEW!)*

In this hexagram we have a powerful trigram hosting a common trigram. Although Mid-Yang is the weakest of all power trigrams, in this particular case he benefits from the masculine identity that he shares with Max-Yang and the proximity of the guest.

This hexagram is the exact Yin Yang opposite of hexagram 37 "Family Members." However, in "Family Members" the hostess is aggressive while the guest is tentative; here the powerful host is tentative while his less capable guest is the most aggressive trigram.

The host is a powerful trigram whose capability is hindered by his own tentative nature. With his main line at position 4, the most aggressive guest has a strong influence on the tentative host. This aggressive influence is exactly what the host needs to overcome his own tentative nature so that his capability could be realized. On the other hand, the power of the host will help the most aggressive (but also most common) guest so that his activities will not be for naught. We have the image of a host with great potential finally liberated from his own drawbacks and becoming effective. Thus, the fitting hexagram name is "Relief."

I-CHING TEXTS AND COMMENTS
(For comparison)

I-Ching reading *(original text in Chinese)*

Translation: Relief. The southwest direction is favorable. (If) there is no place to go, (then it is) good to return to position. (If) there is path to go, (then it is) good to act swiftly.

Comment: We again see "the southwest direction is favorable." This is the direction of All-Yin. If All-Yin is the guest, we would have hexagram 7 "The Army," a powerful force that can, not only relieve the host Mid-Yang from his quandary, but also give him the tremendous power to conquer his adversaries.

The time of Relief, on the other hand, is not completely ideal. The influence of the extremely aggressive guest Max-Yang does help, but Max-Yang (most common) is much weaker than All-Yin (most powerful); therefore the combined outcome is still unclear. If action does not lead to result, Mid-Yang should understand that the power of Relief is not sufficient, and return to where he is. If it is possible to act, he must act quickly, because the influence of Max-Yang, the most common trigram, is short-lived and will lose its impact if he waits too long.

Elaboration on I-Ching reading *(original text in Chinese)*

<u>Translation</u>: Relief. Danger and Movement. Movement relieves Danger. Relief.

Relief is favorable in the southwest direction. Going in this direction gains (support of) the mass. Good to return to position. Because possessing center. If there is path to go, good to act swiftly. Action is fruitful.

When Heaven and Earth are relieved, Thunder and Rain manifest themselves. The manifestation of Thunder and Rain allow the bursting of the buds of the plants and trees that produce the various fruits.

Great is the time of Relief!

<u>Comment</u>: "Danger" and "Movement" are symbolisms for Mid-Yang and Max-Yang respectively. This elaboration explains clearly that the host is relieved from his difficult situation by the action of the guest.

The elaboration also explains the reasoning behind the southwest direction, which is the direction of the mass All-Yin "Going in this direction gains (support of) the mass."

Mid-Yang should return to position (in case the impact of relief is not strong enough) because at least at the original position he possesses center (at line 2). The reason for swift action was given in the I-Ching reading.

The last paragraph elaborates on the great benefits of Relief. The time of Relief is compared to the synchronized action of Thunder and Rain (symbolisms for Max-Yang and Mid-Yang) which connects Heaven and Earth, and gives life to plants and trees.

Symbolisms of I-Ching reading *(original text in Chinese)*

<u>Translation</u>: Thunder and Rain manifest themselves. Relief. The superior man forgives errors and deals gently with criminals.

<u>Comment</u>: "Thunder" and "Rain" are symbolisms for Max-Yang and Mid-Yang respectively. The time of Relief corresponds to when the superior man has just escaped from danger. He must rise beyond the usual of Yin and Yang by forgiving those who put him in trouble and dealing gently with the criminals that have wronged him.

Min-Yang
Min-Yin

41. Decrease

Role	Trigram	Identity	Activity	Ability
GUEST	Min-Yang	Masculine	Highly tentative	Common
HOSTESS	Min-Yin	Feminine	Highly aggressive	Common

YIN YANG LOGIC *(NEW!)*

In this hexagram we have a common trigram hosting another common trigram. Recall from chapter 10 that in this case the hexagram quality depends strictly on the relative ranking of the host and the guest: 1. Max-Yang, 2. Min-Yang, 3. Min-Yin, 4. Max-Yin. Since hostess Min-Yin has lower ranking than the guest, the hexagram has unfavorable meaning. However, since aggressiveness counts as a positive factor, and the hostess is aggressive while her guest is tentative, this is more like a situation of voluntary loss.

Since the two trigrams involved are exact Yin Yang opposites of each other, they have perfect feminine-masculine affinity. In addition, they (the two trigrams in this hexagram) are exactly the same as those in hexagram 31 "E-motions" where the highly tentative Min-Yang suddenly felt an internal vibration in his body at Min-Yin's presence. With her main line (at position 3) in contact with Min-Yang, the feminine-masculine affinity must also cause a reciprocal effect within Min-Yin.

What is this effect? Since Min-Yin is highly aggressive, we expect that she would lose some of her aggressiveness, like an active teenage girl who suddenly stops and blushes when she encounters an awkward but likable teenage boy (Min-Yang). We may say that this interaction causes her to lose her aggressiveness, and name the hexagram as "Loss." However, since the word "Loss" has bad connotation, we will choose a more neutral word to name the hexagram. The choice is "Decrease."

I-CHING TEXTS AND COMMENTS

(For comparison)

I-Ching reading *(original text in Chinese)*

Translation: Decrease. Having faith. Great fortune. No error. Could stay firmly on course. Advantageous to move forward. How can one utilize this situation properly? Use two baskets of grains for worship.

Comment: "Having faith" here means that the hostess believes in the new relationship with the guest Min-Yang. It is correct and quite easy for her to do so because Min-Yang is her match in love, as we have seen in hexagram 31 "E-motions" where Min-Yang hosts Min-Yin. Therefore "Great fortune. No error. Could stay firmly on course."

Once there is the willingness to conform to the time of Decrease, the relationship between the hostess and the guest will be favorable, therefore "advantageous to move forward." The statement "Use two baskets of grains for worshipping" exemplifies the willingness to decrease (losing two baskets of grains).

Elaboration on I-Ching reading *(original text in Chinese)*

Translation: Decrease. Decrease below Increase above. Its Tao moves upward.

Decrease yet has faith, great fortune. No error. Could stay firmly on course. Advantageous to move forward. How can one utilize this situation properly? Use two baskets of grains for worship. The two baskets are in resonance with the time. The decrease of the firm and the increase of the soft also have their own time. Decrease and Increase, Fullness and Emptiness; all happen according to time.

Comment: "Decrease below Increase above" refers to the reciprocal transformation that happens to Min-Yin and Min-Yang. While Min-Yin decreases her aggressiveness, Min-Yang increases his activity.

"The two baskets are in resonance with the time" means that the act of losing two baskets voluntarily fits the time of Decrease. "The decrease of the firm and the increase of the soft" possibly refers to the activities of the two trigrams. Min-Yin, who is aggressive (firm), is encountering Decrease, while Min-Yang, who is tentative (soft), is enjoying Increase.

Symbolisms of I-Ching reading *(original text in Chinese)*

Translation: At the foot of the Mountain there is the Marsh. Decrease. The superior man restrains his anger and suppresses his desires.

Comment: "Mountain" and "Marsh" are symbolisms for Min-Yang and Min-Yin respectively. The superior man must rise above the meaning of the hexagram. He therefore must perform the most difficult Decreases of all: Restraining his anger and suppressing his desires.

Max-Yin

Max-Yang

42. Increase

Role	Trigram	Identity	Activity	Ability
GUEST	Max-Yin	Feminine	Most tentative	Most common
HOST	Max-Yang	Masculine	Most aggressive	Most common

YIN YANG LOGIC *(NEW!)*

In this hexagram we have a common trigram hosting another common trigram. Recall from chapter 10 that in this case the hexagram quality depends strictly on the relative ranking of the host and the guest: 1. Max-Yang, 2. Min-Yang, 3. Min-Yin, 4. Max-Yin. Since hostess Max-Yang has much higher ranking than the guest, the hexagram has very favorable meaning.

Since the two trigrams involved are exact Yin Yang opposites of each other, they have perfect feminine-masculine affinity. In addition, they (the two trigrams in this hexagram) are exactly the same as those in hexagram 32 "Permanence" where the most tentative Max-Yin, by reversing her usual tendency, was able to forge a long term relationship with Max-Yang.

The present hexagram describes this relationship from the perspective of Max-Yang, whose major weakness –as the most common trigram- is his inability to convert (very strong) aggressiveness to results. Despite the fact that both trigrams are common, they are both in favorable positions as the aggressive masculine Max-Yang plays the role of the host and the tentative feminine Max-Yin the guest. These favorable positions work out well for the host Max-Yang, who is like a man too aggressive for his own good, finally finds a good wife (Max-Yin) and settles down. Not unexpectedly, the stability in family life will help Max-Yang focus his great aggressiveness to achieve great successes. Thus, the fitting hexagram name is "Increase."

I-CHING TEXTS AND COMMENTS
(For comparison)

I-Ching reading *(original text in Chinese)*

Translation: Increase. Advantageous to move forward. Advantageous to cross the great stream.

Comment: In the time of Increase, the host enjoys the best of fortune. Therefore "Advantageous to move forward. Advantageous to cross the great stream."

Elaboration on I-Ching reading *(original text in Chinese)*

Translation: Increase. Decrease above Increase below. The playfulness of the people knows no boundary. From above moves down below. Its Tao is of great brilliance.

Advantageous to move forward. "Center and Correct" has glory. Advantageous to cross the great stream. Walks on the great Tao.

Increase is Aggressive and Yielding. The daily advance is without limit. Heaven distributes, Earth produces. This increase is without spatial restriction. Generally, the Tao of Increase operates according to time.

Comment: "Decrease above Increase below" refers to the sacrifice by the guest Max-Yin, and the gain by her partner, the host Max-Yang.

"Center and Correct" refers to lines 2 and 5, as both are centered and fit the Yin Yang property of their positions.

"Aggressive and Yielding" refers to the combination of Max-Yang (aggressive) and Max-Yin (yielding).

The last paragraph elaborates on the greatness of the time of Increase in the relationship between Heaven and Earth.

Symbolisms of I-Ching reading *(original text in Chinese)*

Translation: Wind and Thunder. Increase. The superior man moves toward the good, and corrects the errors.

Comment: "Wind" and "Thunder" are symbolisms for Max-Yin and Max-Yang, respectively. The superior man must rise above the auspicious meaning of this hexagram. He therefore takes advantage of his good luck to move toward the good and correct his errors.

207

Min-Yin

All-Yang

43. Correction

Role	Trigram	Identity	Activity	Ability
GUEST	Min-Yin	Feminine	Highly aggressive	Common
HOST	All-Yang	Masculine	Aggressive	Most powerful

YIN YANG LOGIC *(NEW!)*

In this hexagram we have a power trigram hosting a common trigram. Since the host meets two major criteria (masculine and aggressive) for such a case, the meaning of the hexagram is favorable. However, since the identities of the two trigrams are not matching, the result is less than expected.

The feminine guest Min-Yin is highly aggressive and (with the main line at position 6) not connected to the aggressive and most powerful masculine host All-Yang. Although All-Yang is aggressive, he will judge the guest Min-Yin as being too aggressive (due to the difference in the levels of aggressiveness of the two trigrams) and out of control (main line at position 6, too far from the host.)

Being the most powerful aggressive trigram, All-Yang has the ability to correct the situation. But since the two trigrams are of complementary identities, he finds it difficult to punish Min-Yin severely. His action is more like that of a stern but loving father reproaching his wayward daughter to make her a more worthy human being. The fitting hexagram name is therefore "Correction" or "Corrective Action."

NOTE:

"Correction" is the exact Yin Yang opposite of hexagram 23 "Destruction." The contrast is very interesting. While the ineptitude of a masculine trigram leads to the destructive action by a feminine trigram in "Destruction," the ability of the masculine trigram is the timely solution to the errors made by a feminine trigram in "Correction."

I-CHING TEXTS AND COMMENTS
(For comparison)

I-Ching reading *(original text in Chinese)*

Translation: Correction. Exhibits (the matter) in the royal court. The allegation has gravity. Makes announcement from the city. Not advantageous to employ arms immediately. Advantageous to move forward.

Comment: "*Exhibits (the matter) in the royal court*" *refers to the highest status of All-Yang, the party that initiates the correction process.* "*The allegation has gravity*" *refers to the disconnect between the accused Min-Yin and the correction officer All-Yang. This disconnection signifies the lack of understanding on the part of Min-Yin of the seriousness of the matter.*

"*Not advantageous to employ arms immediately*" *because the host and the guest have masculine/feminine affinity, therefore there is a level of compassion on the part of the host.* "*Advantageous to move forward*" *because the guest is obviously in the wrong, and is much weaker than the host.*

Elaboration on I-Ching reading *(original text in Chinese)*

Translation: Correction means Prosecution. The firm prosecutes the soft. Strong and Playful. Prosecuting yet maintaining tranquility.

Exhibits (the matter) in the royal court. The soft is riding on 5 of the firm. The allegation has gravity. The danger (to the criminal) implied by it has brilliance. Announcement made from the city. Not advantageous to employ arms immediately. This measure will soon lead to dead end. Advantageous to move forward. The development of the firm (lines) will lead to the end (of the culprit).

Comment: "*The firm prosecutes the soft*" *refers to the action of All-Yang against Min-Yin.* "*Strong and Playful*" *refers to All-Yang and Min-Yin respectively.* "*Prosecuting yet maintaining tranquility*" *because the host and the guest have masculine/feminine affinity.*

The explanation for "*exhibits (the matter) in the royal court*" *is given as* "*The soft riding on 5 of the firm*" *(i.e., the only Yin line on top of 5 Yang line). This is more like a memory trick than a valid explanation. In the writer's opinion, it makes more sense to associate the royal court with the supreme power of All-Yang.*

The explanation for "*not advantageous to employ arms immediately*" *is given as* "*This measure will soon lead to dead end.*" *This is ambiguous. We may want to add the reason for the dead end, which is the natural masculine/feminine affinity between the prosecutor and the culprit.*

"*Advantageous to move forward. The development of the firm (lines) will lead to the end of the culprit*" *is in agreement with our explanation in the I-Ching reading.*

Symbolisms of I-Ching reading *(original text in Chinese)*

Translation: The Marsh above Heaven. Correction. The superior man distributes wealth to the people below and dislikes the stagnation of virtue.

Comment: "*Marsh*" *and* "*Heaven*" *are symbolisms for Min-Yang and All-Yang respectively. The superior man must rise above and beyond the confrontational meaning of the hexagram. In order to achieve this goal, he must implement preventive measures so that prosecution is not necessary. Therefore* "*The superior man distributes wealth to the people below and dislikes the stagnation of virtue.*"

All-Yang
Max-Yin

44. Flirting

Role	Trigram	Identity	Activity	Ability
GUEST	All-Yang	Masculine	Aggressive	Most powerful
HOSTESS	Max-Yin	Feminine	Most tentative	Most common

YIN YANG LOGIC *(NEW!)*

In this hexagram the completely helpless Max-Yin (most tentative and most common feminine) again has to play the role of a hostess. This time her guest is the most powerful aggressive masculine trigram All-Yang, whose influence is felt strongly via line 4. The contrast is so great, it makes one wonder if Max-Yin could "survive" this encounter at all.

The easy answer is that Max-Yin won't survive this ordeal. But if this were the case, there would be no changes, and hence no hexagram. Thus, one more time, thanks to the law of Yin Yang reversal, Max-Yin will reverse herself to fit the circumstances. Since All-Yang is aggressive, Max-Yin will reciprocate with aggressiveness. The problem is, All-Yang's aggressiveness is the most well-controlled of all. Max-Yin's simulated aggressiveness, whatever level it turns out to be, will be considered as excessive and therefore inappropriate. Max-Yin is like a shy girl who wants to fit in a party filled with important men; therefore she acts aggressively in an unnatural way. Her behavior will be judged as inappropriate. Thus, the fitting hexagram name is "Flirting."

I-CHING TEXTS AND COMMENTS
(For comparison)

I-Ching reading *(original text in Chinese)*

Translation: Flirting. The female is too strong. Should not marry such a female.

Comment: Max-Yin's unexpected aggressiveness (as implied in the time of Flirting) is definitely shocking in everyone's standard. The advice: "The female is too strong. Should not marry such a female" is only natural.

Elaboration on I-Ching reading *(original text in Chinese)*

Translation: Flirting means meeting. The soft meets the firm. Should not marry such a female. Cannot be together for long.

Heaven and Earth meet each other. All things manifest themselves from this influence. The firm meets "central and correct." All under Heaven can be realized. Great is the meaning of the time of Flirting!

Comment: "The soft meet the firm" means Max-Yin (the soft) initiates the contact with All-Yang (the firm). "Cannot be together for long" because Max-Yin's action is just an extreme reaction to fit the situation, not her real personality. If All-Yang falls for her because of her overly aggressive behavior, he will soon be disappointed.

If we want to stress the analogy, Flirting is the I-Ching presentation of casual sex, which can only take place with a strong come-on gesture from the feminine party. To compare this with the meeting between Heaven and Earth (which are sacred by definition) is completely missing the point.

The writer therefore questions the originality of the second paragraph as it is completely irrelevant. It simply could not have been written by Confucius, who seemed to have exhibited an incredibly profound understanding of the meaning of the 64 hexagrams in "symbolisms of I-Ching reading."

Symbolisms of I-Ching reading *(original text in Chinese)*

Translation: Below Heaven there is Wind. Flirting. The leader of the territory distributes his orders in all four directions.

Comment: "Heaven" and "Wind" are symbolisms for All-Yang and Max-Yin respectively. The time of Flirting is the time where improper interactions may develop and become harmful for the state. Therefore "The leader of the territory distributes his orders in all four directions" as a cautionary measure.

Min-Yin

All-Yin

45. Gathering

Role	Trigram	Identity	Activity	Ability
GUEST	Min-Yin	Feminine	Highly aggressive	Common
HOSTESS	All-Yin	Feminine	Tentative	Most powerful

YIN YANG LOGIC *(NEW!)*

In this hexagram we have a power trigram hosting a common trigram. Although All-Yin is tentative, she can rely on her immense power and the matching identity (feminine just like the guest) to make this a favorable situation.

This hexagram brings out an interesting contrast between a host and a hostess of equal power. Recall that in hexagram 43 "Correction," the guest was Min-Yin and the host was All-Yang. Here we have the same guest who is possibly doing something wrong (highly aggressive with main line at position 6, disconnected from the hostess). The difference is that now All-Yin is the hostess.

Being a tentative trigram, All-Yin will not seek to correct Min-Yin. The immense power of All-Yin is like that of a big crowd. The action of All-Yin in this hexagram can be compared to the gathering of a crowd. When the crowd grows big enough, its sheer number will become a very effective persuasive force that can prevent Min-Yin from continuing with her wayward behavior. The fitting name for the hexagram is therefore "Gathering."

NOTES:

1. "Correction" (hexagram 43) and "Gathering" are two different approaches to solve the same problem. "Correction" is masculine, "Gathering" is feminine. In this particular case, it seems that the feminine approach is superior.

2. "Gathering" is the exact Yin Yang opposite of hexagram 26 "Great Cultivation." Since "Gathering" involves two feminine trigrams and "Great Cultivation" involves two masculine trigrams, one may have the wrong impression that feminine trigrams do not have the potential for greatness. It is therefore necessary to re-emphasize that the Yin Yang theory deals only with the physical world, which is imperfect. It is our imperfect perception that gives "Great Cultivation" more value than "Gathering." From a spiritual standpoint, both hexagrams are equally imperfect.

I-CHING TEXTS AND COMMENTS
(For comparison)

I-Ching reading *(original text in Chinese)*

Translation: Progress. The king goes to his ancestral temple. Advantageous to see the great man. Progress. Advisable to stay firmly on course. Using big animals will be good. Advantageous to move forward.

Comment: Progress is achieved in the time of Gathering because All-Yin is the most powerful feminine trigram, and the wrong-doer Min-Yin is also a feminine trigram.

The ancestral temple was believed to be the place where the mandate from Heaven was communicated to the king. With this mandate the king could rally the people behind him. Therefore, in the time of Gathering, we see "The king goes to his ancestral temple" to ask Heaven for a mandate. "Advantageous to see the great man" because the Mass needs good leadership, which can be provided by the great man. "Advisable to stay on course" because gathering the Mass is not a short term task. "Using big animals will be good" refers to the worship at the ancestral temple, which involves the sacrifice of animals. "Advantageous to move forward" because the Mass acts with noble cause and is more powerful than the guest Min-Yin.

Elaboration on I-Ching reading *(original text in Chinese)*

Translation: Gathering means the Mass (of people). Yielding and Playful. The firm (line) is centered and in resonance, therefore the Mass (can be gathered).

The king goes to his ancestral temple. Great filiality. Advantageous to see the great man. Progress. The Mass is correct. Using big animals is good. Advantageous to move forward. (Acting) in accordance with the will of Heaven.

By observing the Mass, one can see the emotion of Heaven and Earth and of all things.

Comment: "Yielding" and "Playful" are symbolisms for All-Yin and Min-Yin respectively. "The firm (line) is centered and in resonance" refers to line 5; but the logic "therefore the Mass (can be gathered)" is nebulous, as line 5 is not the main line of the guest trigram.

"Great filiality" for the king also means he will get the mandate from Heaven, and can gather the people. "The Mass is correct" and "acting in accordance with the will of Heaven" confirm the correctness of the hostess (in her effort to persuade the guest).

Symbolisms of I-Ching reading *(original text in Chinese)*

Translation: The Marsh above Earth. Gathering. The superior man repairs his weapons of war to prepare for unforeseen contingencies.

Comment: "Marsh" and "Earth" are symbolisms for Min-Yin and All-Yin respectively. The superior man may not be in a power position to gather the mass; therefore he can only resort to other preventive forces, such as the weapons of war.

213

All-Yin

Max-Yin

46. Ascending

Role	Trigram	Identity	Activity	Ability
GUEST	All-Yin	Feminine	Tentative	Most powerful
HOSTESS	Max-Yin	Feminine	Most tentative	Most common

YIN YANG LOGIC *(NEW!)*

The weakest feminine Max-Yin again has to play the role of a hostess, this time her guest is All-Yin, the most powerful of all feminine trigrams. The contrast is so great, it makes one wonder if Max-Yin could "survive" this encounter at all.

We now know that Max-Yin will survive, thanks to the law of Yin Yang reversal, by changing herself in whatever way necessary to fit the circumstances. Since the guest (via line 4) has strong influence on Max-Yin, and the only difference between the two is the distance from the center of power, Max-Yin will be inspired by the guest and will try to increase her own power. This is feasible, because she starts at the lowest position in the power scale, and cannot go anywhere but up. Thus, the fitting hexagram name is "Ascending."

Since Max-Yin only reacts to the guest, and the guest in this case is tentative, ascending is a slow process, but very favorable.

I-CHING TEXTS AND COMMENTS
(For comparison)

I-Ching reading *(original text in Chinese)*

Translation: Ascending. Long term progress. Can be used to see the great man. Has no fear. Advancing southward is favorable.

Comment: Ascending is definitely a time of progress for the most common hostess Max-Yin. However, since her character is weak, at certain point in her progress, Max-Yin will need to consult experts to make the most of her situation. Therefore the advice is "Can be used to see the great man. Has no fear."

In the Later Heaven trigram order, south is the direction associated with Mid-Yin. This direction is particularly favorable because with Mid-Yin as the guest the situation is hexagram 50 "The Cauldron." We will see later that "The Cauldron" is where Max-Yin achieves her glory.

Elaboration on I-Ching reading *(original text in Chinese)*

Translation: The soft in the proper time to ascend.

Flexible and Yielding. The firm is centered and in resonance. Therefore great progress.

Can be used to see the great man. Has no fear. There is (cause for) celebration. Advancing southward is favorable. The will can be realized.

Comment: "The soft in the proper time to ascend" means that this hexagram is the proper time of Max-Yin to ascend from her lowly position. "Flexible and Yielding" refers to Max-Yin and All-Yin respectively. "There is cause for celebration" because this is a very favorable situation for Max-Yin. "The will can be realized" in the southward direction because the resulting hexagram is "The Cauldron" (50), which is the most favorable for Max-Yin.

Symbolisms of I-Ching reading *(original text in Chinese)*

Translation: Wind is born in the middle of Earth. Ascending. The superior man, in accordance with virtue, gathers many of the small to form the tall and great.

Comment: "Wind" and "Earth" are symbolisms for Max-Yin and All-Yin respectively. Since the progress is long-term, the superior man will utilize the opportunities to make even the small become great, by gathering many of the small.

Min-Yin
Mid-Yang

47. Exhaustion

Role	Trigram	Identity	Activity	Ability
GUEST	Min-Yin	Feminine	Highly aggressive	Common
HOST	Mid-Yang	Masculine	Very tentative	Powerful

YIN YANG LOGIC *(NEW!)*

In this hexagram we have a power trigram hosting a common trigram. Mid-Yang is the weakest of the power group. The fact that his identity is opposite that of his guest Min-Yin adds to the misery. By normal I-Ching logic, this is a very unfavorable situation. But exactly for this reason, Mid-Yang can be saved by the law of Yin Yang reversal.

We have seen how the two most powerful trigrams All-Yang and All-Yin dealt with the guest Min-Yin in "Correction" (hexagram 43) and "Gathering" (hexagram 45). They both achieved their purposes to certain extent, each with a different approach.

Being a power trigram, the masculine host Mid-Yang is also supposed to steer the feminine guest Min-Yin away from her wayward path. The problem is, Mid-Yang's power is below those of All-Yang and All-Yin. Keep in mind also that I-Ching asymmetry, which favors aggressiveness, makes Mid-Yang (slightly) less powerful than Mid-Yin at the host position. In summary, as far as the ability to handle chaos is concerned, Mid-Yang is the least effective of the 4 power trigrams. For this reason Mid-Yang will get exhausted in his effort to correct Min-Yin. Thus, the fitting hexagram name is "Exhaustion."

The success of All-Yin (in handling Min-Yin) offers hope, because it does not rule out the possibility of success for a tentative trigram such as Mid-Yang. It also means that the formula for success is to decrease the level of tentativeness.

The time of Exhaustion, then, is not only a great challenge but also a great opportunity for Mid-Yang. Exhaustion may just be the bitter medicine that forces him to decrease his tentativeness. If this happens, he will be able to turn the situation around and achieve great result. If this does not happen, failure is inevitable.

In conclusion, the time of Exhaustion presents a challenge for the greatest. If the host stays the way he is, he will get exhausted (and fails). If he can overcome his own barrier (i.e., his tentativeness) he has a good chance to be successful.

I-CHING TEXTS AND COMMENTS
(For comparison)

I-Ching reading *(original text in Chinese)*

<u>Translation</u>: Exhaustion. Advisable to stay firmly on course. Favorable for the great man. No error. If talking there will be no trust.

<u>Comment</u>: Since there is hope for success, it is "advisable to stay firmly on course." It takes tremendous effort from Mid-Yang to achieve success, therefore "Favorable for the great man. No error." Since excuses are a sign of weakness, and success requires tremendous mental strength in this case, the warning is "If talking there will be no trust."

Elaboration on I-Ching reading *(original text in Chinese)*

<u>Translation</u>: Exhaustion. The firm is rendered ineffective.

Danger and Playfulness. Exhausted but does not lose one's stand. Progress. There is only the superior man.

If staying firmly on course, it is good for the great man; because the firm is centered.

If talking there will be no trust. The mouth has come to its end.

<u>Comment</u>: "The firm is rendered ineffective" refers to the host trigram Mid-Yang, which is ineffective in the time of Exhaustion. "Danger and Playfulness" are symbolisms for Mid-Yang and Min-Yin respectively. "Exhausted but does not lose one's stand. Progress. There is only the superior man" spells out the difficult formula for success in the time of Exhaustion, which can only be realized by the superior man.

"If staying firmly on course, it is good for the great man, because the firm is centered" confirms that Mid-Yang has a chance for success, but the effort required will be tremendous, and can only be realized by great men.

"If talking there will be no trust. The mouth has come to its end" confirms that the time of Exhaustion is not the time for smooth talk or excuses.

Symbolisms of I-Ching reading *(original text in Chinese)*

<u>Translation</u>: The Marsh without Water. Exhaustion. The superior man, in complete disregard of his own life, carries out his will.

<u>Comment</u>: "Marsh" and "Water" are symbolisms for Min-Yin and Mid-Yang respectively. Since the time of Exhaustion requires super effort, the superior man understands that he has to be willing to put even his very life on the line to achieve success.

217

Mid-Yang

Max-Yin

48. The Well

Role	Trigram	Identity	Activity	Ability
GUEST	Mid-Yang	Masculine	Very tentative	Powerful
HOSTESS	Max-Yin	Feminine	Most tentative	Most common

YIN YANG LOGIC *(NEW!)*

Thanks to the law of Yin Yang reversal, when the weakest trigram Max-Yin has to play the role of a hostess, she will modify her own character in whatever way necessary to make the most of the situation. In this case she is hosting the powerful masculine guest Mid-Yang. Max-Yin will play the role of a good hostess so that Mid-Yang's strength can be manifested without the harmful effects.

Mid-Yang's best-fit symbolism is water, which is tentative but extremely powerful. The best role for Max-Yin, then, is a well because this is a place where water manifests only its usefulness (and none of its destructive power). Thus, the fitting hexagram name is "The Well."

The main player at the time of The Well is the guest Mid-Yang, because hostess Max-Yin simply sets the stage for him. Because the guest Mid-Yang is tentative, this hexagram is neither good nor bad. The result depends on how the well is used. For those who are well prepared, the benefit is endless. For those who are not, The Well will be an opportunity lost (and bad consequence, if the lost opportunity was assumed as certainty.)

NOTE:

"The Well" is the exact Yin Yang opposite of hexagram 21 "Biting" where Max-Yang was hosting Mid-Yin. In Biting the extreme aggressiveness of Max-Yang had to be tamed by the painful means of torture conducted by the guest Mid-Yin. In contrast, in The Well, the overly yielding behavior of Max-Yin creates willingness on the part of the guest Mid-Yang. Definitely in these two cases, being feminine is more effective than being masculine.

I-CHING TEXTS AND COMMENTS
(For comparison)

I-Ching reading *(original text in Chinese)*

Translation: The Well. The town may change but not the Well. No loss no gain. People come and go to the well. Drawn near its end and not yet reaching the well, or the bucket is broken: Harmful consequences.

Comment: "The town may change but not the well" because the main line of the guest is at position 5, where it is centered and properly Yang, representing stability and strength.

"No loss no gain" because Mid-Yang is tentative. The outcome depends on how the Well is used.

"People come and go to the well" emphasizes the importance of Mid-Yang, manifesting himself here as water supporting life.

"Drawn near its end and not yet reaching the well, or the bucket is broken: Harmful consequence." is an example of how this hexagram may have bad meaning, mainly for those who are not well prepared and still try to reap the benefits that the well presents to them.

Elaboration on I-Ching reading *(original text in Chinese)*

Translation: The Flexible in Water and Water are moving up. The Well. The well nourishes without limit.

The town may change but not the well, because the firm (line) is centered. Drawn near its end and not yet reaching the well. Not yet fruitful. The bucket is broken. That is harmful.

Comment: "Flexible" and "Water" are symbolisms for Max-Yin and Mid-Yang respectively. "The Well nourishes without limit" elaborates on the immense power of the guest Mid-Yang.

"The town may change but not the Well, because the firm (line) is centered" refers to line 5. The rest of the text has already been covered in the I-Ching reading.

Symbolisms of I-Ching reading *(original text in Chinese)*

Translation: Above Wood is Water. The Well. The superior man comforts the people and encourages togetherness.

Comment: "Wood" and "Water" are symbolisms for Max-Yin and Mid-Yang. The superior man is wise. He understands that the Well has limitless power to comfort the people, and the best way to maximize the benefit of the Well is to have people enjoying its benefit together.

Min-Yin
Mid-Yin

49. Revolution

Role	Trigram	Identity	Activity	Ability
GUEST	Min-Yin	Feminine	Highly aggressive	Common
HOSTESS	Mid-Yin	Feminine	Very aggressive	Powerful

YIN YANG LOGIC *(NEW!)*

In this hexagram we have a power trigram hosting a common trigram. Being the most aggressive power trigram, Mid-Yin happens to be the best player in such a situation. The matching of identities between her and her guest makes her situation even more favorable.

So far we have seen how three powerful hosts deal with the guest Min-Yin, who strays from the correct path. In hexagram 43 "Correction" All-Yang utilizes his aggressiveness and supreme power to correct Min-Yin. In hexagram 45 "Gathering" All-Yin utilizes her understanding and supreme power to call Min-Yin out of harm's way. In hexagram 47 "Exhaustion" Mid-Yang is exhausted because his power is insufficient, and he lacks aggressiveness.

Thanks to the subjective view, Mid-Yin is slightly more powerful than Mid-Yang. In addition, her aggressiveness definitely works in her favor. Since there is no contact between Mid-Yin (main line at position 2) and Min-Yin (main line at position 6), Mid-Yin's action will be decisive. We have the image of Mid-Yin aggressively going after and forcing Min-Yin to change her behavior. Mid-Yin's actions amount to the utilization of force to overwhelm existing activities. Thus, the fitting hexagram name is "Revolution."

Revolution is a very difficult process. This is why most people only believe in a revolution after it has achieved measurable success!

NOTES:

Although hostess Mid-Yin is more powerful than Min-Yin, the difference in power is not great. In addition, the guest is more aggressive than the host. These are the reason why Revolution is usually a very painful process, with significant casualties. As we all know, this is true for most political revolutions.

"Revolution" is the exact Yin Yang opposite of hexagram 4 "Ignorance." Both hexagrams involve methods to improve an existing situation. In "Ignorance" the existing problem was wrong thinking (ignorance), which could be handled by proper training. In "Revolution" the existing problem is wrong action, which has to be corrected by actions.

I-CHING TEXTS AND COMMENTS
(For comparison)
I-Ching reading *(original text in Chinese)*

<u>Translation</u>: Revolution. Only after the day of completion will have faith. Great progress. Advisable to stay firmly on course. Repentance disappears.

<u>Comment</u>: "Only after the day of completion will have faith" because revolution is always thought to be impossible. "Great progress" because the hostess, who initiates the process of revolution, is a powerful trigram, while the guest, who is the victim of the process, is a common trigram.

"Advisable to stay on course" because the guest is also aggressive. If the hostess does not stay focused, the process of revolution may deviate from its intended course.

"Repentance disappears" because repentance is the mental consequence of wrong action, and the goal of revolution is to eliminate wrong action. The success of a revolution, therefore, automatically erases the existing repentance.

Elaboration on I-Ching reading *(original text in Chinese)*

<u>Translation</u>: Revolution. Water and Fire extinguishing each other. The two females are in the same place, but their minds are not in agreement; say "Revolution."

Only after the day of completion will have faith. Revolution will inspire trust. Repentance disappears.

The revolutions of Heaven and Earth form the four seasons. The revolutions by emperors Thang and Wu were in accordance with the Heaven and in resonance with the people. Great is the time of Revolution!

<u>Comment</u>: "Water" is a lesser known symbolism for Min-Yin, used here to contrast "Fire," which is a well known symbolism for Mid-Yin. "The two females are in the same place, but their minds are not in agreement" refers to the action of Mid-Yin, which revolts against Min-Yin.

Emperors Thang and Wu acquired power by revolting against the existing government with the support of the people. That is why the elaboration says: "The revolutions by emperors Thang and Wu were in accordance with the Heaven and in resonance with the people."

Symbolisms of I-Ching reading *(original text in Chinese)*

<u>Translation</u>: Inside the Marsh there is Fire. Revolution. The superior man calculates the calendar and achieves a clear understanding of the time.

<u>Comment</u>: "Marsh" and "Fire" are symbolisms for Min-Yin and Mid-Yin respectively. The advice "The superior man calculates the calendar and achieves a clear understanding of the time" is very profound because the time of Revolution is a very critical time and has to be known with the highest level of exactness.

Mid-Yin

Max-Yin

50. The Cauldron

Role	Trigram	Identity	Activity	Ability
GUEST	Mid-Yin	Feminine	Very aggressive	Powerful
HOSTESS	Max-Yin	Feminine	Most tentative	Most common

YIN YANG LOGIC *(NEW!)*

Thanks to the law of Yin Yang reversal, when the weakest trigram Max-Yin has to play the role of a hostess, she will modify her own character in whatever way necessary to make the most of the situation. In this case she is hosting the powerful feminine guest Mid-Yin. Max-Yin will play the role of a good hostess so that Mid-Yin's strength can be manifested without the harmful effects.

Mid-Yin's best fit symbolism is fire, which is very aggressive and could cause destruction. The best role for Max-Yin, then, is a cauldron because this is the favorite cookware that can safely transform the aggressiveness of fire to the energy required for food preparation without any risk of destruction.

The meaning of this hexagram is very favorable, because the powerful guest Mid-Yin is aggressive (in contrast with hexagram 48 "The Well," which was neutral because the guest Mid-Yang was tentative.)

NOTE:

"The Cauldron" is the exact Yin Yang opposite of hexagram 3 "Difficulties" where Max-Yang was hosting Mid-Yang. In "Difficulties" the overly aggressive behavior of the host Max-Yang did not bring him any immediate result. In contrast, the overly yielding behavior of hostess Max-Yin in "The Cauldron" creates immediate progress and success. This is another case where a feminine trigram is much more effective than a masculine trigram.

I-CHING TEXTS AND COMMENTS
(For comparison)
I-Ching reading *(original text in Chinese)*

Translation: The Cauldron. Great fortune and progress.

Comment: The meaning of this hexagram is good because the powerful guest Mid-Yin is aggressive; therefore the reading is "Great fortune and progress."

Elaboration on I-Ching reading *(original text in Chinese)*
Translation: The cauldron is a symbol. The Wood bends into Fire, the cooking of food. The sages cooked and offered (sacred food) to the King of Heaven. And (sacred) food nourished the benevolent sages.

Being flexible, therefore the ears are quick in hearing and the eyes are clear in seeing. The soft (line) advances upward, possessing center therefore in resonance with the strong (lines). Therefore great progress.

Comment: "The wood bends into fire, the cooking of food" stresses the role of Max-Yin in providing a stage for fire to become a constructive force (cooking food). The importance of this hexagram is elaborated in "The sages cooked and offered (sacred food) to the King of Heaven. And (sacred) food nourished the benevolent sages."

"The soft (line) advances upward, possessing center" refers to line 5, which is the main line of the guest trigram. This line occupies the center position. "Resonance with the strong (line)" happens because line 2, which corresponds to line 5, is Yang; thus lines 2 and 5 are in Yin Yang resonance. However, this resonance is not a valid reason for the great progress of this hexagram. For example, the same resonance exists in hexagram 38 "Difference," where Min-Yin was hosting Mid-Yin, but the result was not great progress. The more meaningful reason for "great progress" is that the powerful guest Mid-Yin is aggressive, as we have mentioned earlier.

Symbolisms of I-Ching reading *(original text in Chinese)*
Translation: There is Fire above Wood. The Cauldron. The superior man keeps his position correct, and secures the decision of Heaven.

Comment: "Fire" and "Wood" are symbolisms for Mid-Yin and Max-Yin respectively.

The decision of Heaven is better known as Destiny. The time of The Cauldron has great promise because the hostess is very flexible. When man is very flexible, the decision of Heaven manifests itself. Since the time of the Cauldron is a very favorable time, the superior man knows that he should not interfere with the situation. If he keeps this position, he will benefit fully from the favorable decision of Heaven in the time of the Cauldron.

 Max-Yang

Max-Yang

51. Thunder
(Double Max-Yang)

Role	Trigram	Identity	Activity	Ability
GUEST	Max-Yang	Masculine	Most aggressive	Most common
HOST	Max-Yang	Masculine	Most aggressive	Most common

YIN YANG LOGIC *(NEW!)*

This is an identity trigram. Recall that the meaning of a hexagram is the situation of the host, which is Max-Yang in this case. For the host position, the appropriate identity and activity are "masculine" and "aggressive." Since Max-Yang meets both standards the meaning of this hexagram is certainly positive.

The guest is a cloned copy of the host. Since Max-Yang is the most aggressive of all trigram, and one of the two most common trigrams (the other is Max-Yin,) the most aggressive masculine Max-Yang guest can be compared to thunder, because thunder creates shock but is generally not harmful at all. In fact, thunder serves one good purpose: It shocks the host (who is also Max-Yang) enough so that he must re-examine himself. This self examination will help host Max-Yang to realize his shortcomings (that he is the most common of all trigrams.) He will therefore happily exercises restraint and pays due respect to the higher forces (i.e., ancestors and the spirits of the land).

I-CHING TEXTS AND COMMENTS
(For comparison)

I-Ching reading *(original text in Chinese)*

Translation: Thunder. Progress. The appearance of Thunder creates apprehension, then cheerful laughters and conversations. Thunder causes fear within one hundred *li*, but one does not drop the cup used in the (spiritual) ceremony.

Comment: Thunder is a helpful shock that forces us to re-examine ourselves and confirms our shortcomings. Therefore "The appearance of Thunder creates apprehension, then cheerful laughters and conversations."

Once our shortcomings are confirmed we will learn to forgo our arrogance and pay due respect to the higher forces of nature. Therefore "Thunder causes fear within one hundred li, but one does not drop the cup used in the (spiritual) ceremony."

Li is a Chinese unit of measure for long distances. Psychologically it is the equivalent of a kilometer or a mile.

Elaboration on I-Ching reading *(original text in Chinese)*
Translation: Thunder. Progress. The appearance of Thunder creates apprehension. Fright leads to Good Karma. Cheerful laughters and conversations. There are clear rules afterwards.

Thunder causes fear within one hundred *li*, (meaning that) it startles the far and frightens the near. Does not drop the cup used in worshipping ceremony. One can preside over worshipping ceremony at the ancestral altar and the rules of the land.

Comment: This elaboration is very much self explanatory. The fear created by thunder forces people to re-examine themselves, therefore "Fright leads to good karma." Thanks to the shock of thunder, people are reminded of the big difference between them and the immense power of the universe. This leads to the idea of universal order, as well as local order. Therefore the elaboration says "there are clear rules afterwards."

"One can preside over worshipping ceremony at the ancestral altar and the rules of the land" because once we realize that thunder is a manifestation of the universe, its appearance will give us a sense of communion with beings in other worlds; leading to our ability to preside over worshipping ceremonies.

Symbolisms of I-Ching reading *(original text in Chinese)*
Translation: Thunder, being repeated, forms Double Max-Yang. The superior man fearfully examines and reduces (his imperfections).

Comment: "Thunder" is a well known symbolism for Max-Yang. It acts like a shock that remind people of their limited existence compared to the vastness and eternity of the universe. To the superior man, thunder is a meaningful reminder of his imperfection. Therefore he fearfully re-examines himself.

Min-Yang
Min-Yang

52. Inactivity
(Double Min-Yang)

Role	Trigram	Identity	Activity	Ability
GUEST	Min-Yang	Masculine	Highly tentative	Common
HOST	Min-Yang	Masculine	Highly tentative	Common

YIN YANG LOGIC *(NEW!)*

This is an identity trigram. Recall that the meaning of a hexagram is the situation of the host, which is Min-Yang in this case. For the host position, being aggressive is preferred. The tentative Min-Yang obviously does not meet this condition.

The saving grace for the host is that the guest, being a tentative and common cloned copy of himself, cannot take any action against him. He can therefore rely on the only property that fits the host position, namely that he is masculine, to neutralize his tentative and common nature and stabilize his position as a host. Since he is the most tentative of all masculine trigram, the strategy that fits him best is to do nothing and interact with no one. Thus, the fitting hexagram name is "Inactivity."

If "Inactivity" can be maintained there will be no error. It can be seen that "Inactivity" is the time when action may lead to calamity, and non-action is the best strategy.

I-CHING TEXTS AND COMMENTS
(For comparison)

I-Ching reading *(original text in Chinese)*

Translation: The back is not moving. Not conscious of the body. Walking inside the courtyard, not seeing anyone. No error.

Comment: The back is the part of the body that best represents non-activity because it is very difficult to move the back. "Not conscious of the body" because although the host's main line (at position 3) is in direct contact with the guest, in the time of Inactivity he will not spend any effort to keep track of the identical guest, who can be considered as a part of his body. The act of "walking inside the courtyard" describes Min-Yang's potential for activity due to his masculine nature and the constraint imposed on this potential, due to the requirement of the time of Inactivity. "Not seeing anyone" is the essence of Inactivity. By not committing himself, Min-Yang cannot make any mistake, therefore "no error."

Elaboration on I-Ching reading *(original text in Chinese)*

Translation: Min-Yang means stopping. Stopping when it is time to stop. Acting when it is time to act. When motion and non-motion are not wrongly timed, their Tao is brilliant.

Min-Yang means stopping at the stopping location. The high and the low are in unison, but not interacting, thus there is no consciousness of the body. Walking inside the courtyard, seeing no one. No mistake.

Comment: This elaboration is self explanatory. The statement "Stopping when it is time to stop. Acting when it is time to act. When motion and non-motion are not wrongly timed, their Tao is brilliant" emphasizes that the right choice in the time of Inactivity is non-action. "The high and the low are in unison, but not interacting, thus there is no consciousness of the body" confirms the inactivity of the host.

Symbolism of I-Ching reading *(original text in Chinese)*

Translation: Two Mountains: Inactivity. The superior man, in his thought, does not leave his position.

Comment: "Mountain" is a symbolism for Min-Yang. In the time of Inactivity the superior man outperforms the requirement of the hexagram meaning by not deviating from his position, even in his thought.

Max-Yin
Min-Yang

53. Gradual Progress

Role	Trigram	Identity	Activity	Ability
GUEST	Max-Yin	Feminine	Most tentative	Most common
HOST	Min-Yang	Masculine	Highly tentative	Common

YIN YANG LOGIC *(NEW!)*

In this hexagram we have a common trigram hosting another common trigram. Recall from chapter 10 that in this case the hexagram quality depends strictly on the relative ranking of the host and the guest: 1. Max-Yang, 2. Min-Yang, 3. Min-Yin, 4. Max-Yin. Since host Min-Yang has higher ranking than the guest, the hexagram has favorable meaning.

The relative positions of the two trigrams are favorable because the masculine host is (relatively) higher than the feminine guest in the aggressiveness scale. Since their identity lines are in intimate contact (host Min-Yang at position 3 contacting guest Max-Yin at position 4), the two trigrams can approach each other despite the fact that both of them are tentative. Understandably, progresses will require time to develop when both host and guest are tentative. Thus, the fitting hexagram name is "Gradual Progress."

Gradual Progress is a favorable hexagram for events that needs time to develop to their ultimate end.

I-CHING TEXTS AND COMMENTS
(For comparison)

I-Ching reading *(original text in Chinese)*

Translation: Gradual Progress. Good for female to get married. Advisable to stay firmly on course.

Comment: The time of Gradual Progress is "good for female to get married" because, for a female, it will take a long time for a marriage to play out its possibilities. "Advisable to stay firmly on course" because impatience will negate the positive meaning of the time of Gradual Progress.

Elaboration on I-Ching reading *(original text in Chinese)*

Translation: Gradual yet progressing. Good for female to get married.

Advances in proper position. Therefore action is fruitful. Advance correctly. Can correct (the situation of) the territory. Its position is that of the firm (line) possessing the center.

Stopping and Flexible. Movements never end.

Comment: "Gradual yet progressing" is the essence of the time of Gradual Progress. "Advances in proper positions. Therefore action is fruitful" because the two main lines are Yang at position 3 and Yin at position 4, both are proper and in intimate contact.

The situation is very sensitive when Min-Yang and Max-Yin interact with each other. We have seen in hexagram 18 "Deterioration" that if Max-Yin is the hostess, the situation will deteriorate (then Max-Yin has to reverse herself to correct the situation). This would correspond to the case of improper advances. Here in the time of Gradual Progress, the situation is favorable. Therefore the elaboration says "Advance correctly. Can correct (the situation of) the territory."

"Its position is that of the firm (line) possessing the center" refers to line 5, which is Yang and occupies the center position of the guest hexagram. We should not pay much attention to this statement, as having line 5 Yang does not guarantee that the meaning of the hexagram is favorable.

Symbolisms of I-Ching reading *(original text in Chinese)*

Translation: Above the Mountain there is Wood. Gradual Progress. The superior man maintains his benevolent virtue and makes ordinary people better.

Comment: "Mountain" and "Wood" are symbolisms for Min-Yang and Max-Yin respectively. Realizing that the time of Gradual Progress is favorable for long-term projects, whose benefits may not be immediately visible, the superior man uses this opportunity to maintain his virtue and improve the virtue of ordinary people. Both are long-term projects.

 Max-Yang
Min-Yin

54. The Marrying Maiden

Role	Trigram	Identity	Activity	Ability
GUEST	Max-Yang	Masculine	Most aggressive	Most common
HOSTESS	Min-Yin	Feminine	Highly aggressive	Common

YIN YANG LOGIC *(NEW!)*

In this hexagram we have a common trigram hosting another common trigram. Recall from chapter 10 that in this case the hexagram quality depends strictly on the relative ranking of the host and the guest: 1. Max-Yang, 2. Min-Yang, 3. Min-Yin, 4. Max-Yin. Since hostess Min-Yin is ranked lower than the guest, the hexagram has unfavorable meaning.

Although these two trigrams are in intimate contact, there are problems with their interaction; that is because the feminine hostess is not as aggressive as the masculine guest. We have the image of an active young girl following an aggressive man. Since the position of the hostess is clearly weaker than that of the masculine guest, she is like a girl who interacts with the man from a weak position (e.g., not as a wife but as a concubine). The literal English translation of the Chinese hexagram name is "The Marrying Young Sister." For brevity it has been changed to "The Marrying Maiden."

Unclear from the hexagram name is the situation of the maiden after her marriage, but from Yin Yang logic we know that her future is not very promising. Thus, at least from the standpoint of the young bride, this is not a happy marriage.

The Marrying Maiden gives us the image of an innocent girl (Min-Yin) running after a mature man (Max-Yang). Why is she doing this? The only feasible conclusion is that she has been cheated or taken advantage of by the experienced man, and the man, after completing his conquest, was trying to leave her. A very sad but realistic picture of humanity, where the innocent keep suffering from the mischief of the experienced.

Understandably, the meaning of the hexagram is bad.

NOTE:
The Marrying Maiden is the exact Yin Yang opposite of the previous hexagram 53 "Gradual Progress." In both cases there is intimate contact between the two trigrams. The main differences are the activity level and the switching of masculine and feminine in the host and guest positions.

Thus, it is not true that all contacts are good! The outcome depends to a large extent on the mutual intentions of the two parties.

I-CHING TEXTS AND COMMENTS
(For comparison)

I-Ching reading *(original text in Chinese)*

Translation: The Marrying Maiden. Action has harmful consequences. No place to go.

Comment: As expected from the unfavorable arrangement of the two trigrams that form The Marrying Maiden, "action has harmful consequences. No place to go."

Elaboration on I-Ching reading *(original text in Chinese)*

Translation: The Marrying Maiden. The great meaning of Heaven and Earth. Heaven and Earth do not interact; therefore the various things do not flourish. The Marrying Maiden. This is the beginning and the end of humanity.

Playful and Aggressive: The Marrying Maiden.

Action has harmful consequences. The position is not proper. No place to go, because the soft is riding on the firm.

Comment: "Heaven and Earth do not interact, therefore the various things do not flourish" is a generic statement that describes the unfavorable arrangement of this hexagram. The interaction between the hostess and the guest is not favorable from a Yin Yang standpoint; hence it is in reverse of the ideal law of interaction as exhibited by Heaven and Earth.

"This is the beginning and the end of humanity" because The Marrying Maiden gives us the dark side of humanity, where the innocent (represented by Min-Yin) are cheated or taken advantage of.

"Playful and Aggressive" are characteristics that describe Min-Yin and Max-Yang respectively.

"Because the soft is riding on the firm" refers to the relationship between Min-Yin (soft) and Max-Yang (firm). The hexagram is unfavorable because the aggressive feminine Min-Yin plays the dominant role of the hostess, while the more aggressive Max-Yang plays the supporting role of a guest.

Symbolisms of I-Ching reading *(original text in Chinese)*

Translation: Above the Marsh there is Thunder. The Marrying Maiden. The superior man, from the distant end, knows the mischief.

Comment: "Marsh" and "Thunder" are symbolisms for Min-Yin and Max-Yang respectively. The superior man knows the laws of karma. Therefore by observing the sad end implied in the time of The Marrying Maiden he knows there has been mischief done in the past.

231

Max-Yang

Mid-Yin

55. Abundance

Role	Trigram	Identity	Activity	Ability
GUEST	Max-Yang	Masculine	Most aggressive	Most common
HOSTESS	Mid-Yin	Feminine	Very aggressive	Powerful

YIN YANG LOGIC *(NEW!)*

In this hexagram we have a power trigram hosting a common trigram. Being the most aggressive trigram of the power group, Mid-Yin is best suited for the hostess position. The hexagram therefore has favorable meaning. However, since the identities of the hostess and the guest are complementary (while being identical is preferred) the great situation implied by the hexagram cannot last long.

We have seen the impact that the most aggressive guest Max-Yang transfers (via his main line at position 4) a degree of extremity to his powerful host or hostess in three hexagrams. In hexagram 16 "Exuberance" the tentative hostess All-Yin gets all excited. In hexagram 34 "Great Energy" the aggressive host All-Yang becomes unusually aggressive. In hexagram 40 "Relief" the tentative host Mid-Yang breaks away from the inactivity barrier and becomes more effective.

In this trigram Mid-Yin is the hostess. Being aggressive powerful, she represents a richness that can be compared, in its brilliance, to that of the sun or, in its productivity, that of a cow. The influence of Max-Yang will push Mid-Yin's aggressiveness one step further, placing her at the zenith of her richness. Thus, fitting hexagram name is "Abundance."

By Yin Yang logic, all extremities will lead to the reverse trend. For this reason, although "Abundance" is an auspicious hexagram, it duration is expected to be short.

I-CHING TEXTS AND COMMENTS
(For comparison)

I-Ching reading *(original text in Chinese)*

Translation: Progress. When a king reaches this point he should not worry. Let him be like the sun at noon.

Comment: The progress comes from the extremely aggressive behavior of the guest, which influences the hostess.

"When a king reaches this point he should not worry. Let him be like the sun at noon" refers to the extreme richness of the time of

232

Abundance. Everyone knows that Abundance will be followed by decline. However, the extreme aggressiveness of the guest may be just enough to keep things the way they are (for a sufficiently long time). The image of a king is meaningful, because the king should be the richest person in the kingdom. He is the proper symbolism for Abundance.

The best way to deal with future decline is to prepare for it. And what is the best preparation that a king can made other than helping at many people as he can? Therefore there is no point for a king to be alarmed at the time of Abundance. He should instead take the opportunity to broaden his ability to help the people, like the sun at noon.

Elaboration on I-Ching reading *(original text in Chinese)*

Translation: Abundance means Greatness. Bright and Aggressive. Therefore "Abundance."

The king has reached this point. Still can make it greater. Has no worry. Like the sun at noon, shining on all things.

The sun of mid-day will go down. The full moon will be eaten off. Even Heaven and Earth have their fullness and emptiness, in accordance with the changes of time. Need we say more about humanity, about the saints and the spirits?

Comment: "Bright" and "Aggressive" are characteristics of Mid-Yin and Max-Yang respectively.

This elaboration confirms that the proper action for the king is to transfer Abundance to the people. It also elaborates on the temporary nature of Abundance.

Symbolisms of I-Ching reading *(original text in Chinese)*

Translation: Thunder and Lightning arriving together form Abundance. The superior man decides criminal cases and punishment with exactness.

Comment: "Thunder" and "Lightning" are symbolisms for Max-Yang and Mid-Yin respectively. The advice for the superior man is most interesting in the time of Abundance "The superior man decides criminal cases and punishment with exactness."

Irrelevant? Not! The time of extreme Abundance is when many people become rebels, with or without a cause. Some are driven by genuine concerns, some revolt against authority simply because they run out of challenging tasks to perform and get bored with their life. It is not an accident that the movement for "the right of criminals" started in the west, where the time of Abundance has been shining off and on for the last century.

The superior man, in anticipation of such activities, guard against future troubles by "deciding criminal cases and punishments with exactness."

Mid-Yin
Min-Yang

56. The Wanderer

Role	Trigram	Identity	Activity	Ability
GUEST	Mid-Yin	Feminine	Very aggressive	Most powerful
HOST	Min-Yang	Masculine	Highly tentative	Common

YIN YANG LOGIC *(NEW!)*

In this hexagram we have a common trigram hosting a power trigram. The host Min-Yang has the benefit of being in close proximity with the guest (via his main line at position 3). Having complementary identity (masculine while the guest is feminine) also helps a great deal. The only problem is that he is a tentative trigram. We therefore expect favorable meaning for the trigram, but the situation is less than ideal.

We have seen how the highly tentative masculine host Min-Yang reacts (via his main line at position 3) to two feminine guests. In hexagram 15 "Humility," he takes a humble stand before the most powerful feminine trigram All-Yin and benefits from it. In hexagram 31 "E-motions," he feels an inexplicable but very positive vibration in the company of his feminine counterpart Min-Yin.

In his interaction with the aggressive Min-Yin, Min-Yang was already on the verge of abandoning his tentative tendency. Mid-Yin is also aggressive like Min-Yin, but –being a power trigram- her aggressiveness leaves a much stronger impression in the host Min-Yang. At the same time, being less powerful than All-Yin, Mid-Yin does not require Min-Yang to be humble in front of her.

The common tentative masculine host Min-Yang is like a shy teenage boy, while the powerful and aggressive feminine guest Mid-Yin is like a girl in her late teens, beautiful and friendly. We can guess the consequence. Min-Yang will feel, not simply a vibration as in the case with Min-Yin, but a full-blown infatuation that throws him completely out of his highly tentative tendency, to the realm of unpredictable activities; like a wanderer who does not know where his next stop will be. Thus, the fitting hexagram name is "The Wanderer."

Despite its chaotic nature, "The Wanderer" is not a bad trigram because confusion is a part of growing up. We therefore expect Min-Yang to gain something out of this extraordinary experience, provided that he does not do anything harmful.

I-CHING TEXTS AND COMMENTS
(For comparison)

I-Ching reading *(original text in Chinese)*

Translation: The Wanderer. Small progress. The wanderer stays firmly on course. Good.

Comment: Small progress is achieved in the time of The Wanderer, because Min-Yin is forced to be resourceful, which is a necessary survival skill that he lacks, being the most tentative masculine trigram. "The Wanderer stays firmly on course. Good" because the risk in the time of the Wanderer is that Min-Yin, because of his lack of experience, will be completely out of control and get himself into trouble. To maintain a good status, he must stay firmly on course.

Elaboration on I-Ching reading *(original text in Chinese)*

Translation: The Wanderer. Small progress. The soft gains center in the outside and is yielding to the firm. Stopping yet brightens brightness. Therefore small progress. It is good if the wanderer stays firmly on course. Great is the time of The Wanderer!

Comment: "The soft gains center in the outside and is yielding to the firm" refer to Mid-Yin (the soft), whose main line is Yin and occupies the center of the guest trigram. As a guest, she is in a yielding position compared to Min-Yang (the firm), who is the host.

"Stopping yet brightens brightness. Therefore small progress." The meaning of Min-Yang is stopping. However, his main line (at position 3) is in contact with the guest, and can learn from her.

Symbolisms of I-Ching reading *(original text in Chinese)*

Translation: Above the Mountain there is Fire. The Wanderer. The superior man, using his brilliance, carefully exercises punishments, not allowing prison related matters to continue.

Comment: "Mountain" and "Fire" are symbolisms for Min-Yang and Mid-Yin respectively. The time of the Wanderer is the time where deviations are most likely to take place. The stability of a territory depends on the effectiveness of its legal system. The superior man realizes that deviations in the legal system cannot be allowed in the time of the Wanderer, that is why "The superior man, using his brilliance, carefully exercises punishments, not allowing prison related matters to continue."

It takes incredible wisdom to see the connection between the time of The Wanderer and the legal system. So profound is the vision of the sage who wrote this symbolism!!!

Max-Yin
Max-Yin

57. The Flexible
(Double Max-Yin)

Role	Trigram	Identity	Activity	Ability
GUEST	Max-Yin	Feminine	Most tentative	Most common
HOSTESS	Max-Yin	Feminine	Most tentative	Most common

YIN YANG LOGIC *(NEW!)*

This is an identity hexagram. Recall that the meaning of a hexagram is the situation of the host or hostess, which is Max-Yin in this case. Being most tentative common feminine, Max-Yin is unique, because she is not qualified to be a hostess in any hexagram. Thus, to face the reality of being the hostess, she must modify herself to fit the situation.

It so happens that hostess Min-Yin has the ideal guest (who is an identical cloned copy of her, just in a different position.) Her willingness to modify herself, then, guarantees that progress can be made. However, since it does not take much to deal with the guest successfully, it is unlikely that the hostess will try anything spectacular. The progress is therefore expected to be small.

Just by the flexible nature of the hostess Min-Yin, she should be able to proceed with whatever plan she has. However, since her ability and her stamina are limited, and since she is willing to listen, she should rely on the advice of others.

I-CHING TEXTS AND COMMENTS
(For comparison)
I-Ching reading *(original text in Chinese)*
Translation: Small progress. Favorable to move forward. Advisable to see the great man.

Comment: Small progress is expected because the hostess will modify herself to fit the guest, and the guest is not very demanding. "Favorable to move forward" because this is a favorable hexagram. "Advisable to see the great man" because the hostess Max-Yin is basically weak, although she is making progress, she could improve on her situation by asking for the opinions of capable people.

Elaboration on I-Ching reading *(original text in Chinese)*
Translation: Double Max-Yin reveals the (cosmic) order.
The firm (line) bends its way to become "Central and Correct," so that the (cosmic) Will is carried out. All of the flexible are yielding to

the firm; therefore small progress can be realized. Favorable to move forward. Advisable to see the great man.

Comment: "*Double Max-Yin reveals the (cosmic) order*" *because the outcome of each phenomenon is a combined picture of the cosmic order and the interference by human beings. When both the hostess and the guest are yielding as in the case of this hexagram, the human factor is reduced to zero, and all we have left is a faithful picture of the cosmic order. This is further explained by "The firm (line) bends its way to become 'Central and Correct', so that the (cosmic) Will is carried out."*

"*All of the flexible are yielding to the firm; therefore small progress can be realized*" *implies that the Will of Heaven favors progress. This is only a speculation. The more feasible explanation for the small progress achieved in the time of Double Max-Yin is that the flexibility of the hostess Max-Yin is reciprocated by her identical guest.*

Symbolisms of I-Ching reading *(original text in Chinese)*

Translation: Double Wind forms The Flexible. The superior man acts according to the (cosmic) order.

Comment: "*Wind*" *is a well known symbolism for Max-Yin. The time of Double Max-Yin requires the complete surrender by human beings to the Will of Heaven; that is why "The superior man acts according to the (cosmic) order."*

Min-Yin

Min-Yin

58. The Playful
(Double Min-Yin)

Role	Trigram	Identity	Activity	Ability
GUEST	Min-Yin	Feminine	Highly aggressive	Common
HOSTESS	Min-Yin	Feminine	Highly aggressive	Common

YIN YANG LOGIC *(NEW!)*

This is an identity hexagram. Being highly aggressive, the hostess fits her position; therefore progress is expected. However, the guest (who is an identically aggressive cloned copy of the hostess, just in different position) strays too far from the host; which is potentially a problem. The kind of problem that the guest may create cannot be too serious, because she, too, is a common trigram. However, the risk of straying from one's proper course exists because both trigrams are aggressive. It is advised therefore that the hostess is careful in her action, so that she stays firmly on course.

In summary, progress is expected in the playful time of Double Min-Yin, but it is advisable to stay firmly on course.

NOTE:

In Double Min-Yin, we have the image of two active young girls, possibly identical twins, one running without looking back (the guest, with main line 6 far away from the host), the other running after the first (the hostess, with main line in contact with the guest), trying to catch her. Obviously this is a joyous time, the time of Playfulness.

These lines were written several days after the final of the 2002 Worldcup Football (or Worldcup Soccer, depending on where you live). It was estimated that one quarter of the world's population (counting also babies) was watching the game on TV, and many world events had to be delayed until the game was over.

There have been wars after games; there have been games that prevented wars. This shows how important Playing is to humanity. A society that does not pay attention to the games that people play is a society in trouble.

I-CHING TEXTS AND COMMENTS
(For comparison)
I-Ching reading *(original text in Chinese)*
Translation: Progress. It is advisable to stay firmly on course.

<u>Comment</u>: Progress is guaranteed in the time of Double Min-Yin, because Min-Yin is aggressive, and her main line is in good contact with her identical guest. She must stay firmly on course because this is a playful time, which may be very distracting.

Elaboration on I-Ching reading *(original text in Chinese)*
<u>Translation</u>: Double Min-Yin means "Playful." The firm at the center, the soft at the edge. While playful, it is advised to stay firmly on course to fit the will of Heaven and the realization in Man. When playfulness leads the way, people forget their toils. When playfulness interferes with mishaps, people forget (the possibility of) death. Great is the stimulus of Playfulness on the people.

<u>Comment</u>: "The firm at the center, the soft at the edge" refers to the fact that the two center positions 2 and 5 are occupied by Yang lines (the firm), which are not the main line for either the hostess or the guest. The main lines for the two trigrams are Yin (the soft) in positions 3 and 6, which are the two edges.

Playfulness has its own importance, and therefore has to be accompanied by mindfulness. The advice is therefore "While playful, it is advised to stay firmly on course to fit the will of Heaven and the realization in Man." The importance of playfulness is emphasized in the following: "When playfulness leads the way, people forget their toils. When playfulness interferes with mishaps, people forget (the possibility of) death."

Symbolisms of I-Ching reading *(original text in Chinese)*
<u>Translation</u>: Adding one Marsh to the other: The Playful. The superior man discusses and practices with friends.

<u>Comment</u>: "Marsh" is a well known symbolism for Min-Yin. The superior man takes advantage of the playfulness of the time of Double Min-Yin by getting together with friends. Important matters could be discussed in a relaxed atmosphere.

Max-Yin
Mid-Yang

59. Dispersion
(Sacrifice)

Role	Trigram	Identity	Activity	Ability
GUEST	Max-Yin	Feminine	Most tentative	Most common
HOST	Mid-Yang	Masculine	Very tentative	Powerful

YIN YANG LOGIC (NEW!)

In this hexagram we have a power trigram hosting a common trigram. Mid-Yang is the weakest of the power group. The fact that his identity is opposite that of the guest (Mid-Yang is masculine, guest is feminine) adds to his quandary. By normal logic, the situation is very unfavorable. But for this very reason, the law of Yin Yang reversal comes to Mid-Yang's rescue.

Max-Yin is a common feminine guest. With her main line (at position 4) in contact with Mid-Yang, Max-Yin makes the masculine host aware of the fact that she is the weakest feminine trigram. Being a powerful masculine trigram, Mid-Yang is willing and able to help Max-Yin. In fact, Mid-Yang will be very effective in his effort to help Max-Yin because both sides agree on the same (tentative) approach. (This is in contrast with the limited result obtained by All-Yang in hexagram 9 "Small Cultivation" despite the fact that All-Yang is more powerful than Mid-Yang. The difference is that All-Yang's approach is aggressive.)

However, since Mid-Yang's approach is tentative, it will require considerable effort on his part to achieve the great result implied by the hexagram. In other words, he has to sacrifice for Max-Yin's sake. Since the most fitting symbolism for Mid-Yang is water, the symbolism for the sacrifice by Mid-Yang is the dispersion of water. Thus, the fitting hexagram name is "Dispersion."

In conclusion, Dispersion is a time of great challenge and opportunity. Great success is within reach, but sacrifice is the order of the day.

NOTE:
"Dispersion" is the exact Yin Yang opposite of hexagram 55 "Abundance" where Mid-Yin was hosting Max-Yang. In "Abundance" the hostess benefits from the aggressiveness of the guest Max-Yang. In "Dispersion" the host has to sacrifice for the sake of the most tentative guest Max-Yin.

I-CHING TEXTS AND COMMENTS
(For comparison)

I-Ching reading *(original text in Chinese)*

Translation: Dispersion. Progress. The king goes to his ancestral temple. Advantageous to cross the great stream. Advisable to stay firmly on course.

Comment: Progress can be made in the time of Dispersion because the host Mid-Yang share the same quality (of being tentative) with the weak guest who is asking for his help.

"The king goes to his ancestral temple" because the temple is a symbolism for sacrifice, which is necessary in the time of Dispersion.

"Advantageous to cross the great stream. Advisable to stay firmly on course" because once the determination to sacrifice has been made, the power of the host Mid-Yang should be sufficient to achieve great success in this rather trying situation. It is important, however, to stay firmly on course because the challenge of the time of Dispersion is great.

Elaboration on I-Ching reading *(original text in Chinese)*

Translation: Dispersion. Progress. The firm arrives and knows no limit. The soft (line) in proper position in the outer (trigram) is in agreement with the one above.

The king goes to his ancestral temple. The king is still at the center.

Advantageous to cross the great stream. Riding on Wood is fruitful.

Comment: "The firm arrives and knows no limit" refers to the main line of the host, which is Yang (the firm) and occupies the strong center position 2.

"The soft (line) in proper position in the outer (trigram) is in agreement with the one above" refers to line 4, which is Yin (soft) and is in close contact with the host trigram. It is also in (Yin Yang) agreement with the line above it, but this point should not be considered as a key factor as the progress is due to the resonance between Max-Yin and the host, not with another line within herself.

"The king is still at the center" is a valid explanation given for "The king goes to his ancestral temple," as the center position for Mid-Yang (line 2) is not very strong. An understanding of the Will of Heaven (passed down from the ancestral temple) is necessary for the king to continue with his effort to help Max-Yin in the time of Dispersion.

Symbolisms of I-Ching reading *(original text in Chinese)*

Translation: Wind flowing above Water. Dispersion. The ancient king offers his sacrifices at the royal temple.

Comment: "Wind" and "Water" are symbolisms for Max-Yin and Mid-Yang respectively. Since the time of Dispersion requires a clear commitment to sacrifice, it makes sense for the ancient king to offer his sacrifice at the royal temple.

241

Mid-Yang

Min-Yin

60. Self-Restraint

Role	Trigram	Identity	Activity	Ability
GUEST	Mid-Yang	Masculine	Very tentative	Powerful
HOSTESS	Min-Yin	Feminine	Highly aggressive	Common

YIN YANG LOGIC *(NEW!)*

In this hexagram we have a common trigram hosting a power trigram. Min-Yin has the benefit of being close the guest (thanks to her main line at position 3) and being aggressive. The fact that her identity and that of the guest are complementary also helps a great deal. We therefore expect a favorable meaning for this hexagram.

We have seen how the highly aggressive hostess Min-Yin reacts (via her main line at position 3) to two masculine guests. In hexagram 10 "Stepping cautiously," she takes proper care in her interaction with the most powerful masculine guest All-Yang. In hexagram 41 "Decrease," she loses some of her aggressiveness in the presence of her tentative masculine counterpart Min-Yin.

Although the masculine guest Mid-Yang is not as threatening as All-Yang, the fact that he is a power trigram forces Min-Yin to pay attention to her actions. Since Mid-Yang, who is somewhat similar to her masculine counterpart (Min-Yin) by being tentative, she will also sacrifice some of her aggressiveness in his presence. This interaction is therefore the intermediate between "Stepping cautiously" and "Decrease." We have the image of an active young girl who voluntarily controls her own behavior in the presence of the powerful guest. Thus, the fitting hexagram name is "Self-Restraint."

NOTE:

"Self-Restraint" is the exact Yin Yang opposite of hexagram 56 "The Wanderer" where Min-Yang was hosting Mid-Yin. In "The Wanderer" the host Min-Yang, because of his proximity with the aggressive and powerful guest Mid-Yin, was influenced by her and became restless, which was uncharacteristic of him. Here in "Self-Restraint" we have the hostess Min-Yin, because of her proximity to the tentative and powerful guest Mid-Yang, is influenced by him and restrains her aggressiveness.

I-CHING TEXTS AND COMMENTS
(For comparison)

I-Ching reading *(original text in Chinese)*

Translation: Self-Restraint. Progress. Painful self-restraint cannot stay firmly on course.

Comment: The high level of aggressiveness is the reason that makes Min-Yin a common trigram. By restraining her aggressiveness, she certainly will achieve progress. However, since her basic character is playfulness, painful self-restraint is very unnatural for Min-Yin, and she therefore cannot continue with it for long.

Elaboration on I-Ching reading *(original text in Chinese)*

Translation: Self Restraint. Progress. The firm and the soft are separate, and the firm gains center.

Painful self-restraint cannot stay firmly on course. Its Tao has reached its end.

Playfulness advances to Danger. Appropriate position leading to self-restraint. "Center and Correct" therefore well connected.

Heaven and Earth self restrain, therefore the four seasons form. Self-restraint within control will not harm property, will not hurt the people.

Comment: "The firm and the soft are separate and the firm gains center" is ambiguous because here we have Min-Yin (the soft) in direct contact with Mid-Yang (the firm). It is more appropriate to say "The firm is separate from the soft and gains center," which is a good description of the situation because the main line of Mid-Yang (the firm) is at the most powerful position (line 5) and therefore has a strong influence on Min-Yin (the soft).

"Painful self-restraint cannot stay firmly on course. Its Tao has reached its end" because painful self-restraint is against the playful nature of the hostess Min-Yin.

"Appropriate position leading to self-restraint" refers to the correctness of line 3 (main line of the hostess, in direct contact with the guest) and line 5 (main line of the guest, not in contact with the hostess but occupying the most powerful position).

The last paragraph praises the role of self-restraint in the operation of nature as well as in the conduct of human affairs.

Symbolisms of I-Ching reading *(original text in Chinese)*

Translation: Above the Marsh is Water. Self-Restraint. The superior man controls numbers and measurements, and deliberates on virtue and conduct.

Comment: "Marsh" and "Water" are symbolisms for Min-Yin and Mid-Yang. "The superior man controls numbers and measurements" because these are the criteria used to evaluate the effectiveness of the process of self-restraint. He also "deliberates on virtue and conduct" because these are the focus in the time of Self-Restraint.

Max-Yin
Min-Yin

61. Central Harmony

Role	Trigram	Identity	Activity	Ability
GUEST	Max-Yin	Feminine	Most tentative	Most common
HOSTESS	Min-Yin	Feminine	Highly aggressive	Common

YIN YANG LOGIC *(NEW!)*

In this hexagram we have a common trigram hosting another common trigram. Recall from chapter 10 that in this case the hexagram quality depends strictly on the relative ranking of the host and the guest: 1. Max-Yang, 2. Min-Yang, 3. Min-Yin, 4. Max-Yin. Since hostess Min-Yin has higher ranking than the guest, the hexagram has favorable meaning.

This hexagram is the best situation that two trigrams with the same identity (both feminine or both masculine) and ability (both powerful or both common) could find themselves in: In perfect contact (with the main line of the host at position 3, that of the guest at position 4) and at proper positions (with the host being aggressive, the guest tentative).

In the imperfect world of Yin and Yang, it is impossible to achieve the Middle Way, the best possible situation is to get close to it. In this respect, this hexagram is only second to hexagram 11 "Great Harmony." Since the harmony implied by this hexagram happens at the center, where the two main lines interact, the fitting hexagram name is "Central Harmony."

I-CHING TEXTS AND COMMENTS
(For comparison)

I-Ching reading *(original text in Chinese)*

Translation: Central Harmony. Good (even for) pigs and fish. Advantageous to cross the great stream. Advisable to stay firmly on course.

Comment: The time of Central Harmony is a very favorable time; therefore it is "Advantageous to cross the great stream." However, as we all know, it is very difficult to maintain the happy center; therefore it is "advisable to stay firmly on course."

Elaboration on I-Ching reading *(original text in Chinese)*

Translation: Central Harmony. The soft at the inner, and the firm possessing the center. Harmony could change a country for the better.

Good (even for) pigs and fish. The trust can encompass pigs and fish. Advantageous to cross the great stream. Riding in the hollow of the wooden boat.

In Central Harmony, it is advised to stay firmly on course, in resonance with Heaven.

Comment: "The soft at the inner and the firm possessing the center" means the two Yin lines (the soft) occupy the center positions of the hexagram (line 3 and 4), while the two center positions 2 and 5 are occupied by Yang lines (the firm). These should be considered as a memory trick more than a valid reason for the favorable meaning of the hexagram. That is because, for example, the same conditions are met by hexagrams 29 "Danger" (Double Mid-Yang).

It is obvious that "Harmony could change a country for the better."

"Advantageous to cross the great stream. Riding in the hollow of the wooden boat" appeals to a symbolism of Max-Yin, which is wood. This again should be considered only as a memory trick than a valid reason. It is "advantageous to cross the great stream" simply because the time of Central Harmony is a great time where all factors are favorable for serious undertakings.

"In Central Harmony it is advisable to stay firmly on course, in resonance with Heaven" refers to the mutability of Central Harmony. One must realize this great opportunity by acting in resonance with Heaven, otherwise it may slip away.

Symbolisms of I-Ching reading *(original text in Chinese)*

Translation: Above the Marsh there is Wind: Central Harmony. The superior man contemplates on prison-related matters and delays death penalties.

Comment: "Marsh" and "Wind" are symbolisms for Min-Yin and Max-Yin respectively. In the time of Central Harmony there exists a deep mutual understanding among people who are significantly different from one another. The superior man, in his effort to outperform the meaning of this hexagram, turns his attention to the outcast of the society, namely the criminals. That is why in the time of Central Harmony "The superior man contemplates on prison-related matters and delays death penalties."

Max-Yang

Min-Yang

62. Small Extremity

Role	Trigram	Identity	Activity	Ability
GUEST	Max-Yang	Masculine	Most aggressive	Most common
HOST	Min-Yang	Masculine	Highly tentative	Common

YIN YANG LOGIC *(NEW!)*

In this hexagram we have a common trigram hosting another common trigram. Recall from chapter 10 that in this case the hexagram quality depends strictly on the relative ranking of the host and the guest: 1. Max-Yang, 2. Min-Yang, 3. Min-Yin, 4. Max-Yin. Since host Min-Yang has lower ranking than the guest, the hexagram has unfavorable meaning.

This hexagram is the exact Yin Yang opposite of the preceding hexagram. The two are similar in two ways. First, host and guest trigrams are of the same identity (both masculine or both feminine). Second, they are of the same ability level (common). The problem with the present hexagram is that the positions of the two trigrams are not proper (with the host being tentative and the guest aggressive).

Under the influence of the most aggressive Max-Yang, the host Min-Yang is inclined to deviate from his tentative nature and act aggressively, which would be a mistake. However, since Min-Yang is in close contact with Max-Yang and understands the situation, he is not expected to make serious errors. In summary, Min-Yang will make the mistake of acting aggressively, but his mistake will not be too serious. Thus, the fitting hexagram name is "Small Extremity."

Since the host position favors aggressiveness, Small Extremity is not a bad situation. However, since the aggressiveness of Min-Yang is a borrowed effect, he must realize that he can only utilize it to achieve small results. Attempts at big projects are doomed to fail.

NOTE: Small Extremity and Great Extremity (28) are similar in all three properties: 1. Host and guest trigrams are of the same identity (both masculine or both feminine), 2. Host and guest trigrams are both common, 3. Host trigram is tentative, guest trigram aggressive. Thus, it is not by accident that they share the name "Extremity." The difference is that in Great Extremity host and guest trigrams are far apart (main lines at positions 1 and 6), whereas in Small Extremity they are neighbors (main lines at 3 and 4).

I-CHING TEXTS AND COMMENTS
(For comparison)

I-Ching reading *(original text in Chinese)*

Translation: Small Extremity. Progress. Advisable to stay firmly on course. Can achieve small matters, not important matters. The flying bird leaves sound. Not appropriate to be high; appropriate to be low. Great fortune.

Comment: *Progress is achieved in the time of Small Extremity because the host position favors aggressiveness, and Min-Yin becomes aggressive by the influence of the guest Max-Yang. However, he must keep in mind that this is a borrowed effect, therefore "Advisable to stay firmly on course. Can achieve small matters, not important matters."*

"The flying bird leaves sound" refers to the geometrical image of the 6 lines, which suggest a flying bird. We see the body of the bird clearly (Yang lines 3 and 4), but only blurred images of its two flapping wings (Yin lines 1, 2 and 5, 6). The induced aggressiveness of Min-Yin is compared to the impact of such a flying bird: The (insignificant) sound created by the flapping wings.

"Not appropriate to be high; appropriate to be low" is the proper advice for the time of Small Extremity. If this advice is followed, the result is "great fortune," which has to be understood in the relative meaning of smallness in the time of Small Extremity.

Elaboration on I-Ching reading *(original text in Chinese)*

Translation: Small Extremity. The small is in extreme (i.e., committing error) but may progress. In the state of extremity, it is advised to stay firmly on course, act according to time.

The soft (lines) gain center, therefore is favorable in small matters. The firm (lines) are in inappropriate positions, and not possessing the center, therefore cannot achieve important matters.

There is the image of a flying bird. The flying bird leaves sound. Not appropriate to be high, appropriate to be low. The high is in reverse, while the low is yielding.

Comment: *"In the state of extremity, it is advised to stay firmly on course, act according to time" spells out the limit of the time of Small Extremity.*

The statement "The soft (lines) gain center, therefore is favorable in small matters. The firm (lines) are in inappropriate positions, and not possessing the center, therefore cannot achieve important matters" should only be considered as a memory trick, not as a general rule, because, for example, the same conditions are met in hexagram 30 "Brightness" (Double Mid-Yin), with clear potential for great success.

The last paragraph explains the image of the flying bird and the reason why it is more proper to be low than high. These are in agreement with our discussion in I-Ching reading.

Symbolisms of I-Ching reading *(original text in Chinese)*

Translation: Above the Mountain there is Thunder. Small Extremity. The superior man acts in excess of (required) humility, mourns in excess of the sorrow, and spends in excess of his saving.

Comment: *"Mountain" and "Thunder" are symbolisms for Min-Yang and Max-Yang respectively. The superior man must be willing to exercise controllable excesses to fit the requirement of the time of Small Extremity. This is why "The superior man acts in excess of (required) humility, mourns in excess of the sorrow, and spends in excess of his saving."*

Mid-Yang

Mid-Yin

63. Completion
(In Correct Order)

Role	Trigram	Identity	Activity	Ability
GUEST	Mid-Yang	Masculine	Very tentative	Powerful
HOSTESS	Mid-Yin	Feminine	Very aggressive	Powerful

YIN YANG LOGIC *(NEW!)*

In this hexagram we have one power trigram hosting another power trigram. Since the hostess is aggressive and the guest is tentative, there is a power conflict. In power conflicts the meaning is favorable if the host or hostess is more powerful than the guest. Thanks to the subjective view, Mid-Yin appears more powerful than the guest. The meaning of the hexagram therefore is expected to be favorable. However, there is a limitation. Since the host position prefers masculine over feminine, there is a side effect.

These two trigrams are exact Yin Yang opposites of each other; therefore there exists a very strong relationship between them. Since the aggressiveness of Mid-Yin is proper for her position as the hostess, so is the tentativeness of Min-Yang for his position as the guest, the outcome of this interaction is expected to be favorable.

In hexagram 22 "Decoration," Min-Yin's achievement was superficial because the guest (Min-Yang) was too tentative and (with his main line at position 6) too far removed from her. In hexagram 55 "Abundance" her achievement was the best possible because the guest (Max-Yang) was extremely aggressive and (with his main line at position 4) in direct contact with her. This hexagram corresponds to the intermediate case because the guest Mid-Yang, despite being tentative (like Min-Yang), is more capable than either Min-Yang or Max-Yang. This means Mid-Yin's achievement will be more than superficial, but not too great. A reasonable estimate is that she has completed the task required of her. Thus the fitting hexagram name is "Completion."

"Completion" is not a great achievement, but it has the psychological effect of complacency that most likely will lead to serious problems.

I-CHING TEXTS AND COMMENTS
(For comparison)

I-Ching reading *(original text in Chinese)*

Translation: Completion. Progress for the small. Advisable to stay firmly on course. Favorable in the beginning, but becoming chaotic at the end.

Comment: "Progress for the small" because completion is a positive result, but cannot be considered great. "Advisable to stay firmly on course" because in the time of Completion it is easy to lose one's focus and stray into errors. It is obvious that the time of Completion is "favorable at the beginning." However, the big risk when a project is completed is that everyone will become complacent, and there is no follow up to take care of loose ends. Therefore "becoming chaotic at the end."

Elaboration on I-Ching reading *(original text in Chinese)*

Translation: Completion. Progress. The small is progressing.

Advisable to stay firmly on course. The firm and the soft are correct and in appropriate positions.

Favorable in the beginning because the soft gains center.

The end, because of the stopping of activities, becoming chaotic. Its Tao has come to the end.

Comment: "Advisable to stay firmly on course" for reasons cited in I-Ching reading above.

"The firm (lines) and the soft (lines) are correct and in appropriate positions" could mean all lines in Completions are in the proper Yin Yang positions for them (Yin on Yin positions, Yang on Yang positions). It could also mean Mid-Yang (the firm) and Mid-Yin (the soft) are in appropriate positions according to their tentativeness (as guest) and aggressiveness (as hostess). However, it is not that important to know whether the elaboration means the first or the second.

"Favorable in the beginning, because the soft gains center" refers to line 2, which is the main line of the hostess at the center position. This should only be considered as a memory trick because, for example, in hexagram 36 "Dimming" (Mid-Yin hosting All-Yin) the soft also gains center yet the situation is difficult.

"The end, because of the stopping of activities, becomes chaotic. Its Tao has come to the end" elaborates on the impact of completion, which leads to complacency, which in turn leads to non-action and chaos.

Symbolisms of I-Ching reading *(original text in Chinese)*

Translation: Water on top of Fire. Completion. The superior man is worried about calamity, therefore he is on guard.

Comment: "Water" and "Fire" are symbolisms for Mid-Yin and Mid-Yang. The superior man, with his wisdom, understands that Completion will leads to complacency and future trouble. This is why "The superior man is worried about calamity, therefore he is on guard."

 Mid-Yin
Mid-Yang

64. Incompletion
(In Disorder)

Role	Trigram	Identity	Activity	Ability
GUEST	Mid-Yin	Feminine	Very aggressive	Powerful
HOST	Mid-Yang	Masculine	Very tentative	Powerful

YIN YANG LOGIC *(NEW!)*

In this hexagram we have one power trigram hosting another power trigram. Since the host is tentative and the guest is aggressive, there is a power conflict. In power conflicts the meaning is unfavorable if the host or hostess is less powerful than the guest. Because of the subjective view, Mid-Yang appears less powerful than the guest. The meaning of the hexagram therefore is expected to be unfavorable. However, there is an upside to the problem. Since the host position prefers masculine over feminine, there is a positive future.

These two trigrams are exact Yin Yang opposites of each other; therefore there exists a very strong relationship between them. In addition, they are both power trigrams. Power trigrams of opposite identities will cooperate with each other. However, since the tentativeness of Mid-Yang is unfit for his position as the host, so is the aggressiveness of Min-Yin for her position as the guest, the outcome of this interaction is expected to be unfavorable.

In hexagram 47 "Exhaustion," Min-Yang's was in a desperate situation because the guest (Min-Yin) was too aggressive and (with her main line at position 6) too far removed from him. In hexagram 59 "Dispersion" he had to sacrifice but was able to achieve good result because the also tentative guest (Max-Yin) was in direct contact with him (via her main line at position 4). This hexagram corresponds to the intermediate case because the guest Mid-Yin, despite being aggressive (like Min-Yin), is more capable than either Min-Yin or Max-Yin. This means Mid-Yang situation is not desperate, but not that good either. A reasonable estimate is that he has not completed the task required of him. Thus the fitting hexagram name is "Incompletion."

"Incompletion" is not as bad a situation as it sounds. The reason being that if the identity property is considered, then Mid-Yang (masculine) and Mid-Yin (feminine) are in their proper places. The situation is more like a case where all the pieces are in, but they are out of order. Since both trigrams are powerful, it is very feasible for them to eventually put the pieces together successfully. Thus, Incompletion has the promise for great future success.

I-CHING TEXTS AND COMMENTS
(For comparison)

I-Ching reading *(original text in Chinese)*

Translation: Incompletion. Progress. The small fox has yet crossed the stream. He wetted his tail. No place to go.

Comment: Progress is made in the time of Incompletion because there are still things to take care of. "The small fox has yet crossed the stream" contains the essence of the time of Incompletion, when the goal has not been achieved.

"He wetted his tail. No place to go" refers to the troublesome situation in the time of Incompletion. One is stuck with the existing project (i.e., wetting own tail) and is not free to move to the next project (i.e., no place to go).

Elaboration on I-Ching reading *(original text in Chinese)*

Translation: Incompletion. Progress. The soft gains center. The small fox has yet crossed the stream. Still not escaping the center. Wetted his tail. No place to go. No continuation to the end. Although not in proper positions, the firm and the soft are in resonance.

Comment: "The soft gains center" must mean the main line of the guest Mid-Yin at position 5, which is the most favorable position in hexagram configuration.

"The small fox has yet crossed the stream. Still not escaping the center. Wetted his tail" refers to the main line of the host Mid-Yang at position 2, which is a center position. The fact that Mid-Yang's main line is Yang and yet it is a tentative trigram suggests the image of the main line being trapped at the center position, which is the image used here.

"No place to go. No continuation to the end" because (due to the lack of aggressiveness by the host) everything is out of order. Order has to be established first before any positive result can be realized.

"Although not in proper positions, the firm and the soft are in resonance" refers to the fact that both Mid-Yin (aggressive in the guest position) and Mid-Yang (tentative in the host position) are in the wrong positions. However, since their identities are in proper positions (masculine Mid-Yang as host, and feminine Mid-Yin as guest) and of comparable strength, they are "in resonance." We therefore expect that they will be able to sort out the disorder in their relationship and will be successful eventually.

Symbolisms of I-Ching reading *(original text in Chinese)*

Translation: Fire on top of Water: Incompletion. The superior man carefully differentiates things according to their locations.

Comment: "Fire" and "Water" are symbolisms for Mid-Yin and Mid-Yang respectively. In the time of Incompletion, the wise superior man realizes that disorder is the main reason behind the trouble at hand. He therefore starts the process of improvement by differentiating things according to their locations.

LAST WORDS FOR THE FIRST VOLUME

Ending note: The I-Ching as the new hope for the social sciences

The importance of subjectivity in the social sciences was finally recognized in the 20th century, but even at the time of this writing the scientific community still cannot come up with any efficient procedure to deal with subjectivity. One reason for this difficulty is the belief that subjectivity is so random that it is completely outside the realm of science.

In this respect, the I-Ching is superior. Thanks to the completeness of the trigrams, subjectivity is reduced to the very manageable set of 64 hexagrams. With the assurance that no interaction could lie outside the realm of the 64 hexagrams, suddenly there is hope that the social sciences can finally be systemized and understood in their totality without having to resort to the various *ad hoc and conflicting* empirical theories that are flooding these fields today. This is a great step forward in our search for an ultimate understanding of man's nature and his place in the universe.

APPENDIX I
A critical review of the two existing scientific paradigms
(that they are both incomplete)

The description of existing science requires two paradigms that are diametrically opposite to each other. At one extreme is classical physics, which claims that all physical phenomena are completely deterministic. At the other extreme is quantum mechanics, which claims that all physical phenomena are indeterminate.

Since these two hypotheses are mutually exclusive of each other, at least one of them has to be wrong or incomplete. We will argue that both hypotheses are incomplete.

In order to show that a hypothesis is incomplete we only need to present a single case where it does not work. We will choose a property of light called "polarization," which is the orientation of light in the plane perpendicular to its direction of propagation. For reference purposes we will call the direction of light propagation the z direction, the traverse plane the x/y plane.

Light polarization has been investigated quite extensively. In polarization experiments, one or more polarizing filters are placed in the path of photon propagation. A polarizing filter is a specialized filter that has a preferred direction, which can be changed by simply rotating the filter in the x/y plane.

Direction of light
propagation

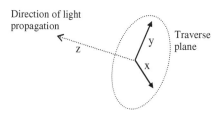

Traverse
plane

Figure 1a: The traverse plane x/y (in complex notations) is formed by two equivalent dimensions (x and y). The equivalence of x and y is reflected in a property of light known as polarization.

Let θ_1 and θ_2 be the preferred directions of two polarizers placed parallel to each other. If we shine a beam of light perpendicular to polarizer 1, it is well known that the light coming out of polarizer 1 will be at half the intensity of the incoming light. Let N_0 be the number of photons in the incoming light beam, N_1 and N_2 the number of photons coming out polarizers 1 and 2 respectively; it is well known that the following are true if N_1 is sufficiently large:

$$N_1 = N_0/2 \qquad (1a)$$
$$N_2 = N_1 \cos^2(\theta_2 - \theta_1) \qquad (2a)$$

Although the long-term photon count can be predicted precisely with equation (2a), it is impossible to predict if a particular photon will be absorbed by the polarizer or passes through it when the two polarizers are not lined up at the same angle <u>and</u> not lined up perpendicular to each other (i.e., $\theta_2 \neq \theta_1$ and $\theta_2 \neq \theta_1 \pm \pi$). Proponents for classical physics may attempt to argue that photons happen to be extremely sensitive, and our experimental conditions are not well controlled enough to make the action of each photon predictable. However, the simplicity of the experiment makes this argument untenable as it is very difficult to see how any improvement in the experimental set up can produce the desired predictability. The inability to predict how individual photons behave, then, is a powerful case against the position of total determinism (held by classical physics).

On the other hand, also from equation (2a), if the two polarizers are perfectly aligned (i.e., $\theta_2=\theta_1$), all photons that pass through the first polarizer will also pass through the second polarizer, because:

$$N_2 = N_1\cos^2 0 = N_1 \times 1 = N_1 \qquad (3a)$$

If the two polarizers are lined up perpendicular to each other (i.e., $\theta_2=\theta_1\pm\pi/2$), None of the photons that pass through the first polarizer will pass through the second, because:

$$N_2 = N_1\cos^2(\pi/2) = N_1 \times 0 = 0 \qquad (4a)$$

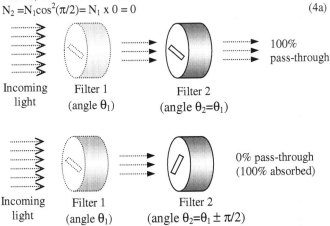

Figure 2a: Experiments with polarizing filters confirm that light has a preferred angle in the traverse plane (x/y plane). If the second filter is lined up exactly as the first, all photons coming out of the first filter will pass through the second. On the other hand, if the second filter is lined up perpendicular to the first, none of the photons coming out of the first filter will pass through the second.

The absolute certainty implied by (3a) and (4a) negates the position (held by quantum mechanics) that all physical phenomena are indeterminate.

Thus, we are forced to conclude that absolute determinism and absolute uncertainty are only partial descriptions of physical phenomena. In other words, both paradigms are incomplete.

APPENDIX II
The incompleteness of Einsteinian Spacetime

The mainstream theory of space and time at the time this discourse is written is that of Einstein. According to Einstein's theory, time is a space-like dimension. This leads to the possibility for time travel, which is in conflict with the very foundation of determinism. Einstein's theory is a part of classical physics, which is based on determinism. Since the conflict is internal, Einstein's theory of space and time is a paradox that can never be resolved.

Einstein recognized that there had to be a connection between space and time, but he still followed the traditional practice of assuming that the three spatial dimensions are equivalent. We will now use the very theory of Relativity to show that this view is incorrect.

Let (x, y, z) and t be the space and time measured in a given coordinate system, and (x', y', z') and t' the space and time measured in a second coordinate system moving in the z direction with velocity v. It is known from Einstein's Special Relativity theory that:

$$x' = x \tag{5a}$$
$$y' = y \tag{6a}$$
$$z' = (z-vt)/[1-v^2/c^2]^{1/2} \tag{7a}$$
$$t' = [t-vz/c^2]/[1-v^2/c^2]^{1/2} \tag{8a}$$

It is clear from (5a), (6a), and (7a) that the two dimensions x' and y' in the traverse plane (i.e., the plane perpendicular to the direction of motion) are equivalent, but distinctly different from the dimension of motion z'. In addition it is clear from (7a) and (8a) that the time dimension t' is entangled with the dimension of motion z' via the velocity v. The only way for x', y', z' to be equivalent to one another and for time to be detached from space is that there is absolutely no motion (v=0). However, it is known from modern physics that the state of absolute motionlessness can never exist. In other words, it is impossible to have v=0. Thus, in reality the dimension of motion is always entangled with time, and therefore different from the other two spatial dimensions.

APPENDIX III
The entanglement of space and time

We will choose photons as our subject of investigation in this discussion because photons do not possess mass, and this simplifies the analysis a great deal. The investigation of massive particles (i.e., particles that possess mass) such as electrons, protons are more complicated and will have to be delayed to a future opportunity. However, with proper modifications, the essence of the ensuing discussion is also applicable to massive particles.

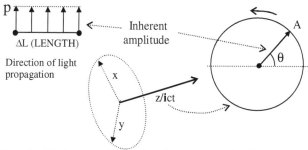

Figure 3a: The long-term ratio for lengths is a pure number, but the long term ratio for many repeat experiments with photons is a function of space and time and has to be represented geometrically as a rotating radius of a circle to reflect the equivalence of space z and the modified time ict.

255

If we measure many length segments with a ruler whose resolution is 1mm, the actual lengths of all segments measured as 1000mm could be anywhere between 999.5mm and 1000.5mm. As far as the ruler is concerned, all these lengths are equivalent. Thus, the distribution for all segments measured as 1000mm will be uniform (see left picture of figure 3a.)

By extending this logic to the case of photons, we would expect the distribution of photons to be constant everywhere along the z direction. To test this hypothesis we devise a simple thought experiment. We place a photo-sensitive plate a distance D away from a well controlled light source. We will then aim the light source directly at the plate, turn the light source on at time $t=0$ and turn it off at time $t=t_1$. By varying the distance D but keep t_1 constant, we will have a set of photo sensitive plates filled with photon dots. This allows us to track the number of photon dots N as a function of the distance D. Not surprisingly, we will find N stays more or less constant; which confirms that the number of photons does not change along the path of light propagation.

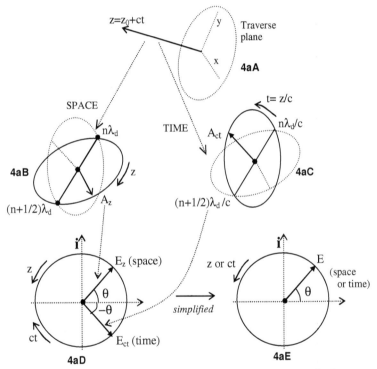

Figure 4a: The long term ratio for many repeat experiments with photons is a function of space and time and has to be represented geometrically as a rotating radius of a circle to reflect the equivalence of space z and the modified time ict. Note that the traverse plane (x-y) has not been included.

But there is an important difference between resolution limit in length measurement and resolution limit in photon detection. Length resolution could be changed (by using a more precise ruler, for example,) but photon resolution (i.e., the wavelength λ_d) is whatever it is. The reason why photons have various wavelengths is outside the scope of this appendix, but it is clear that the situations at z and at $z+\lambda_d$ are the same. In other words, in addition to having a uniform magnitude A, photon distribution must possess a second characteristics which repeats itself with spatial increments of $n\lambda_d$ where n is an integer. By symmetry consideration, the only geometrical presentation that meets these requirements is an arrow of fixed length rotating at constant speed in such a way that each full revolution corresponds to one wavelength λ_d.

To complete the picture we have to include time; that is because the spatial direction z of light propagation is connected to time by the relationship:

$$z = z_0 + ct \tag{9a}$$

Where z_0 is the measure for z at time t=0. Thus, in the direction of motion, space and time are coupled:

$$\Delta z = c\Delta t \tag{10a}$$

Since $\Delta z = \lambda_d$, we find $\Delta t = (\Delta z)/c = \lambda_d /c$. Time, then, must also have an equivalent amplitude that varies exactly like that of space. We say that the temporal amplitude and spatial amplitude move in sympathy. Geometrically we can present the situation for time in a plane perpendicular to that for space (figures 4aB and 4aC). Since space and time are perfectly symmetrical, a simpler geographical representation is shown in figure 4aD, where the clockwise and counter clockwise directions are used to differentiate space (z) and time (ct). In fact, it is sufficient to show only one arrow (representing space or time), with the understanding that it constitutes only half of the total picture (see figure 4aE).

APPENDIX IV
The Central Limit Theorem and macroscopic existence

The Central Limit theorem (CLT) has been discussed in detail in an earlier book by the writer "The End of Probability and the New Meaning of Quantum Physics." For the purpose of understanding the Yin Yang theory, all we need to know about CLT is:

"Given a random distribution A. If a distribution B is formed by taking N samples from A each time, and if N is large enough, then B will approximate a normal distribution with the same average value as A."

The normal distribution is also known as the Gaussian distribution (in honor of the great German mathematician Karl Gauss). Since the graph of this distribution has the shape similar to a bell, it is commonly referred to as the bell curve.

The amazing fact is that we start with the original distribution, which could be extremely random, and end up with the bell curve, which is well ordered. But what is a well ordered entity? The answer: A macroscopic existence!

Since the bell curve is achieved by an averaging process, and not all averaging processes are the same, the key word to remember is "randomness level." Each averaging process has a characteristic randomness level. The higher the randomness level, the larger the sample size N has to be; otherwise the bell curve cannot be formed by the Central Limit Theorem averaging process.

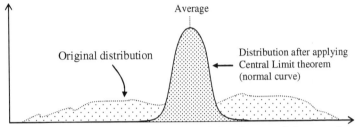

Figure 5a: The Central Limit theorem is definitely one of the most beautiful theorems of mathematics. It transforms (almost) everything to a normal curve. Here a very random looking distribution has been transformed to a Gaussian curve thanks to the action of the Central Limit Theorem. Surprisingly there are not that many applications for this powerful theorem. But that will change.

We finally find the answer to the so-called time puzzle: Since the CLT process requires certain conditions to be successful, it is possible for a CLT process to fail. When the CLT process fails, the macroscopic entity ceases to exist while it parts go on living.

INDEX

33643232R00148

Made in the USA
Lexington, KY
03 July 2014